HENRY'S DAUGHTER

D0557995

7 20715 50569 9

Linda F. Radke, President
Five Star Publications, Inc.
PO Box 6698
Chandler, AZ 85246-6698
480-940-8182
www.HenrysDaughter.com

Library of Congress Cataloging-in-Publication Data

Norman, Mildred, 1920–

Henry's daughter: my journeys through the 20th century / by Mildred Norman.
    p. cm.
    ISBN-13: 978-1-58985-056-9
    ISBN-10: 1-58985-056-4

1. Norman, Mildred, 1920–   2. Iowa – Biography.   3. Arizona – Biography.
I. Title.

    CT275.N6944A3 2007
    977.7'033092—dc22
    [B]
                                   2006037366

Printed in the United States of America
Editor: Nancy Miller
Cover Design: Kris Taft Miller
Interior Layout: Raphael Freeman, Jerusalem Typesetting
Project Manager: Sue DeFabis

HENRY'S DAUGHTER
My Journeys through the 20ᵗʰ Century

by
Mildred Norman

[handwritten inscription: Merry Christmas & a good story, Love, Anne & Vincent]

FIVE STAR PUBLICATIONS, INC.
Chandler, AZ

This Book is Dedicated to
My Children
Nancy, Mary Patrice and Jon
and My Grandchildren
Sha, Shelby, Amy, Michael and Ben
My Great Grandchildren
Courtney, Arah, Caitlin, Mason,
Collin, Audrey and William

Table of Contents

PREFACE

I've had fun writing this book. It is amazing how many things you remember when you sit down at your computer and start writing about any phase of your life. One memory leads to another and another and another and the anecdotes and people in your life come cascading back.

I had to make a decision early on about what I would write. I would love to have told you more about my parents, my siblings, my extended family and the many wonderful friends I have had throughout my life. But I wanted even more to tell you about the many changes which occurred from the time I was born in 1920 until the present 2006. More advances have been made in technology, science, politics, economics, health care, religion and social changes than in any other span of eighty-six years in the history of the world. It has been fascinating to be a part of this development so I have chosen to tell about how these changes and the major events like World War II have impacted my life.

Because I made that choice it meant that I did not develop the characters of many people who were very important to me. I also did not try to describe the places or beautiful scenery I was privileged to see because I could not do it adequately even if I tried. Instead my book is pretty much anecdotal and is intended to tell you something about my life and times. It is my story based on my experiences related to the social changes, politics, religion and the technological changes that touched my life directly.

I mention people in the book who have influenced me greatly. Many real names are included, but if I tell personal experiences, I use fictitious names. Many of these people are no longer living and I have lost track of many others. The book is not a picture of all the changes in the world but just a snapshot of what has happened to me. It's been a great life!

My good friends, Mary Joy and Jerre Stead, and my grandson, Michael Bankoff, have given me lots of encouragement. I gave them the first part of what I wrote and they kept encouraging me to write more. As I gave them additional parts, they would always say, "Keep going." Without them this might have been just a story of how I grew up in Parkersburg, Iowa. Thanks Mary Joy, Jerre and Michael!

I also want to thank my daughter, Nancy Miller, for editing the whole thing. It was a daunting task. And thanks to my daughter, Mary Bankoff, for coming up with a name for it. Much appreciation to Linda Radke and all the great folks at Five Star Publications, Inc.

Mildred Norman
June 2006

HENRY'S DAUGHTER
Introduction

A few years ago when Ben, my youngest grandson was ten, I told him that we ate a lot of popcorn when we were kids. He gave me a very quizzical look and said, "Gran, I didn't know you had a microwave." I thought, this kid doesn't have a clue about how we lived. I really ought to tell him about it before I die because I have had a very interesting life. It covers a span of Americana that should not be lost for my descendants because there will never be another time like it.

Let me start by briefly covering the whole territory. I was born and raised in Parkersburg, Iowa – a small town of 1200 souls if we were all at home. We called it P'Burg and lustily sang our school song which was *On Dear P'Burg*, to the tune of *On Wisconsin*. My birthdate was February 6, 1920 so you can figure out this huge number if you have a calculator.

My father, Henry Dresselhuis, was a blacksmith who emigrated to the United States from Holland when he was twenty-one years old. My mother, Grace, was born in Iowa; both of her parents were German immigrants. There were ten children in our family, but one son was stillborn, one son died at three months, and a third son died at eighteen months. The survivors were what my father called his "one and a half dozen children" – one son and a half dozen girls.

While I was growing up, going to college was a given. Dad started many conversations with, "When you go to college…" Becoming a first grade teacher was always a goal and I wanted to get married and have a family.

But I never dreamed that I would have three careers or would live in eight states and Germany. In my wildest imagination I never thought that a Rockefeller would be my friend, or that I would play bridge with two of the Nurenburg trial judges, or that I would attend a party in Berlin for General Lucius Clay. It didn't occur to me that I would someday be elected to public office, or that politics would play a major role in my life. Meeting governors, a president, a vice president, generals or a burghermeister would have been fantasy.

We thought World War I was the war that ended all wars, so we didn't foresee the biggest war in history, nor did we have the slightest clue about how technology would change our world. Living in the twentieth century has been exciting, eventful, horrific, dynamic, challenging and always interesting. I hope you enjoy reading about it.

CHAPTER ONE
Growing Up in Parkersburg

Our family was considered "Dutch" because my father came from Holland. There were only five Dutch families in P'Burg and the surrounding community, and practically all of the rest were Germans. We were rather typical of communities all over the Midwest, except that there were also Swedes, Norwegians and Danes in surrounding states like Minnesota and Illinois. We were one hundred percent Anglo-Saxon, with two Jewish families, which meant nothing to me. The only hint of prejudice in Parkersburg was the notion that being Dutch was better than German because of World War 1, no doubt. My dad always marveled at the wonderful "melting pot" in the United States.

We were the Dresselhuis family, and we lived in a two story white frame house with a basement, just one block off Main Street. The downstairs and the upstairs combined probably didn't consist of more than 1200 square feet but the nine of us didn't question its adequacy. It was home. We could cut through the driveway between the Blair's and McDowell's, and across the alley and be downtown in less than a minute. The school was one block south of us and our church just three blocks northeast. We knew every house and every family in town. My sister, Frannie, can still relate who lived where and even track a succession of families in the rental properties.

My mother was pregnant nine times in fifteen years. My sister, Etta, was born in 1909, my brother, George, in 1910 and my sister, Gertrude, in 1911. During the next six years one son named Edward was stillborn and another son, also named Edward was born but died when he was eighteen months old. (They were named for my dad's father, Eddo.) We heard the story about him many times. He had the measles, and probably pneumonia. Dad came home in the middle of the afternoon to see how he was doing. He and Mama had a cup of tea and then went in to check on him. Little Edward was sleeping, but as they watched, he threw back his hand and was dead. They never got over grieving for him.

My sister, Edene, was next in line. She was born in 1917. I came along three years later in 1920. Twins, Alyce and Edward, were born in 1921 but Edward died when he was three months old. He had been very small and sickly from birth. Following Dr. Bruechert's advice, Mama had repeatedly soaked him in olive oil and fed him goat's milk, but he didn't make it. I think I remember a small coffin with the baby, which sat on our dining room table, but I was only a year and a half old at the time. Our baby sister, Frances, was born in 1924. And so we had a family of nine people in that small house.

The seven children were always referred to by our parents as "the three big ones" and "the four little ones." That six year gap between the two groups (when two children died) made the division very reasonable. Once when we were snowed in and had nothing better to do, we figured out that the initials of the three big ones from the top down spelled "EGG" – Etta, Gertrude, George. The four little ones from the bottom up spelled "FAME" – Frannie, Alyce, Mildred and Edene. The EGG group was so much older that they all graduated and left home when I was still very young so I don't really have as many memories of them as I do of our FAME group.

Our Town

With seven churches we were a very religious community. Our entire family could be found in the Christian Reformed Church whenever the doors were opened. We also had Methodists, Baptists, Catholics, two breeds of Lutherans – the regulars and a Missouri Synod kind, and even a Congregational church, although we were never quite sure if they were really Christians. In spite of all that, we also bore a slight resemblance to *Peyton Place*.

To know our town, you had to know Main Street. It was an important aspect of our social life. In the wintertime the stores were open on Saturday night, but in the summer they also opened on Wednesday nights. In the winter, especially if the roads were bad, just the men folk came to town. But in the summer the whole family came in to trade their eggs at one of the two grocery stores for staples like sugar, flour, or baking soda – whatever food they didn't grow or raise on the farm. The men folk took care of their "business" (the eggs), and then the sinners among them would go to the pool hall. The church goers sat in the back of the store, sat on the curbs out front or stood in clusters on the corners. They all talked and watched the people go by.

The mothers with their babies and young children stayed in the cars which were parked head first to the curb and watched the people. Married women without children also had to stay in the cars or they would be deemed to be "street walkers." In town most of the men worked in the stores or

3

businesses. The majority of women, unless they were pregnant, sick or too old also took part in the festivities. They would go down to "pick up a few groceries," but they really went to socialize and to hear the latest gossip.

The kids and teenagers loved those Wednesday and Saturday nights the most. On Saturday evening, you'd get all dressed up, meet your best friends and then just walk up and down the street, talking and watching all the sights. After the crops were sold in the fall, some of the farmers would buy new cars. Sometimes our banker would be standing on the corner in front of the bank. "There goes John Schmidt in his new Ford. He doesn't even know he's broke." But the banker knew he had just spent all of the corn crop money without paying back the loan for his seed corn.

Wednesday nights were even better. If you were anybody at all, you played in the band. We had a bandstand on wheels, which was usually parked right next to the water tank just off Main Street. Every Wednesday afternoon the Mayor would round up a bunch of men and they would drag the bandstand out into the intersection on Main Street. Everybody in our family played in the band. My dad would leave work early so we could eat in time for all of us to be at the schoolhouse by six-thirty. We had uniforms. They consisted of white starched pants, a white shirt (also starched) with a red handkerchief in the pocket, and topped off with a red and white sailor hat, with a crease in the top. Later we added red capes with white linings.

All day Wednesday we would be ironing pants and shirts – mama washed them for us. Occasionally someone left the red handkerchief in their pocket, and the whole wash load of pants and shirts would come out bright pink. That meant a trip to the grocery store for Clorox. It also meant the whole contingent from our family looked pretty pink the next Wednesday. It took about four weeks of repeated Cloroxing for it to gradually disappear.

At least four Dresselhuis kids played in the band at the same time. We would eat early, get all dressed up in our uniforms and go up to the school. We'd get our instruments and music, and then congregate on the corner. Miss Townsend, our director would get us all in perfect alignment and we would march down the hill to the bandstand. Our town was bounded on the southern edge by Highway 20, which was up the hill. The whole town sloped downhill, and the school was about midway. Downtown was further down the hill, and the railroad track on the northern edge of town was way down the hill.

The band concert was a really big deal. All the farmers, townspeople and everyone's kids gathered around the bandstand. We played a variety of King marches, medleys of popular and semi-classical tunes, and occasionally, if we had practiced hard enough on Monday night, we would play John Philip Sousa's *Stars and Stripes Forever*. It was a real crowd favorite, but a terrible workout for those, like me, who played the clarinet.

We didn't know the word "culture" in P'Burg, but I guess those band concerts were as close as we got, except for the high school orchestra, which performed at special occasions in the wintertime. We also gave junior and senior high school plays, had an all high school operetta every year, plus declamatory contests annually. You volunteered and had to memorize a dramatic or humorous "oration." The English teacher was the sponsor and she coached you. She also chose a board of judges. The declamatory contest was a very popular public event. I always volunteered and learned my "piece," but I would be a nervous wreck standing backstage on the night of the performance. I would pray that I would make it out to the big X marked in the middle of the stage and please, dear God, don't let me forget the words with all the movements and gestures Miss Myers had taught me. I always did humorous pieces and sometimes I won or placed. My brother, who later became a lawyer, usually won the dramatic class during his days at P'Burg High.

Schools today could take a lesson from our school in Parkersburg because we used it from seven in the morning until nine at night. When I started school we were all in one building and we had a total of around 300 kids in grades one through twelve. Later, they added a kindergarten, but only our baby sister could take advantage of it. When I was in the fifth grade, a big new addition was built with a really nice gym and a stage. It was a two story affair and above the gym was a big assembly hall for the high school and several classrooms. The old and new buildings were connected – it was absolutely marvelous. The gym in the basement of the old building became a shop for the manual arts classes. Girls weren't allowed to take "shop" but my brother built a cedar chest which one of my sisters still has.

It must have been quite a juggling act to schedule all of our activities – and without a computer yet! The same kids played in the band, the orchestra, sang in the boys glee club, the girls glee club, the mixed glee club, they were the actors and actresses in the plays, the operettas, the declamatory contests, and they played on the girls basketball team, the boys basketball team, or the baseball team. We didn't have "after school programs" like they have now, but we had to be at some type of practice by quarter of eight every morning.

We stayed after school for basketball, baseball, or music group practices, and after supper we had practices for the plays, operettas or declamatory contests. In our family we couldn't go to anything at school on Thursday nights, because we had Catechism at church. The teachers were well aware of this – there were absolutely no exceptions, so they scheduled around it. Seven kids who participated in everything couldn't be ignored. It sounds like an impossible schedule, except the activities at school were the only attraction in town.

One big advantage in our family was that when you got to high school you no longer had to work in the garden. But starting in the seventh grade, you worked part time in Wayne's grocery store. It was during my stint at the grocery store that my sex life started. The store had a large basement where extra groceries were stored. If you needed something from the basement you went down a long flight of wooden steps and reached for the dangling cord to pull on the light.

We closed the store each evening at seven (except Wednesdays and Saturdays); it was dark by then in the wintertime. One night Wayne asked me about five minutes to seven if I would go down to the basement and turn off the light. I thought he was testing my courage, because occasionally, you saw a rat in the basement. I didn't want to look like a scaredy-cat so I said, "Sure." Proceeding very cautiously down the steps, I had no idea that Wayne was following me. Just as I reached the bottom of the stairs, he grabbed me and kissed me passionately. It scared me to death. I broke loose, ran up the stairs, grabbed my coat on the way through the store and ran all the way home.

I couldn't tell my mother or anyone what had happened but I was petrified. I thought that if a married man kissed you, you probably would have a baby. The timing was especially bad because a girl at our church – a Dutch girl yet – was having a baby, and she wasn't married. She was only sixteen years old, and she had been the hired girl at a farmhouse where the wife was dying of cancer. I had no

7

idea how all of this had happened, but my parents had been talking in Dutch in very low tones for months. We always knew it was some kind of gossip if my parents talked Dutch, and most of the Dutch language we learned was from our eagerness to figure out what they were saying.

I watched my stomach for months with great fear and trepidation. I had seen hundreds of pregnant women at church – everybody had big families and my mother would always announce at Sunday dinner who was newly pregnant. She had this uncanny ability to discern it about eight months before the birth. No one will ever know how much agony I secretly endured, before I finally decided there was no baby in my stomach.

Another bastion of culture in our town was the movie house which had movies on Friday and Saturday. As Christian Reformers, we were taught from the cradle on that movies were the work of the devil. When I walked past the movie house I would stay near the curb as far from the building as possible. I worried about the Hunnerbergs who owned the movie house. They were a very nice family and I didn't want them to miss out on heaven. I never really thought about what was happening in there until I was in the sixth grade. My sister Gertrude was home from college for the weekend and she told me that if I had a quarter she'd take me down and we'd sneak into the show. So much for the devil; I had a quarter and I couldn't wait to do it.

At seven we told my mother we were going over to Smutney's. They had one daughter my sister's age and one my age. I was so excited that I don't remember that the lie bothered me a bit. The movie house was right in the middle of Main Street on the left hand side. It was Saturday night so I stood guard looking for people from our church while my sister bought the tickets – ten cents each and a nickel profit for her. We entered the movie house and the very first thing

I saw was *Rebecca of Sunnybrook Farm*. I couldn't believe my eyes. I stood stock still as if I were frozen. Rebecca was riding in a carriage and the big wheels were going around and around. She was talking out loud!

My sister pushed me into this dark space and maneuvered me around until I was sitting in a chair. It wasn't until afterward that I learned there were rows of red seats on either side of an aisle and the seats folded up and down. During the show I was utterly fascinated. I couldn't believe what was happening. I wept at Rebecca's trials and tribulations, and was absolutely enthralled when it all ended happily. It was the most stunning moment of my life.

Occasionally, we would have special cultural events from the outside world. Sometimes a hypnotized man sat in the drugstore window, and everyone in town would go by to see him. We would try and get his attention by pounding on the window, waving and yelling, but he would be transfixed – nothing could distract him. It was quite amazing.

Sometimes the Chautauqua would come to town offering lectures and performances by well-known people. A big tent would be set up on the school playground or in a field on the edge of town. They were quite popular. When I was only a baby, Dad took my brother George to hear William Jennings Bryan. George was only nine years old at the time but when they walked away he asked Dad, "What does Mr. Bryan do for a living?" When Dad told him he was a lawyer, George said, "That's what I'm going to do when I grow up." And he did.

Years later, when William Jennings Bryan died, my dad made a special trip home at ten in the morning to tell my mother. Mrs. Oelman, our elderly neighbor, was sitting on her porch as usual – keeping track of the neighborhood. She called to my dad, "Henry, what are you doing home at this time of day?"

"I came to tell Grace that William Jennings Bryan died."

She said, "Oh, he must have lived north of town. We always lived south."

There was no airport anywhere near Parkersburg in the 1920s, but about once each summer, a biplane would fly over town and a man would do stunts on the lower wing. Everyone would come running out of their houses over this miraculous event. It was akin to the halftime shows at the Super Bowl today – really special. That's about all of the culture I can remember in Parkersburg.

The Sporting Life

Sports were also a big part of our lifestyle in P'Burg, and, of course, they centered on our high school. In the fall and spring the boys played baseball. They played the teams of the other high schools in the county, but I remember them primarily as a terrible embarrassment. Our family owned three lots which adjoined the baseball field up on the highway. My dad dug up every inch of those lots and planted a huge garden every year. We all had to work in the garden which put us in full view of the high school boys, who practiced and played, so I never appreciated baseball as a child. The players probably didn't even notice us, but we were humiliated.

However, in spite of the embarrassing moments, gardening had its upside. I didn't think so at the time, but it really was quite a sight to watch Dad push the fork in deep along a hill of potatoes, and then turn it over exposing seven or eight potatoes. We would crouch down on our hands and knees, pick up the potatoes, shake off the soft black dirt and put them in a small pile. Then we would follow Dad and crawl down to the next potato hill.

We'd work until dark in the fall and then load up our loot

in the very ungainly coaster wagon Dad had made for us and start the procession toward home, about four blocks away. The baseball players would be long gone by then. We'd cross the highway and look longingly toward the filling station. If Dad had sufficient cash on hand, and he usually did in the fall, we would stop at the station where they had candy bars and pop for sale for five cents each. We would each get to spend a nickel, and it was agonizing to decide whether we wanted the delicious, thirst quenching pop or the delicious sweet candy. You could choose between Babe Ruth, Hershey or Butterfinger. Personally, it wasn't too hard for me. To this day I would choose chocolate anytime, anywhere even if I were out in the desert dying of thirst.

Gardens were a very real part of our environment in P'Burg. Everyone had one in their back yard – we had no apartments or condos. Even the retired farmers had huge gardens. They would plant enough potatoes in long, long rows to last the whole year. Everyone planted enough vegetables to be able to can in Mason jars what they couldn't eat during the summer months. We all strung green beans with a needle and a double strand of thread and hung them up on the back porch to dry. They would last through the winter. We also cut up the extra cabbages and put them with alternating layers of salt into big crocks which were kept in the basement. We did the same thing with beans which we "snippled" – that's a Dutch word for what we now call a "French cut."

Potatoes, carrots and turnips were kept in piles on the basement floor. They were somewhat shriveled by spring but we ate them anyway. We were lucky in our family because we had "the lots," so Dad didn't have a very big garden at home – just lettuce, radishes and green onions. It meant we had a place to play.

We had basketball at P'Burg High School and everyone

11

loved it. People came from near and far to witness the games. It would take a three day blizzard, six feet of snow and below zero weather before anyone even thought of canceling a game. If the snow plows could get through, we played. My brother was just entering high school when I started first grade, and he played in the old gym in the basement. There were bleachers at one end which seated about twenty-five people. Most of the townspeople were crowded around the edges or out in the hall. Both the boys and girls had teams, and one year my sister Edene was on the team that won the State Championship! The whole town went crazy.

I never saw a black person until I was six years old when a work crew laid the pavement on the street in front of our house. A black man named Jim was on the crew. All of the children would run alongside the workers fascinated by what they were doing. Jim would proudly show us his right hand which had two thumbs on it. I thought all blacks had two thumbs until I was in the fourth grade.

My oldest sister, Etta, was working in Des Moines when I was in the fourth grade. My two younger sisters and I were thrilled to visit her apartment for a week in the summer. This was a really big deal because we seldom left Parkersburg and a big city like Des Moines was almost beyond our comprehension.

On Saturday she took us down to tour the State Capitol. The gold dome and marble steps were quite impressive. A group of about twenty black children arrived at the same time we did for the tour. We were utterly fascinated at the sight of such small colored people. We followed them in awe and tried to check their hands for a second thumb. I was confused when none of them had one, but rightly concluded that Jim must have been different.

My next encounter with Negroes (that's what we called them then) was when I was in high school. I would occasionally go to Waterloo with my date on Friday night to go to the show. They had Negroes who worked in the Rath Packing Plant and the John Deere factory, so I learned that they were rather ordinary in the big cities. It never occurred to me that they might have special problems. Probably because of Dad's "melting pot" mentality, I never felt any prejudice. It was just a difference, but it certainly didn't matter.

However, we had our own brand of prejudice. The "town folk" looked down on the "country kids" when they first came to high school. They had all gone to one-room country schools through the eighth grade, and they carried their lunch in a brown paper sack. We didn't say or do anything against them, but we certainly didn't accept them. Assuming they didn't know much, we simply ignored them.

Everyone had their own circle of friends and the country kids weren't a part of ours. It probably took them a year or two to find their niche. We gradually included most of them, but if they weren't extroverts, really smart or good athletes they may have never found it. We just didn't notice – a lot like prejudice today.

Cars were a rather scarce commodity in P'Burg when I was very young. I remember that we still had posts in front of the churches and on Main Street so that horses could be tied up. Most of the Christian Reformers were farmers and as a very small child I remember the horses tied up in front of the church stamping their feet in the snow and snuffling loudly. They were very impressive. Gradually they disappeared and were all gone by the time I was in junior high.

Almost everyone walked wherever they had to go which wasn't that hard since Parkersburg was probably six blocks long from the north to the south and eight or ten blocks wide from east to west. It was only the richest ones who had cars and they only used them for occasional trips out of town. The family across the street owned the Ford garage and they even made a trip to California in their car one summer! Two of our neighbors were retired farmers and they had cars. The men would go out to the farms they still owned once or twice a week to check on the renters.

Aunt Minnie lived in Cedar Falls, which was eighteen miles away, and she had a black Model A Ford. We knew when she was coming because when she turned off the highway on the south side of town and started coming down the hill, she would put on the brakes. You would hear this loud whirring sound which gradually decreased as she went slower and slower, and then ended when she came to an abrupt stop right in front of the house. When she left, one of us would help her "start" the car. This meant you put the crank in a shaft just below the radiator, gave it one big turn at a time until it started the engine at which time you jumped out of the way lest you get run over!

Uncle Albert had a Whippet that was the joy of his life. Occasionally my dad would pay him fifty cents or a dollar to take us somewhere – usually to the Bible Conference at Cedar Falls in the summertime, or to see Aunt Ada and Uncle Ole, who lived near Wellsburg about twenty miles away. We loved those trips, although Uncle Albert was a real showoff, and we had some pretty harrowing rides. Uncle Albert's wife died before I was born and left him with three small children. Aunt Minnie took baby Gertrude to live with her, but Uncle Albert remained on the farm with Edward and Lyda. When Edward was eighteen and Lyda was twenty-one, Uncle Albert sold the farm and they moved to town.

Uncle Albert didn't see that an education was necessary but my Dad insisted that Edward and Lyda go to high school. It was difficult for them, but they always came to our house to do their homework and they both graduated. In fact, Lyda got her Ph.D. and became a professor at the

University of Minnesota in Duluth, and Edward had a very successful career in the Army.

Sometimes we would go with Mama on the train to see Aunt Ida and Uncle Harm in the tiny town of Stout. I remember that it cost twelve cents each way, and apparently one child could go free because only one of us could go per trip. Stout was on the Illinois Central and it was a very short walk from the train station to Aunt Ida's house. Uncle Harm was always sitting in the doorway of the front porch smoking his pipe. His feet would be propped up on the porch railing and you had to step over them to get into the house. He was friendly but he never moved. He kept his eyes on the bank down on the corner. He was a director and probably a part owner. He kept track of every single person who entered or left the bank and if he couldn't figure out why they were there he would walk down and find out.

Aunt Ida was wonderful. She had been married previously with five children, and they lived on a farm. When the youngest child was just a baby, her husband didn't come in for supper one evening, so she took a lantern and went to the barn. He was dead – hanging from a rafter. She had to sell the farm and go live in nearby Stout, where she worked as a "hired girl" doing housework and taking care of children. She met Harm, whose wife had died in childbirth and left him with eight small children. They married and she raised the whole bunch of them. Aunt Ida was always smiling and laughing and never had anything but good things to say about Uncle Harm and the whole bunch of kids.

FIRE!

We were a very law-abiding community. Apparently, citizens pretty much looked after each other in the daytime, but we had a Night Marshall, Mr. Lumley. I'm not sure what he did, except that he would stay around Main Street most of the time. It was one block long with stores on both sides. Often he would be in the pool hall until it closed. I guess that is where all the crooks were – everyone knew it was a den of iniquity. I followed the same pattern as when I walked by the movie house, walking on the curb as far from the building as possible. If I were feeling especially brave, I might sneak a look over my shoulder to see what kind of sinfulness was going on in there. I never saw anything except our town drunks and ne'er-do-wells playing pool, but I assumed it was an awful place.

The Night Marshall would go into high gear whenever we had a fire. Mary, the telephone operator, would be notified by a frantic family member. She had control of the fire whistle and she would set off five alarms if the fire were in town and six blasts if it were in the country. Mr. Lumley would hear it and go into action immediately. He would hurry over and open the fire station. Meanwhile Mary would call the volunteers. Not all of them had telephones, but they would hear the whistle. The sound of that whistle – especially the ones at night – also sent our family into high gear.

Fires during the night were among the very most exciting things that happened in Parkersburg. In snow, sleet, rain or good weather everyone in our family would jump out of bed and into whatever clothes were nearby and we'd take off. My dad was at the head of the pack and my mother stayed home to make cocoa for our return. It probably started when there were only a few children, and you had to be six or seven years old to be eligible to attend the fire. I'm sure Dad really missed those excursions when we finally all left the nest.

We never owned a car so we went on foot. If the fire was in town, we'd start for the downtown fire station, but sometimes the fire truck had left the station before we got organized and we would see it coming up the hill, and we'd follow it. It was so old and decrepit that we had no trouble keeping up with it. In fact, sometimes it broke down and we had to help push it, or other times there would be so much snow on the road that we had to push to keep it moving. If it was navigating on its own, we'd find out where the fire was and by cutting through neighborhoods, we usually could beat it to the scene.

We only lived a block from the downtown fire station so we often made it to the station before they took off. If it was icy, they couldn't back it down out of the station because the driveway was on a slope. We might have to throw sand or try and hold it back as they rolled it down.

Town fires were especially sad because we always knew the people. Thankfully, injuries were rare, and no one ever died in a fire in Parkersburg. If it was a night fire in the winter time, whole families would be running around in the snow and freezing cold. It must have looked comical. Screaming women with their hair in curlers, worried men, older couples and children in their nightgowns were all a familiar sight. "Two-ton Tina" rushed out of her kitchen with a pan of milk, threw it out on the snow, and then went back into the burning house to replace the empty pan on the kitchen table!

The children were always the first concern, and neighbors took them in. Retrieving clothes, bedding, pictures and furniture was the next priority. Dad made us stay back unless we were high school age. All of this happened before the fire truck got there.

When the fire truck arrived, we all greeted it with whoops and hollers and stepped back to let the fireman take over. Usually the house was practically gone by then. These fires often started from overheated stove pipes. The men folks had huge decisions to make about just how much fire to leave in their pot bellied stove on nights when the temperature might drop to thirty below zero. Some mornings our water pipes froze, and we often had thick frost on the interiors of all of the windows, but our house never burned down. We did have a fire once, but that is another story.

If the fire was in the country, it was a different routine. We would call Mary, the telephone operator, and ask where it was. Sometimes we just couldn't go but my Dad knew the territory very well and he would know how close the farm was to the railroad track. If it were possible to get there, we would all run two blocks down the hill to the railroad station. We would find the handcar which was always parked there, move it to the proper track, jump on and take off. It had a big handle you had to push back and forth to make it go. We would take turns on level ground, coast down the hills and pump hard, even getting off to push going up hill. Sometimes we would go five or six miles to a fire.

All the men smoked in those days, and often the fires started from cigarettes or pipes. Sometimes lanterns were mistakenly left behind in the barn and started fires when they blew over. In the summertime, fires might start from internal combustion in the haystacks. The fire truck may or may not make it depending on the distance and the condition of the roads but often the volunteers would come in their cars and try to help. If it was a haystack or a hay barn you just stayed back and watched it burn. If it was the big barn the whole emphasis was on getting the animals out. My Dad was especially good at this because he had an affinity for animals, especially horses. If it was the house, it was the same routine as in town.

Fortunately, we didn't have more than one or two big fires a year but they were so impressive that I still have vivid memories or them. Things are so entirely different now but to this day every time I see a fire truck I have a terrible urge to chase it.

Our House

We thought our house was truly "modern" because we had running water (cold only), electricity and an indoor bathroom. The running water was there before I was born, but I can dimly remember when I was about four, they strung the electric wires for our electricity. I was in the fourth grade when we got the bathroom. Sitting on that stool for the first time was lovely – quite an improvement over going to the "outhouse," the two-holer located about fifty feet behind our house. Daytimes weren't so bad, but I remember that rain or snow we each had to make a trip out there before we went to bed. It was probably psychological, but we never had to go during the night!

We couldn't get the bathroom until my brother went to college. We just had four small bedrooms for the nine of us, but he always had his own private bedroom – something I never attained. When all of us were at home, Mama and Dad had one room, George had the second one, my two oldest sisters had the third and we four little ones had the fourth. We had two double beds with barely an aisle between them.

The advantage was that we had lots of fun jumping from one bed to the other. Sometimes this caused the slats to be displaced and the mattress fell down. It was quite a job to lift the mattress and get the slats back in place. Often Mama would hear the commotion and shout from below, "Girls get in bed!" Each bedroom had a tiny closet for four girls to share, which was no problem since we had so few clothes. But we were happy and the world continued to turn.

My parents often had friends or neighbors in for coffee in the evenings. Before television this was a very common practice. Sometimes we four little ones would sneak down the stairs as quietly as possible to see and hear what was going on. We'd take turns peeking around the corner of the stairway. If Dad saw us, he'd just look away, but my mother would sternly order us back to bed.

My fondest memory is all of us around the dining room table. We ate two meals a day there, dinner and supper seven days a week. We did our homework there, and we played countless games of Monopoly, Rook and Old Maid there. All the neighbor kids came, and Mama made cocoa and sometimes popcorn for us. For some reason, regular playing cards were banned – we never learned to play bridge. I guess it was because of their association with gambling that they were considered evil. We never questioned it.

In the evening Dad would usually be in his place by the kitchen table. He would help Mama by peeling the potatoes, apples or carrots for our next day's meal, and he always read the *Waterloo Daily Courier* (except during the Depression when we couldn't afford it). On Thursdays the church paper, *The Banner*, would arrive in the mail and he read it cover to cover.

At least three or four nights a week Father Mauer would join Dad and sit across the table. Father Mauer was the Catholic Priest who lived on the corner two doors away from us. He and Dad could talk for hours; he'd usually still be there when the rest of us went to bed. They loved to talk about politics and religion. As good friends, they respected each other in spite of all their differences.

Dad loved to read. At least once a week, two or three of us would go to the library and get books for him. He would read in *The Banner* about special books he wanted – books like Spurgeon's sermons, which were about 800 pages long and weighed a ton. He would write down exactly what he wanted, and we would give the slips of paper to Mrs. Chamberlain, the librarian. She would usually have to order the book, and in about two weeks, it would arrive. She probably spent a large portion of her budget on Dad's books, but she never complained. Dad probably read more books than any other person in town and might have been the best educated, in spite of his lack of formal training. The day I graduated from college it occurred to me that Dad knew a lot more than I did.

Mama also enjoyed reading, although she never had much time. The romance novels were her favorites; she loved Grace Livingston Hill and Kathleen Norris. We strongly suspected that Dad read them, too, but we could never prove it.

One of our favorite pastimes as kids was "trading." One of the sisters would say, "Let's trade," and we'd all run to our respective hiding places and retrieve our treasures. We'd have an assortment of things like a pair of beads, a bracelet, a fur muff, a pretty shell, or even a piece of candy. Frannie had a small round red purse with a little chain on it. Edene had a bright red silk scarf and we could bargain for hours as we traded back and forth. Once in awhile especially after Christmas or a birthday some new items would appear but usually it was the same old stuff we traded back and forth. The little red purse might change hands several times but eventually Frannie would get it back and Edene would periodically get the red silk scarf. I would trade anything and everything for a piece of chocolate, even a dried up piece of fudge. (Mama occasionally made fudge but unfortunately it was usually either too hard or too soft). When I went to college I was quite a good debater, probably because of the skills I honed in those trading sessions.

In the summertime Mama would send us to Dad's shop with a syrup pail of coffee in the morning and in the afternoons a pail of tea. Sometimes he would reach in his pocket and divide the pennies he had among us. We would go to Mrs. Christopher's Restaurant and buy candy. She had a counter in the front of the restaurant with row after row of penny candy. You could buy a licorice pipe for a penny, two chocolate stars for a penny, six white hearts with "Love Me" or "I love you" written in red on them, a penny gum ball or any number of other goodies. It would take forever to make your big decision but she never ran out of patience. She was the combination cook, server and cashier; she might look over her glasses at her waiting customers, but she never admonished us and we were completely oblivious to how busy she was.

When I was in the third grade, Etta bought our first radio. She had graduated from high school and was working to save money to go to college. It really was a wonderful thing for her to do but at first I hated it. It sat against the wall in the living room and when we first turned it on the static was terrible. I was scared of it and wished they would haul it away. Alyce, Frannie and I hid out, but the rest of them figured out how to hook up the antenna and it settled down and was really quite nice. It soon became a very important part of our lives. Dad absolutely loved Henry Aldrich and *Amos and Andy*, laughing until he cried. We all enjoyed *Fibber McGee and Molly* but the really big show was the *Firestone Hour* on Wednesday night.

Dad would come home from work early, and after supper, we all gathered in the living room. We could hardly bear the ecstasy when Thomas L. Thomas started by singing, *If I Should Tell You How Much I Love You*. Years later when I was singing in the Valley Presbyterian Church choir in Scottsdale, Arizona, Thomas L. Thomas was a winter visitor one Sunday. He was a friend of our choir director. After church the girl next to me said, "Did you ever hear of Thomas L. Thomas? He's the man talking to Ralph." I swooned.

A grown woman in my forties, I was still overwhelmed. I staggered out to him and jabbered, "Oh Mr. Thomas, you have no idea how our family loved you." I went on and on and all the time I was circling around them babbling. I made a complete fool of myself, but he just smiled and nodded and kept talking to Ralph. I was so happy!

On Saturday afternoon we often listened to Opera. The big orchestra impressed me the most. On Sunday afternoons Dad would listen to Father Coughlin, a pretty radical priest from Detroit, I think. I'm sure Dad didn't agree with him at all, but he found him very interesting.

Our Meals

All of our meals started and ended with a long prayer from Dad. The opening prayer was in Dutch and the closing one in English. We were supposed to keep our eyes closed, but we would sneak looks to check out what we were going to eat and would hope that Dad would say "Amen" before it got too cold. He always prayed for the "Yerden, Eirotten and Hottentotts." Translated that is "the Jews, the Heathen and the Hottentotts." When I acquired a Jewish son-in-law years later, I told him that the reason he was so wonderful was because Dad had prayed for him long before he was born. I didn't question it at the time, but I guess it was because of the Boer War in South Africa, that the Hottentotts were included. Clearly, the Jews and the Heathen were Biblical.

After supper, before the closing prayer, Dad also read an entire chapter of the Bible. We liked it when he turned the huge Bible toward the back because most of the chapters in the New Testament are shorter. The Old Testament was okay if he stayed with Psalms or Proverbs, because many of them are short, but Isaiah had interminable chapters, and if he turned to the front we knew we would hear endless lists of unpronounceable names. If he thought our minds were wandering, he would ask one of us to tell him what he had read. If we didn't know, we had to stay after and read the whole chapter for ourselves. We were glad if we had play practice, a basketball game or Catechism, because he would skip the questions.

Our food did not vary very much. It was probably standard for all the families in town – maybe in the whole Midwest. We had our big meal at noon. We always had potatoes with fresh vegetables in the summer and in the winter the snippled or dried beans, the sauerkraut from the crocks in the basement or the corn or kale which my mother had hot packed during the summer in Mason jars. We had very little fruit, except for apples. Everyone had at least one apple tree and my mother used them in a variety of ways. We had applesauce on the table for practically every meal. Once in awhile she would make Waldorf salad with apples, walnuts from our tree and a mayonnaise she made herself.

Our meat was almost always side pork – a fatty kind of bacon which was cut in thick slices and fried. We called it "speck." Occasionally a farmer would give Dad a chicken, and Mama would make wonderful chicken and dumplings. If the butcher had liver, he would give it away so sometimes we would have it. For dessert we had baked apples or some kind of pudding – tapioca, rice, chocolate or bread pudding, except on Sundays when we had Pie!

Suppers were almost always the same – fried potatoes, fried eggs and fried side pork. If there were no leftovers, Mama would make soup. It was usually made from dried peas or beans and was really very good – I still make both kinds. Occasionally, it was "calmalkbrey" a concoction made from barley and buttermilk. We put dark Karo syrup in it when we ate it, but I still don't like it. My sister, Edene, in Grand Rapids made it for me last week. It's only tolerable if you put at least a half cup of syrup into each serving. It's

amazing how healthy we have all been. Our plain food undoubtedly was better for us than all of the fast foods kids
eat today.

The best part of our meal was the conversation, not the
food. We'd talk about our daily activities – mostly school,
but we weren't allowed to criticize our teachers. Dad would
say, "Just listen to them. That's how you learn." But our big
discussions were about politics. My earliest memories are
about Al Smith who was running against Herbert Hoover.
That was in 1928 so I was eight years old. I remember Dad
predicting, "He'll never win because he is a Catholic," and
he was right.

My most vivid memories are of our endless discussions
about Franklin Delano Roosevelt. I was twelve years old
when he was first elected, and he was still President years
after I graduated from college. We talked about him inces-
santly. The "New Deal" was a very big deal for us. We dis-
sected the farm plans, the PWA (Public Works Administration), the REA (Rural Electrical Administration), the CCC
(Civilian Conservation Corps), and bank closures. Dad
didn't express his opinions very often, but he always started
arguments. And he would always throw in, "When you go
to college." He revered education; it was always a given that
we would go to college even when we didn't have a penny to
our names. He really appreciated being an American citizen
and education and politics were an important part of it.

Mama wasn't particularly interested in all this talk. In
the summertime when the windows were open she would
say, "Don't talk so loud. The neighbors will think we are
fighting." To this day we all still love politics. Some of the
highlights of my life have revolved around my involvement
with politics.

Sunday dinners were so special. Dad would do the
shopping on Saturday night. His trip to the grocery store

was momentous because he would pay the grocery bill for the week. If it was a big enough bill, the store owner would give him a sack of assorted candies. When we were little, that was one of the biggest events of the week.

If any of us know any diplomacy today, it is because of the skills we learned in dividing up that candy. Mama would not allow us to fight over it or she would confiscate it, and dole it out piece by piece during the next week as rewards for being especially good. So we had to be able to talk ourselves into getting what we most coveted. For me it was always chocolate. If there was only one piece of chocolate in the whole bag I would surrender my rights to everything else. Sometimes I might even throw in some unrelated treasure I had in the bargaining process. Because of my enthusiasm for chocolate I probably got taken many times but I still don't regret it.

Dad also visited the butcher shop every Saturday night. He would come home with a huge piece of beef, which would completely cover a large platter, which we called "the meat platter." We were always impressed when he would announce, "That cost seventy-five cents!" My sister, Edene, remembers a time when he came home from his shopping trip, deposited the groceries on the table and the meat on the platter. Then he reached into his pocket and drew out a dime which he also put on the table. "Look at that," he said, "we have every thing we need and I still have money left over!" That was my dad. How things have changed!

That piece of beef was the centerpiece of those spectacular Sunday dinners. After his shopping trip on Saturday night Dad would peel potatoes, carrots and onions for Mama. Early Sunday morning she would brown the meat, put it in a large roasting pan and surround it with the potatoes, carrots and onions which had resided in a large pot of cold water overnight. Until I was about ten years old, we had a coal burning cook stove which was all we had for cooking or heat in the kitchen. Dad would really have to "stoke" it up so the oven would stay warm while we were at Sunday school and church.

When we got home from church we would all help to "dish up." Mama made delicious gravy while the rest of us would set the table and get out the ever present applesauce. We also had fresh white and dark brown Dutch bread, which Mama had baked on Saturday. She also made pies on Saturday – apple, mincemeat, which she had canned herself, or custard. For a special treat, she would send one of us down to the basement to get a quart jar of pears or peaches that she had also canned. The number of jars available depended on how often Dad had been able to buy an overripe cheap lug on his Saturday night shopping trips during the fall months.

We never knew when he might be so fortunate, but when he could buy discounted fruit, we all had to go into high gear. The fruit had to be canned that same night, because it would be spoiled by Monday and, of course, we wouldn't can on Sunday. We all knew the routine. The empty Mason jars were brought up from the basement and washed in water heated in the tea kettle. The fruit had to be washed, then peeled, quartered or sliced. Mama boiled it with the exact amount of sugar, which only she could determine, and then put it into the jars and sealed. By the time we went to bed the jars were all lined up cooling off on the kitchen table. It was really special when we had them for Sunday dinner dessert the next winter.

One Saturday night I was really sick to my stomach and threw up several times. The next morning Mama decreed that I would stay home from church and Edene would stay with me. Actually, I had recovered by then, but I didn't argue. Shortly after everyone had departed for church, Edene and

27

I decided to go down to the basement and get a jar of pears. We thoroughly enjoyed eating them at first, but we still had lots left over by the time we were really full. However, we were forced to eat the whole jar or we would be caught with the evidence. When the family returned from church Mama was delighted that I had recovered. She said, "We'll celebrate. Edene, go down to the basement and get a jar of pears!"

Doing the dishes was a horrible chore. Mama put the tea kettle on while we ate, so we had hot water. We used her homemade soap – made out of lye and I don't know what else. There were two big pans – one to wash and one to rinse. These huge pans had to be hauled out from the "pantry" – two shelves at the top of the steps leading to the basement. When I was little, the two older sisters, Etta and Gertrude always did the dishes. Later it befell the little ones – the FAME group – to accomplish this horrendous task. There were three jobs – clear the table, wash the dishes, and dry, which had to be scheduled among the four of us so that it came out even. Dad figured out the rather complicated logistics. Actually, it wasn't that bad – we would do "girl talk" and every once in awhile Dad would say, "You mustn't talk about other people." But if we persisted in quieter voices he would say, "What did you say?" and we would remind him that he wasn't interested in gossip.

When my grandmother died, my grandfather came to live with us. Grandpa Bulthuis would sit in the chair next to the table, and Dad could retire to the living room to read the *Waterloo Courier*. Grandpa would regale us with stories of his youth. Gerrit Belthuis was my mother's father, born near Hamburg, Germany. When he was eighteen years old he wanted to marry a girl on a neighboring farm and go to America. Her father refused to allow his thirteen-year-old daughter to wed, so Grandpa went to sea! He sailed on a clipper ship across the Atlantic for five years. He would tell us about the storms, almost getting swept overboard or shipwrecked, about climbing up on the masts in the storms – even about trying to capture the peas as they rolled back and forth on their tin plates. At the end of the five years he went back to Germany, married my grandmother, and together they sailed for America. Like many other immigrants they went to Iowa because they had friends who had preceded them there.

Our Neighborhood

We had wonderful kids in our neighborhood. The McDowell's lived directly across the street from our house. They had two girls – one my age and one Gertrude's age. They had twin boys but they weren't born until I was in high school, so they were never part of our gang. The five Engelkes kids lived three houses south of the McDowell's. Their ages corresponded roughly to ours. Since their dad was the undertaker, there were often dead bodies in caskets in their living room. I always went through the back door when I went to their house and never went near the living room.

A few years ago my sister, Frannie, confided that she and Anna May, the youngest Engelkes, used to go in and hold funeral services for the dead. Frannie would play the piano, which was right next to the casket, Anna Mae would sing, and they would say comforting words about the dead and quote whatever Bible verses they knew. They would even rearrange the clothing or hair of the dead person. Mrs. Engelkes was a very hard working woman and she probably had no idea they were doing this.

The Bailey kids were also a part of our very tight group who constantly played together. There were two of them, a boy a year older than me and a girl Alyce's age. Down on the corner the Methodist preachers came and went, but the Pritchard family lasted the longest, and three of their five kids were a part of our gang.

In the summertime we played outdoors all of the time except when you had to do chores at home. One of our favorite games was Tin Can Off. We put a tin can on our cistern near our back door. One player would knock it off with a big stick and then the person who was "it" would run to retrieve it while all the rest of us ran to hide. The trick was to run in "free" while the "it" person was out looking for you. Another favorite was Simon Says. Everyone stood in a row with an "It" person out front. The "It" person would tell you to "take three steps forward" or "two steps back." If you remembered to say "May I?" you got to do it. If you forgot, you were penalized. The "It" person had unlimited power I guess. The person who crossed the finish line first was the winner.

We also played Count to Ten, Tag, Hopscotch and Annie Annie Over. Later we learned to play tennis. All of us "babysat" to earn money. We would earn between twenty-five and fifty cents for an evening or afternoon, and you not only took care of the children but you did dishes, ironed clothes, or did housework while you were there. The parents played bridge or drove to Waterloo for dinner and a show. But baby-sitting would earn the dollar or two you needed for a tennis racket. We also bought roller skates with our money. They cost about a dollar with four wheels and clamps, which fastened them to your shoes.

When we were in high school we had town tennis tournaments and one year Alyce and I won the championship. We could really serve those balls. When I went to college I learned you were supposed to circle the racket over your head before you brought it down to hit the ball. We didn't serve that way in Parkersburg. We just brought the racket straight up and then smacked it straight down but we could really serve a mean ball. I never could change.

In the winter time we played Fox and Geese. There was a big vacant lot next to the Bailey's house. I remember so well how gorgeous new snow looked if we went out early Saturday morning. We would get in a long line and then shuffle around in a big circle to make a path in the snow. The object of the game had something to do with getting into the middle of the circle. I don't remember the details but I do remember how beautifully the snow would glisten in the sunshine.

Modernizing our House

As we grew up our modern house became more and more modern. The bathroom was the real biggie – going from "outhouse" to "in-house" was nothing short of a miracle. And the "bath" situation also changed dramatically. Before the bathroom, we took baths in a big round tub which Mama brought up from the basement every Saturday night and put in the middle of the kitchen floor. She would fill not only the tea kettle but every available pot and pan with water late in the afternoon, and put them on the cook stove to heat the bath water. We all had baths, starting with Frannie, the youngest, and ending with Dad. Between baths Mama would dip out some of the water and add some hot water, but it never got completely changed. Mama would personally scrub you until you were eight or nine and then you got to do it yourself.

The wood burning cook stove was replaced by a gas stove. I missed the old cook stove. When we got up on cold winter mornings you could put your feet on the oven door and be warm and toasty as you put on your socks and shoes. Sometimes, when you came into the kitchen, there would be one of the pool hall regulars sitting by the oven with a cup of coffee. Dad would walk down to the Post Office every single day except Sundays. Occasionally, there would be a hung-over drunk who had not made it home the night before slumped in front of the pool hall half frozen. Dad would bring him home, thaw him out and send him home.

The old cook stove also had a tank on one end that heated our water, providing a constant supply. Mama always had irons on the top of the stove which she used almost daily to keep our clothes ironed. She had one handle and three irons. One was used until it cooled off, and then was replaced with a hot one. She must have gotten an electric iron at the same time she got the new stove.

When you graduated from the fourth grade girls had to iron at least one night a week after school. We all hated it. Maybe that's why we volunteered for every play, musical group, or athletic team that came along. If you got home early you probably had to iron! To this day I avoid ironing. If it doesn't come out of the dryer ready to wear or I can't send it to the dry cleaner, forget it.

Mama was so proud of that new stove. Its main attribute was that it was clean – no more ashes all over the place, no pails of cobs and coal, no bin of ashes to empty – it was wonderful. That new stove was probably also very dangerous. It had a tank of gas attached at one end and you had to pump it up for pressure. A gauge told you how much pressure you had to pump but I don't believe you could tell when the gas was running low. Sometimes it would run out just as we were preparing a meal. Mama would have to remove the tank and one of us would have to run two blocks to the gas station for a refill. It was also tricky to learn how to make popcorn on this modern device.

It may have been even earlier that we replaced the wash machine. The old one had a handle on it that you had to move back and forth to operate. There was an old chair with no back next to it which you sat on when it was your turn to be the operator. The "new" one still had the old wringer on it, but it was electric. Dad did the electrical work – probably used an extension cord from the kitchen. I was traumatized because my mother sat in the kitchen with her hands over her ears saying, "Henry, you have no idea what you are doing. You are going to burn the house down." She apparently thought it was going to start with an explosion. I was probably six or seven years old. When I went to bed that night I couldn't sleep waiting for the explosion.

Our first icebox was just that – a wooden box with shelves and a compartment at the top for ice. Underneath was a dish pan which had to be emptied regularly or the melted ice ran all over the kitchen – everything in the kitchen in those days made a mess! *The Ice Man Cometh* was a reality – he came twice a week. If the chunk he hauled in was too big he would take out his handy dandy ice pick and chip away until it fit. Poor mama lived with this particular mess until after I left for college.

Replacing the pot-bellied heater in the dining room was another one of the great modernization steps which took place through the years. I was in junior high when this transformation occurred. The old heater was another dangerous mess; it had to be fed cobs and coal with the resulting messy ashes. It also had stove pipes which had to be taken down and cleaned every spring – talk about dirty!

On terribly cold days and nights in the winter, Dad would "stoke" up the fire until the stovepipes were red hot. They ran through a hole in the ceiling to the hall in the upstairs and out through the roof. Those pipes were the only source of heat we had upstairs in the winter until Dad cut a hole in the dining room ceiling just above the stove and installed a small register. On the top side it was in the bathroom and was a real Godsend for us when we got up in the

33

freezing cold mornings. In really cold weather, Dad would get up in the night to keep the fire going. It was a miracle the house never burned down.

The replacement stove was a floor furnace. It was quite elegant – a shiny brown metal square about five feet tall with a grate on top. It had a stove pipe – for the fumes I guess – and it burned oil. We had a barrel of oil just outside the window and the barrel and the stove were magically hooked up to each other. It was a wonderful improvement. With the old stove we had to hang a bedspread between the dining room and the living room on cold days in order to stay warm in the kitchen and dining room. Now we could use the living room. And again Mama could say "It's so clean."

In the summertime the floor furnace could be moved to the "backut." I was grown before I realized that it was really the "back hut." (Horserporters was another word I didn't learn until I was grown. A horserporter was an elastic band you fastened around your waist. It had four pieces of elastic dangling from it and each piece had a fastener on the end. You used it to hold up your stockings but I was probably forty years old before I realized that a horserporter was really a "hose supporter.")

The backut was sort of a combination entry way and storage room attached to the back of the house. The storage room held everything that wouldn't fit into the house and that was a lot! For years Mama would say, "Henry, I've got to have shelves in the backut" and finally he built them, but it was still a mess.

"When I die," Mama would say, "I don't want you to have a sale. I don't want everyone in town to see this mess." And we didn't.

The storage room had walls and a window. Dad screened in the entry room and in the winter he covered all of the screens with black tarpaper which looked terrible but it kept out the cold. My mother kept a pair of clean overalls on a chair in the entry room. In the summertime, Dad was required to change from the oily black overalls he wore in the blacksmith shop into the clean ones before he could enter the house. Poor Mama, she was always battling the dirt. With seven kids, the appliances she had, Dad's occupation and the severe weather it was a constant battle.

Mama always dreamed of having a downstairs bedroom off the dining room. She had had all of her children in the dining room. Apparently they brought down a bed as the time approached. Dr. Bruechert would come and after "it" happened, a neighbor who had a telephone would call Aunt Minnie and she would arrive in her Model A. But sadly, the modernizations did not include a downstairs bedroom.

Mama did the washing on Monday year round. Even after she got her updated wash machine it was still a horrendous job. I don't know how she did it. It started before we even got out of bed. First of all she had to build a fire in the wood burning stove down in the basement. Then she had to carry buckets of water from the faucet at the far end of the basement to the big boiler on the stove. She would come up and get us all off to school while the water heated. Next she had to ladle the water from the stove to the machine. She used the lye soap she had made herself.

The modern machine didn't have cycles so she had to time how long it washed. Then she had to dip the clothes out of the water and put them through the wringer which was a part of the machine. This was a really dangerous contraption – sometimes hands were "caught" in the wringer and smashed pretty hard. From the wringer they went into a big tub of cold water. They were swished around by hand to remove the soap water, the wringer was moved to the other side of the tub and the clothes were put through the wringer again. They dropped down into the clothes basket.

Mama would carry this big basket up the steps, through the kitchen and backut to the long clotheslines outside. She did this even in the wintertime when the clothes froze almost immediately as she hung them.

When we came home from school we had to help carry in "the wash." In the winter it was hard to bend the big, frozen sheets. We carried them to the dining room where Mama hung them on ropes she put up temporarily or draped them over the chairs. As soon as the laundry got in the house everything became limp and, of course, it was still half wet. The only redeeming feature of the whole operation was that everyone in town – in the known world I guess – was doing exactly the same thing so Mama just took it for granted.

And before, during and after the modernizations Mama's big goal was "keeping it clean." We had the usual daily and weekly chores like dishes, ironing, mopping the steps and around the edges of the living room rug. But the real biggie was the annual Spring Cleaning. Mama did ninety percent of this herself and it was awesome. It would occur when the weather turned nice, usually in May. Mama would announce that the time for cleaning had arrived and we would be grateful that we could rush off to school.

No piece of furniture, no curtain or drape, no rug, no wall, no floor, no anything escaped the Spring Cleaning. The nine by twelve living room rug was rolled up and taken outside, spread on the grass and beaten furiously with a configuration of circular wires attached to a handle. All the quilts, the blankets and the drapes were spread out on the clothes lines outside to air out. They too were beaten half to death. The curtains were washed, starched and ironed. All of the woodwork and the walls were washed down. Every floor upstairs and down was scrubbed. Mama had a big plan in her head and managed to accomplish it in two days. We helped her carry out the rug before school and returned it to its place after school. We were also responsible for bringing in the bed clothing – that's what we called the quilts and blankets and we made up the beds again. We all heaved a sigh of relief when it was over because we didn't bother Mama with anything during the two day ordeal.

Other annual activities were painting and wallpapering which would happen sporadically, probably when she could afford the paint or wallpaper. The front porch and steps got painted every summer. They always needed it because the whole family gathered there after supper every night all summer long. We didn't mind the painting because the results were so fantastic. We used dark gray paint and each board was literally transformed when you spread the thick paint over it. New paint on the steps was especially enchanting.

The wallpapering was something else again. Only the kitchen had wallpaper but because of the coal burning stove it had to be replaced every year. Mama always picked out very cheerful paper full of brightly colored flowers. You didn't take off the old paper unless it was very loose because the plaster was bad and it would come right off with the paper. Mama made the paste. She cooked a concoction which was mainly flour and water. We had wooden "horses" which supported two or three long boards. This make-shift table was used to unroll the paper, cut it to size and apply the paste. The paper was thin and tore very easily so you handled it very gingerly.

The ceiling was the biggest challenge but it was the dirtiest and had the most plaster problems so it had to be done. Two people stood on the planks and ran back and forth with the paper over their heads trying to get it to stick. It was an unbelievable process because it kept tearing and falling down. But by the end of the day the whole room looked great! I still like wallpaper.

One summer my sister Gertrude and I were doing the wallpapering. She was home for vacation after teaching her first year of school in a little town near Des Moines named Redfield. She had used an old towel as a turban to cover her hairdo and had on an old dress and apron, which were already covered with paste. In the middle of the ceiling part there was a knock on the front door. We assumed it was a neighbor and Gertrude got down to let them in. To her horror it was a representative from the college over in Grundy Center where she had applied for a job. She didn't make any excuses. She invited him in, they sat down and with her hands folded in her lap she answered all of his questions. Mama always had the coffee pot on the back of the cook stove so I took them each a cup of coffee. To our utter amazement she got the job.

The Great Depression

The depression was called "Great" compared to other depressions, but I can't remember anything great about it. My first memory of it was when my father came home from one of his early morning visits to the post office, and told my mother that the bank went broke. In 1929 I was nine years old, in the fourth grade. I rushed for school early to go by the bank. I wanted to see if it was just a pile of rubble, or only partially broke. That tells you worlds about our level of sophistication or lack thereof.

The biggest impact of the depression was my mother's forced employment. She left home for intermittent, long periods. Dr. Bruechert arranged for her to take a course in practical nursing. Often when we came home from school, we would find her waiting with her nurse's outfit on for Dr. Bruechert to pick her up to take her to a new patient. The patients had cancer or some other terminal disease, and

Mama was their one person Hospice. Most of them lived in the country in the surrounding area and some of her "cases" would last for months.

She not only took care of all their physical needs and gave them medications, she listened, talked, sang, played the organ (if they had one), and read to them – most often the Bible. She usually slept on a cot in the same room with the patient, and cared for them twenty-four hours a day. For all of this she was paid the grand sum of seven dollars a day. But that was huge for us.

As a blacksmith, my father was entirely dependent on the farmers, and during the Depression, they had nothing. The prices for corn, hogs, and other farm products were so low that the farmers sometimes ate their hogs and burned the corn for fuel. When they couldn't afford to take their livestock to market, they had very little cash. Dad was often paid with meat, chickens or eggs, so we never went hungry, but Mama's nursing money paid the light bill, the interest on the house, and took care of the ever present need to give money to the church.

We got a telephone about this time, so Mama could be contacted by the doctor or her patients; but this created another bill. Her salary was a godsend. My dad must have worried terribly about money, but I never remember him complaining. One time when Mama was home between cases she said, "Henry, why don't you send out bills?"

"Grace, if they had money to pay me they would pay me. A bill would just be another worry for them so why should I spend the postage?"

Mama would get one day off, usually a Sunday when family or relatives could take up the nursing duties. We would watch all Saturday afternoon for her return about four or five o'clock. On Sundays she would play the organ at church which was much appreciated by the congregation because if she wasn't there they had to sing without any accompaniment.

After church everyone stood around out front and visited with friends for fifteen or twenty minutes even if we stood in the snow. It was a wonderful, weekly opportunity to talk. The women talked to each other mostly about their children and the men folks talked about the weather and the crops. The children and youth did the same kind of thing. The little ones hung onto their mother's skirts, older ones ran in circles through and around the conversing groups. Teenagers stood in groups by gender and eyed each other. Many a romance started there. Most of the town girls in church married country boys and many of the country kids married each other. Mama must have really enjoyed the visiting after spending a full week with a sick patient.

After church we would have our usual Sunday dinner and then Mama and Dad would sit down and plan their finances. Sometimes one of us would get to pick out a new dress from the Sears catalog – they cost three or four dollars. It was a real thrill when it was your turn. Between three and five Mama would be picked up and returned to her case. We hated seeing her drive off.

Mama's nursing career started in the early thirties and life on the home front was not easy without her. My sister Etta had graduated from high school in 1928. She spent the next two years working for the law firm in town. Her paychecks undoubtedly kept us going because Dad's cash income was dwindling fast. In 1930 a neighbor girl who was in Washington helped arrange for Etta to take a federal test. She passed it and joined the neighbor in Washington so she was not there during the hardest years although her cash contributions helped pay those ever present bills.

George graduated in 1929. He had worked hard in the

grocery store and the restaurant and had saved $300 so he could fulfill his dream and go to Law School at Drake University in Des Moines. When the bank went broke he lost every penny of it. He had no hope of recouping any of it because he was under eighteen, so any proceeds were going to go to our father's "note" on our house. Our local entrepreneur who sold insurance and real estate had sold George a life insurance policy when he was in the seventh grade and had his first grocery store job. George cashed it in, but it wasn't enough.

Our local attorney came to the rescue. He had a connection with Meredith Publishing Company in Des Moines. They made a trip to Des Moines and Mr. Meredith told them his father-in-law needed a chauffeur and George got the job. He earned his board and room plus fifty dollars a month and that put him through law school. He lived over the garage and had some interesting experiences as a chauffeur. One winter he drove Cap Howell to Florida and he witnessed the attempted assassination of Franklin Delano Roosevelt and the killing of Mayor Cermac of Chicago.

I'm not sure just when the depression ended but things gradually improved for us. However, I know that I was a junior in college before Dad was finally able to pay off the "doctor bill" which had been a part of our lives since before I was born. I was home on vacation when Dad came home during the day with a ten dollar bill.

"Grace, go and give this to Dr. Bruechert. It is the last money I owe him." Mama was so excited. She went upstairs and put on her Sunday hat and got her purse. She didn't change from her "house dress" but she had me go with her and we walked around the entire block so she could enjoy the moment – they were finally free of all debt. Then she calmly removed her hat and walked the two blocks to the doctor's office to get her final receipt.

But no matter how tough things were, we always managed to help others who needed it more. My Uncle Joe had a grocery store in the small town of Greene. Mama helped them when Aunt Bertha died of cancer. Uncle Joe lost the store and he and Ivan, their only child went to Waterloo to find work at John Deere's or Rath Packing. They ended up in long food lines and only one small room to live in. They would make the thirty mile trip to come see us when they could afford the gas, and Mama and Dad would share whatever food we had with them – potatoes, sauerkraut, beans, or canned fruit.

And we always shared with Tante Riek. She was an elderly Dutch widow who lived down by the town's water tank. She lost her savings when the Bank went broke and lived very frugally in her very small house with her Dutch Bible and a smile on her face. She would be so thrilled when we arrived with a syrup pail of soup or beans or whatever Mama could put together.

One time a neighbor stole precious coal from our limited supply in our basement. Dad heard a noise in the night and went down to investigate. He saw the neighbor go across the lawn and into his back door with a sack of our coal on his back. He was younger than Dad and had no children but a very complaining wife. Dad decided, "I guess he needs it worse than we do" so he didn't do anything about it.

Toward the end of the Depression a farmer on the edge of town talked Dad into forming a partnership and getting some John Deere farm machinery on consignment. They knew some farmers who desperately needed it who would be able to mortgage their land to buy it. Dad had known the farmer and his family for years and assumed he was trustworthy. Unfortunately the farmer sold the machinery, collected the money and left town leaving Dad with the unpaid bills from John Deere. He probably could have forced the wife to sell the farm but he "didn't want to cause her more trouble then she already had." It took him years and years to pay off the "machinery" bills but eventually he did.

When Dad was seventy-three years old and dying of cancer, the prodigal farmer returned. He sat at Dad's bedside and gave him forty dollars (he said it was all the money he had) and asked Dad to forgive him – which he did. My dad was something else!

The Depression must have been a nightmare for both of my parents, but I don't remember that they ever complained. They continued to thank God for their blessings! Mama must have hated to leave us to go nursing and Dad must have worried about unpaid bills constantly but he never talked about it. He prayed to God and trusted that Franklin Delano Roosevelt was going to make things better and in the meantime he managed with what he had. At mealtime we followed the Bank closings and all of the New Deal Plans with great expectations and eventually they all paid off.

Dad was depressed himself only once during the Depression. Our electricity was turned off because we couldn't pay the bill. We girls hung sheets and blankets at the windows so our friends and neighbors couldn't see that we were using kerosene lamps and candles. He had a stricken look on his face. Mama was off nursing. But our misery didn't last more than a few days. My brother arrived home from college with four dollars to pay the bill and the lights came on again. I suspect that Mr. Streever, who managed the electrical company, had alerted George in Des Moines and he came through for us.

The Christian Reformed Church

Our church looked like most of the other churches of that era. It was a long, narrow frame building with a bell tower and a steeple. It had a shingled, peaked roof and long narrow windows on both sides which had rounded tops on them. Ours had one unique feature which made it rather special. The basement was partly above ground and the main floor was higher than most so we had very wide, sloping concrete steps going up to the entrance. They were almost as wide as the building so they were very impressive. I go back to Iowa for a visit every summer and I still see some white wooden churches like it in rural areas. However, most of them, like the one in Parkersburg have been replaced.

We all knew every nook and cranny of that church – partly because of Spring Cleaning and partly because we spent so much time there. My sister, Frannie, told me that one time she asked Dad if she could stay home from church. She said he looked at her very sternly and said, "Don't ever ask me that again." She didn't. It never occurred to the rest of us to even ask.

The spring cleaning was a repeat of what we did at home – everything in the whole place was washed and scrubbed from top to bottom. Often I was on the mop brigade along with some sisters and friends who had to "clean the benches" (pews). We each had our own bucket of warm soapy water, a cloth and a brush. Every inch of every wooden bench had to be thoroughly cleaned.

If you didn't clean benches you were a go-fer for the women who were scrubbing every inch of the kitchen to a fare thee well or washing the windows which entailed going up and down tall ladders. They also scrubbed all the floors upstairs and in the basement on their hands and knees. The few men who showed up did odd repair jobs mostly to doors and windows or to the plumbing – one sink in the kitchen and one toilet in a closet in the basement. (We were all trained to "go" before we went to church). There was a small furnace room but the janitor, a retired farmer, wouldn't allow anyone in there even during spring cleaning. Air conditioning, of course, didn't exist.

The physical attributes of the church were easily remembered, because we had ample time to study them on Sunday mornings. Sunday school was from nine-thirty to ten-thirty and we were all there. We sat in small circles in various corners of the basement. As you grew older you moved around to a new circle with the same bunch of kids until, if you were a Dresselhuis, you went off to college. No adults went to Sunday school, but then most of the country kids didn't even go to high school.

Right after Sunday school we all trooped upstairs for Church which started at ten-thirty and lasted until noon. Until I was in the sixth grade, the entire morning service was in German. Most of the members had emigrated from Germany, lived on farms and had never learned English. During World War I, before I was born, the church had been forced to conduct their services in English. The Minister couldn't speak it himself but he read sermons in English.

After the war Dad insisted that English be retained "for the sake of our children" but he lost his battle. All of our lives we heard occasional references to "the Church Trouble," because my dad was so upset that he left the Christian Reformers and took his family to the Baptist Church. He returned only when the minister begged him to and the Consistory (the governing body) compromised with him – morning services would continue to be in German and evening service would be in English. That arrangement continued until the American born generation finally took over control of the Consistory.

Getting through those long unintelligible services was agonizing. You had to be creative. In the summertime, you could count the flies on the wall but that didn't take much time. You could squirm around and count how many women were breast feeding their babies, or try to find a bright color in the clothing of any of the congregants but if you got too wiggly Dad, who kept his arm stretched out on the back of the seat behind his row of children, would give your arm a good pinch.

The old reliable time-consumer was the *English Hymnal.* There would be two copies on every bench and you had to trade off with your sisters. When you finally got a turn you had all kinds of possibilities. You might go to the alphabetized list of hymns in the back and locate each page number from one on up. Or you might pick a particular hymn and count how many capitalized words there were in each verse and determine which verse "won." Or you might look at the index and find which hymn name had the most words, which one the least, how many had two word titles, how many with three words, etc. You would hang onto the Hymnal until the sister sitting next to you and whose turn it was next would kick you so hard in the shins that you would reluctantly give her the book and go back to counting how many people in front of you had black hair, or gray hair or bald heads, or whatever.

My mother was the organist and she never liked the psalms that were sung from the *German Psalter.* There were so many whole notes which the congregation dragged on and on. My dad didn't help. He loved to sing everything and anything and the whole notes didn't bother him a bit. He didn't sing well but he loved it and sang loud and clear, anyway. He led the congregation even when he was taking up the collection because he knew all the words of everything we sang. Sometimes Mama would lean up over the top of the organ and glare at him when he sang too slow, but he never even noticed. And she knew they would follow his singing, not her playing.

46

Obviously the English services at night were much better. If it weren't for them I probably would never have gone to church again when I grew up – I could count flies at home. The sermons were long and filled with theology which didn't interest me at all. Dad thought a sermon shorter than forty-five minutes was not acceptable and he didn't want to hear "stories." We often heard references to "hell" and "fiery brimstone." I was curious but not particularly frightened. And we also heard about Heaven, a place where the streets were paved with gold and everything was perfect. Occasionally there would be a disparaging remark about "the Romans" (Catholics). Dad never commented on that but it seemed strange to me because of his close relationship with Father Mauer.

When I was five or six I worried a great deal about just who God was. We heard that He created the earth and had existed forever but we also heard that he was born in Bethlehem and the shepherds came. I found it very confusing but was too embarrassed to ask any questions. Finally, finally I caught on about the Trinity, the three-in-one concept. I could buy that.

Mama really loved playing the organ at the night services. When I was very little the organ was a "Pump" organ. She had to pump like mad with both feet for the more boisterous hymns like *Onward Christian Soldiers* but she made it. She also loved the more sentimental, soothing ones like *In the Garden* and *There'll be no Disappointment in Heaven*. She would sing along with her real favorites. Playing that organ was one of the greatest joys of her life. And the organ, like our appliances at home, evolved through the years. By the time I was in high school we had a very nice one which may have been close to state of the art for the times. And now when I visit Parkersburg, they have a lovely organ in a new church and a very accomplished young organist who is the great granddaughter of one of Mama's best friends.

And then there was Catechism. The classes coincided with the school year and you started attending when you started school. The classes were held on Saturday afternoon until you were in high school and then you went on Thursday night. You literally learned the short version of the *Heidelberg Catechism* when you were in grade school and the long version when you were in high school. We went through the same material every year. I can still remember the very first question and answer in the short version –

Q. What is the sole purpose of Man?
A. To glorify God forever.

Learning the long Catechism for the Thursday night sessions was really agony. The answers were whole paragraphs long. We would wait until after school on Thursday and then study like mad and practice with each other until it was time to go. We had five or six paragraphs to learn each week and you had no idea which ones you might be called upon to recite so you had to learn them all. It was really the only studying I ever did until I got to college. My brother and the three sisters ahead of me in school all did exceedingly well and I just coasted by in high school. The teachers apparently assumed I knew as much as my siblings and I guess I could ramble on enough in the essay tests to convince them I knew what I was talking about. Without Catechism I may have flunked out of college the first year but I certainly didn't appreciate it at the time. We all dreaded Thursday nights.

But we had other special events at Church which were really great. Every Christmas Eve we had a program which was the highlight of the year. My mother saved to buy material to sew for the "little ones," so they would have a new dress for the Christmas program. Right after Thanksgiving the Sunday school teachers would pass out little Recitations which we were to learn. We had weekly rehearsals starting the first part of December. On the Big Night we would get up one after another and recite our verse. No one ever clapped in the Christian Reformed church and sometimes disasters occurred – like the time one little girl lost her pants. She was three years old and she calmly reached down to retrieve them and then just kept skootching them up for the rest of the piece.

After three or four "pieces" there would be a song by three or four of us. I particularly liked the Sino song – *Jesus Loves Me this Sino*. (I was twenty years old before I realized the song was supposed to be *This I Know!*) The congregation especially enjoyed it one time when our little group sang one song and my mother was playing another. Mama switched back and forth but never managed to get it all together although we did finish more or less at the same time – we quit singing when she quit playing.

The big highlight came just after the last recitation was spoken and the last song had been sung. Then it was time for "The Sacks." Two or three benches had been pushed together in the afternoon to make room for the huge pile of big brown paper sacks which had been filled with peanuts, nuts, hard candy, two or three chocolates, an orange and an apple. They were heavenly. Mr. Alspach, probably the oldest member of the church and a seemingly permanent member of the Consistory, stood by the big pile with a list and called out family names and numbers. Actually the families were solicited ahead of time and they had to pay twenty-five cents for each Sack. Dad always managed to pay for one for each child plus Mama got one free. It was her annual pay for being the Organist.

You never knew where your name was on the list so you held your breath until finally it was your turn to go collect your treasure. The first thing I would do would be to check to see whether I had two or three of the chocolates. It didn't really matter because the contents were bait for our "trading" sessions for days to come and I was likely to end up with all of the chocolates anyway. Actually, they were pretty bad chocolates – just a big mound of white sugary globs covered with a very thin coating of chocolate, but I couldn't be happy until I had all or most of them.

Trading and eating our Christmas sacks took up most of our Christmas vacation. We all kept them with us day and night except Gertrude. She would stash hers away and after everybody else had eaten theirs, she would bring hers out and eat it in front of us. We hated it and called her "prissy." She maintained her reputation year around because on the Fourth of July Dad would bring home a whole gallon of ice-cream from the creamery. Gertrude would announce, "I really don't care for ice cream." We couldn't believe it!

Another big happening at our Church was the annual Mission Feast. I strongly suspect it was organized for the missionaries, but the food, the Feast part was what I remember the best. In either case, it was a day long affair in the summertime and consisted of three church services and two meals. A bonafide missionary was present for the occasion and he spoke at a service at ten-thirty in the morning, another one at two in the afternoon and a third one at seven in the evening. During the intervals we ate and ate and ate.

Mission Feasts were always held on a weekday and some men and women had to come the day before to prepare. The men set up long tables on "horses" with boards in the church basement. The women covered all of the tables with white butcher paper and then set them with the cheap white china dishes and the silverware which were kept in the kitchen cabinets and drawers. We could probably seat about a hundred people. All of the men and the elderly women ate first.

The women who were kitchen workers and the kids were at the second seating.

The amount of food we had was unbelievable: fried chicken, sliced ham, beef and pork plus, applesauce and pie plant (rhubarb) sauce, plus potato salads, Jell-O salads with bananas, baked beans, homemade breads and cookies, spice cakes, applesauce cakes, chocolate cakes, white cakes, apple pies, berry pies, lemon pies, pie plant (rhubarb) pies, chocolate pies, cherry pies and lemonade to drink. Such a spread! I have since been to some of the finest restaurants and hotels in the world but I have never seen a more appealing outlay of food. My favorite, next to the chocolate pie of course, was the Jell-O with bananas on top. We never could afford bananas at home so this was a very special treat.

All summer long we would have to save pennies for Mission Feast. When Papa (that's what we called him when we were very little) gave us pennies to deliver coffee or tea to him at the shop, he would admonish us to "save one for Mission Feast." We would turn in our little pile at the afternoon service and the missionary would explain that they would all go to help the Rehoboth Indian children. All my life I thought these children were in India. Years later, in 1969, when we were moving to Phoenix, I was driving down Highway 40 in northern New Mexico when all of a sudden I saw a small white church with a big sign that said, "Rehoboth Indian Mission Church." I couldn't believe it.

I slammed on the brakes, brought the car to a halt on the shoulder and kept repeating, "I don't believe it, I don't believe it."

My son and my daughter were with me. They had been snoozing but they woke up and said, "What's the matter, what's the matter?" I had to explain all about the Mission Feasts and the pennies, but I finally reconciled myself to the fact that Indian children in New Mexico probably made good use of my pennies and we drove on.

Sunday school picnics were also annual affairs at Church. I remember them as being embarrassing because we didn't have a car. We would all go stand in front of the Church with our bowl of potato salad, a pie or whatever and wait for someone to come pick us up. They always would come but the wait was not fun. The picnic would be at the Cattle Congress Grounds in Cedar Falls which was eighteen miles away. It was fun and again the food was great. We played games all day long. We could see the Cedar River at the edge of the Grounds but we were not allowed near it. I was always anxious about whether or not we would get our ride home again so those picnics aren't especially memorable for me. Except for the food I would rather have played with the neighbor kids back home.

One of our ministers along the way had a daughter who was a school music teacher somewhere in the east. She would come home for the summer and would form a Children's Choir for the Church. They were a riot. The daughter's name was Evangeline. She had short, dark hair and wore dark rimmed glasses. When we annoyed her she would click her heels. When she wanted our attention she would say, "Look at my baton." At first I had no idea what her baton was but we soon learned. We reported every Saturday afternoon for practices for the performances we would give at evening services about once a month as long as she was home.

Believe it or not she would stand on top of the Communion Table just below the Pulpit to direct our choir of eight or ten children, aged from seven to twelve. She would move back the front pew to make room for us, pull the Communion Table forward and tower high above us. The boys had to help her get up on the table. Our big number was

My Task. My most vivid memory of it all was that we had to hang on to the "T...A..." for what seemed like an eternity and we were all bright red in the face. Then she would whip her big long baton down with a flourish and we would all vehemently come forth with a mighty "SK" which almost blew the front row out of the church showering them with our spittle. It is pretty amazing that with that kind of a start I continued to sing in church choirs wherever I was for the next fifty plus years!

We had some real characters in the church. One of them was our janitor, who was a retired farmer. He took his duties very seriously and one of them was to maintain a proper temperature in the church. I'm sure it was a challenge, especially in the winter time when the temperature might be thirty degrees below zero. Sometimes you could see your breath inside the church. I remember one Sunday morning when our family fought our way through a blizzard to get to church. The janitor had not made it, so the church was freezing cold. The Minister had us come to his house next door where Mama played their organ and the minister conducted the entire service, including his forty-five minute sermon in his living room. Only our family was present but I'm sure the minister knew that my dad expected it.

But I remember the janitor best for how he carried out his duties on hot, humid summer Sunday nights. I don't know just what level of heat inspired him but sometimes right in the middle of the sermon he would get up and walk to the back of the church. In the very southwest corner of the church he kept a long pole with a notch on the top. He would take his pole, go down the aisle, reach over the worshippers and endeavor to place the notch on his pole in a small hole in the window frame. Sometimes he would have to make several stabs before he got the notch in the hole, but when he did he could pull open the top part of the rounded window which was hinged about one foot down from the top. There would be a collective sigh of relief when he was successful.

Everyone in the church would follow his every movement as he moved from one window to the next, up one side and down the other until all twelve windows were open. Even when he walked across the front of the church right in front of the pulpit the Minister never missed a beat. The janitor's wife sat with a tight smile on her face looking straight ahead. Everyone else was transfixed with the drama unfolding before them.

The church also played a part in our New Year's celebrations. All the neighborhood kids would come to our house. We would play Monopoly and Mama would make cocoa and popcorn. Shortly before midnight we would get all bundled up and go to our Church to ring the bell. We would take Dad's round watch on a chain with us and exactly at midnight we would ride up and down with the rope as we rang the bell for about five minutes. On the way home we would sometimes stop at the Catholic Church and attend their Mass. We would sit on the back rows of the small church and watch in wonderment. Father Mauer looked so different in his fancy white robes. And it was all so completely different from what we saw and heard in our church. He was running back and forth lighting candles and talking in Latin. It was very impressive.

Music was always a big deal in our family. We had an old pump organ which Mama played regularly and one or more of us would join Dad who would sing along with whatever she was playing, mostly hymns. Sometimes she would branch out and her repertoire would include *Oh Danny Boy*. We loved it. When Etta graduated from High school and was working for the law firm she bought Mama a piano. Nothing was more appreciated or better used than that piano. The sing-alongs were more and more frequent and we discovered that little three-year-old Frannie could play. She wasn't tall enough to even see the keyboard but she could pick out *I Was Born on a Farm Down in Iowa, Yankee Doodle Dandy* and other tunes. She went on to be quite a child prodigy and still plays beautifully.

Dad really loved to sing. Almost every day after dinner which we had at noon, he would sit on a newspaper on the piano bench next to either my mother or sister, Frannie, and they would play and sing several hymns before he went back to work. After we all went to bed at night he would sit in his big chair with a hymn book and sing every verse of all of his favorites. He'd sing the soprano part of the first verse, the alto part of the second verse, the tenor for the third verse and the bass for the fourth verse. Then he'd move on to the next hymn even if there were more verses. Many a night his hymn singing lulled me to sleep, and I'm sure my siblings had the same experience. And all those sessions enabled him to sing all the words to every hymn in church every Sunday even if he was passing the collection plate.

And we all played various instruments. George bought a violin while he was in junior high with money he earned working at the grocery store. Gertrude and Edene played it after he graduated. The school furnished the rest of the instruments we played. I played the clarinet and the cello. The others played the flute, the marimba, the French horn, the oboe and Edene was the Drum Major of the Marching Band for her last two years in high school.

When I was a junior our marching band won the County and Regional Contests and progressed to the State Contest in Iowa City. It was a life changing experience for me. I was so excited to find myself marching in the huge football stadium at the University of Iowa that I could hardly toot my clarinet. Everyone else must have been equally overwhelmed because we made fools of ourselves that day. We started out just fine and marched the length of the football field. When we approached the end, Otto, our Drum Major at the time signaled for us to turn around. At the whistle he turned but the kids in the front row were apparently semiconscious. They kept going straight ahead until they reached the stands and in a matter of seconds we all plowed right into them except Otto who marched the full length of the field all alone in the opposite direction. We did not win the contest.

Later I was standing on Iowa Avenue looking up at Old Capitol and down at the Iowa River and I made up my mind that I would go to the University of Iowa. Almost everybody in Parkersburg who went to college went to the State Teachers College in nearby Cedar Falls and I wanted to be a teacher but I decided then and there that I would go to the University of Iowa.

Parkersburg Folks

Percentage wise we probably didn't have any more strange characters than any other town, but they were memorable. One of my favorites was Miss Kieve Cow. I have no idea what her real name was. Although we thought she was old, she was probably in her middle forties when my friends and I started noticing her. She lived west of Main Street in a very neat house all by herself. She had a brown cow with a bell hanging from her neck in the back yard. Every spring she would lead that cow on a short rope all across town to Johnson's Dairy where we all bought our milk. The cow would stay there for three or four days and then we would see Miss Kieve Cow leading the cow back home.

Another character was Nettie Buss. She was born and raised on a farm near Parkersburg. She was engaged to a neighbor boy named Elmer. Both of them were the youngest children in their respective families. They couldn't get married because they had to help their parents with the farms. They were probably in their thirties when both of Nettie's parents died. She bought a nice small house in town which had an indoor bathroom. Elmer stayed on the farm but every Saturday night he would come to town and take a bath in Nettie's bathtub.

We know this because we spied on them. Elmer would arrive about seven o'clock in his Model A and carry his clean clothes on a hanger into the house. We would sneak around and observe that they sat at the kitchen table for awhile and had a cup of tea. Then the light would go on in the bathroom and we would get close enough to hear the water running. Nettie would put the dishes away in the kitchen and then sit in the living room and knit. Pretty soon Elmer would emerge all clean from head to toe. He would give her a little peck on the cheek and she would go to the door with him and watch as he drove off in his spiffy car. He would give a quick honk as he drove off which probably meant, "See you next Saturday night." (Ben, my grandson, is going to find it hard to believe that this was how his Gran actually spent her Saturday nights during her teen years!) As far as I know, they never did get married.

I only remember two crimes that were committed in Parkersburg as I grew up. When I was about four years old the first one occurred. The Methodist minister, his wife and their son Warren lived on the corner just across from the Catholic Priest who lived two doors south of our house. Warren wanted to go camping for a week one summer with some friends, but his parents would not consent to it. They did allow him to sleep in a tent in the back yard.

One evening Dad built a big bonfire to burn the leaves he had raked. All of the kids in the neighborhood were there and we roasted marshmallows. I was sitting in the wagon and all of a sudden Warren grabbed the handle and pulled the wagon right through the fire. Dad jumped up and shouted angrily at Warren. I wasn't hurt but it was scary. About a week later, Warren left his tent late at night, went into the house, got his shotgun and stood at the bottom of the steps. He called to his parents and when they appeared, he shot them both. His father died instantly. Warren jumped in their car and drove off, but ran into a ditch just outside of town and was captured. His mother recovered and spent the rest of her life living very close to the state prison where Warren died years later.

The second tragedy in nearby Stout made the front page of the Chicago newspaper. At breakfast one morning in the house next door to Aunt Ida and Uncle Harm, a man shot his wife, sister-in-law, son, daughter and himself. The son was in the freshman class of our high school. I only remember him as one of the country kids who brought his lunch in a brown sack but we were all shocked and saddened. The Superintendent came into our Assembly Room and removed his desk. The other kids in the row stood up and moved their desks forward to fill in the gap. The whole thing was unbelievable.

There were also a few *Peyton Place* happenings in Parkersburg. They consisted primarily of married men running around with married women. We kept regular track of three couples who met in the same places and one unmarried man who met a married woman with children. I don't think any of them knew they had an audience and actually I never saw anything but very passionate kisses. I never suspected what might be happening when they lay down in the grass. My sex education didn't progress that far until I went to college.

Most of our teachers were not very memorable – except our chemistry teacher. We had no laboratory but he would stand in front of the class, hold up a beaker and pour various ingredients into it which caused it to bubble and steam very impressively.

Our high school principal was a quiet motivator. She would write quotations on the blackboard which she changed twice a week. I can still quote, "The heights of great men reached and kept were not attained by sudden flight but they, while their companions slept, were toiling upward in the night." I still find that pretty impressive. It was in this environment that I drifted along until high school graduation.

Everybody was my friend and the teachers all appreciated the fact that I was one of those smart Dresselhuis kids so I got good grades with very little effort. I could walk from our Assembly Hall in a crowd of kids with my book open and scan the chapter I should have studied. I also had the gift of gab so I got by just fine. In fact, I graduated second in my class. My good friend Leonard who was one of those country kids who brought his lunch in a brown bag was first. Dad may have been disappointed because I was the first one not to be first but he didn't say a word and it didn't bother me. I knew Leonard was smart and he actually studied, so he deserved it.

I was sad to be leaving high school but happy at the same time because I was going to go to the University of Iowa. It was May of 1937 and the whole world lay ahead of me.

CHAPTER TWO
Life at the University of Iowa

*H*ow in the world could I afford to go to college? My brother and two of my sisters had paved the way. Just like them, I got a scholarship and some jobs. George had already graduated from Drake University and was a married, struggling lawyer in Odebolt, Iowa. Gertrude had graduated from Iowa State Teacher's College and was teaching in Redfield, Iowa. Edene was a student at Calvin College in Grand Rapids, Michigan. Etta, the oldest sister, was working in Washington, D.C. She never went to college but probably got a better education than any of the rest of us as an Air Force wife who lived all over the United States and in two foreign countries.

I couldn't possibly have done it today because tuition runs in the thousands and living expenses and books are out of sight. But in 1937 I had to pay fifteen dollars a semester over and above my scholarship and fifteen dollars a month for half my room and board. My used books cost two or three dollars each and after the first semester I often shared that expense with other girls at the house who were taking the same courses. If a book cost more than three dollars we had to go to the library to read it.

Many people helped me along the way. My parents gave me great moral support and inspiration simply by expecting me to do it. My teachers, the principal and the superintendent in Parkersburg all helped by getting me the scholarship. Gertrude's fiancé, Mike, helped tremendously. It was the summer before his senior year in medical school and he had a great relationship with the dean of men who was in charge of the National Youth Administration money. (This was one of Franklin Delano Roosevelt's great programs which we so often discussed around our dinner table and was responsible for getting thousands of Depression kids through college.)

Mike was such an outstanding success that the dean really admired him. He was only six years old when his parents died, so he and his younger brother grew up in an orphanage. Fortunately, they grew up in a loving, caring atmosphere. He was brilliant and the staff at the orphanage was responsible for helping him get to the University. Because of Mike's influence the Dean allocated ninety dollars a year to a job at the University library where I would work for twenty-five cents an hour.

Mike was also responsible for getting me into a cooperative dormitory like the one he lived in. The University owned a group of about ten large old homes near the campus in Iowa City which they used to house needy students. It was a wonderful plan. Each of us paid fifteen dollars a month and worked two hours a day cooking and cleaning.

After high school graduation I spent the summer working in the Chevrolet Garage. Our music teacher had married the garage owner and she hired me for a dollar a day to do the office work. I made out all the bills, answered the telephone, talked to the customers and made the bank deposits across the street from the garage. The five dollars I made each week was a fortune to me. I spent some of the money for yarn and knitted my basic wardrobe that summer – a blue skirt and top, and a green skirt and top. My mother sewed two dresses for church and parties for me and my sister Etta generously sent me five dollars for new underwear. I could go to Trey's Store and buy panties for thirty-nine cents, bras for forty-nine cents, a slip for sixty-nine cents and have enough left over to splurge on a pair of silk stockings. I was as happy as any rich kid in the world. And so I went off to college very confident that everything was under control. And it was.

My friend and neighbor, Jimmy Engelkes, was also going to the University, so early in September his dad drove us to Iowa City and dropped us off. I had not slept a wink the night before we left. I was scared to death. How could I possibly do this? What was I thinking of to leave my home, my family, my friends, all of Parkersburg? Had I lost my mind? Mike was the only person I knew in Iowa City and he was going to be in medical school way across the river. I felt trapped because I knew I couldn't change my mind.

But when Mr. Engelkes dropped me off and left me standing on the curb with my one suitcase, I looked up at Coast House proud, happy and excited. It was thrilling to think, "I'm a student at the University of Iowa." I spent the next five wonderful years there. Sometimes it was very tough and I wasn't sure that I could make it but someone always came through to help me.

The Coast House

Coast House was a marvelous place. It had been a beautiful, privately owned mansion in its day. In the entry was an elegant staircase winding up to the second floor, with high ceilings and lovely hardwood floors throughout; all of the rooms were big. It was located on a corner near the University President's home. Directly across the street was a wooded ledge about thirty feet wide with a very picturesque bench overlooking the Iowa River far below.

Thirty girls lived at Coast House. The first floor had a living room, dining room, kitchen, a bedroom and a half bath. The second floor had five bedrooms and a full bath. The third floor was really an attic, but four girls lived up there. I was assigned to the biggest bedroom on the second floor along with four other freshman girls. We had two sets of double bunk beds and one single bed. The room had a pretty windowed alcove with a desk in it. Two dressers and a very small closet provided plenty of storage for our limited wardrobes. I had a top bunk of my own but we shared everything else.

The bathtub in our second floor bathroom was the only one in the house. We signed up for one bath a week but of course it didn't mean you had any privacy. The door was always open and girls came in and out to use the toilet or put on their makeup in front of the only decent mirror in the house. If you wanted a second or third bath during the week you could stay up late, get up early or come home between classes. It worked because we all got along. We knew we really had no choice. Most of us came from very large families so it was the same old thing – get along or be miserable. It is truly remarkable and wonderful that we became lifelong friends.

We were all in the same boat – working girls, but poor as church mice. And we all worked at the house. Our housemother was a graduate student who had one of the bedrooms on the second floor to herself. She assigned all of the work and we shifted around every week or two. You might be on the cooking detail for breakfast, lunch or dinner, you might have to clean the two bathrooms or you might have to mop floors or dust.

If we had a big snow storm we would all be out shoveling snow and throwing snowballs. The Tri-Delt Sorority House was right next door to us and they probably felt sorry for us. Actually, we looked down on them. We thought they were real snobs. If we came out of the house to walk down to the campus and a Tri-Delt came out at the same time we would wait until they got started down the walk. We didn't want to know them but they probably thought we were standing in awe of them.

My first semester was wonderful with so many new friends and experiences. It was such freedom walking around the campus, going to my job at the library on the Iowa River, going up the big hill to the Old Capitol Building, the showpiece of the campus, and just knowing I was actually a student at the University of Iowa. One of my favorite activities was bridge. At night when we finished with our studying I went around to the various rooms looking for three others who would play bridge. The game fascinated me early on when I observed the girls from Des Moines and Cedar Rapids playing it. It was so unlike Rook or Old Maid. You really had to use your head. We would throw down a blanket on the cold hardwood floors in the halls or living room and go at it. I felt so mature when I realized that bridge really wasn't evil.

But most of all I loved the socializing with the other girls. You got to know them better. And I finally learned more about sex. No one talked openly about the subject in those days and I certainly wouldn't ask any questions for fear I would look stupid. But I listened carefully and gradually caught on to what the birds and bees were all about. A senior at the house got pregnant, moved out and got married. That was the opening that caused enough talk that I finally received my sex education.

And I didn't forget my strong religious background. On the five block walk down to the campus we always passed a Presbyterian Church. I started attending it from the first

Sunday I was there and after a few weeks I joined the choir. I thought they sounded marvelous and I was halfway in love with the bass soloist who had an absolutely gorgeous voice. I was a member until I graduated.

I also attended the Young People's Meeting on my first Sunday night at the church. Expecting it to be something like Catechism at home I was amazed, confused and disillusioned when I walked in and found to my horror that they were playing Ping-Pong in church on Sunday! I left those sinners immediately and cried all the way back to Coast House when I realized what they were doing in God's House on Sunday! I never went back to the Sunday night orgies.

Then I had a rude awakening. The semester ended at the end of January and the grades came out. I got a D in Botany which was a four-hour course. I got a B in English and the rest were C's. English was only a three hour course so my grade point average was less than two points. To remain at Iowa, a two point average was the minimum required, so I was truly devastated. I cried and cried. Going back to Parkersburg and having the whole town know that I had flunked out of the University was unimaginable. Didn't these people in Iowa City know that I was a Dresselhuis, that I was smart and that I always got good grades?

It was a life changing experience when I realized that I was going to have to actually read all of the assignments, pay attention in the laboratory, and actually cut up frogs. Worst of all, I had to quit playing so much bridge. Learning to study was not an option. I was a junior before I made the "Smarty Club" which meant you had all A's and B's but I never made Phi Beta Kappa.

The Social Scene

But I did fall by the wayside when it came to movies on Sunday. It took more than a year because at first I never even considered it. For one thing, I seldom had the ten cents for the ticket. But I also thought God might strike me dead. We didn't even think of such a thing in Parkersburg and I certainly had taken Parkersburg with me when I went off to college. But gradually I came to realize that the girls who did go were not bad people and that I would never get to see a show unless I went on Sunday because I was working, in class or studying from morning to night Monday through Saturday. Friday and Saturday nights I usually babysat for various professors kids for ten cents an hour.

Then one day I got a call and was asked if I would be part of an advertisement for *Goodbye Mr. Chips,* a movie starring Greer Garson. I would be part of a group of five students who would see the show free on a Sunday afternoon and then our comments about it would be part of an ad for the show. I couldn't resist, but feared I was on the road to hell. Afterwards I started to realize that I wasn't really a different person because I had attended a show on Sunday.

The shows were so romantic and so beautiful – no profanity or sex scenes in those days. Instead of bedroom scenes, couples just disappeared into the sunset. They had really wonderful love stories, suspenseful plots, beautiful clothes, enchanting scenery and they almost always ended happily. One of my favorites was *Rebecca,* the Daphne du Maurier story directed by Alfred Hitchcock. The Nelson Eddy-Jeannette McDonald ones were also great favorites. He was so dashing, she was so beautiful and they sang those stunning duets. It didn't seem odd that she was always out in the woods in an evening gown. I would swoon every time they opened their mouths. How could such joy possibly be sinful? So if I had the ten cents for the ticket I went to the movies on Sunday afternoon with only a small pang of guilt. It probably happened less than ten times during my entire college career.

I didn't date a lot in college partly because I didn't have time but also because I didn't meet anyone who particularly appealed to me until my last semester in school. The eighteen- and nineteen-year-old boys in my classes all looked like fraternity men to me and I was scared of them. I knew from our bridge sessions that they all smoked and drank and were "fast." They loved to party with sorority girls and they probably wouldn't look at me twice because I lived in a co-op. It didn't matter because I didn't like them anyway. When I did date it usually was someone who pushed me around the dance floor at the Union, stepped on my feet and was totally boring. I always had a baby-sitting job when he called again – at least that was what I told him.

My observations weren't entirely true – we had a beautiful girl at our house named Georgia and she dated men from all over the campus. She even dated Nile Kinnick – the biggest of all of the BMOC's (big men on campus). I remember sneaking down to the kitchen on some false pretense when I learned that Nile and Georgia were making popcorn there. It didn't occur to me that he was from a little town in Iowa just like I was and that his parents and surroundings were not unlike my own. I was awestruck to be in the same room momentarily with him.

To this day Nile Kinnick is the only Hawkeye who ever won the Heisman Trophy; he had a four point grade average, was the speaker at our Commencement, and today the stadium is named for him. Tragically his fighter plane went down in World War II. They did not locate his plane until 2004 – another one of the millions of reasons why I hate war.

I will remember Nile best for the winning pass he caught in a game with Minnesota. It was the fall of 1939 and our team made history as the Ironmen. I was sitting in the student Knothole Section at the end of the stadium where you could buy a seat for fifty cents, a small fortune and the reason I didn't attend many games.

Lots of the girls had steady boyfriends. One of my best friends met her future husband on the first day of Matriculation Tests which all freshmen had to take in the field house the first week of school. When we were seniors I sang at their wedding and we still are very good friends. But my social life centered mainly around the exchange dinners we had every other Wednesday night with one of the four men's coop dorms. Half of their men would come to our house and half of us would go to theirs. Sometimes we would have a party with them on Friday night. If it was at our house we pushed back the furniture in the dining and living rooms after dinner, played some records, popped some popcorn and even served some Cokes. We had a dozen marvelous records of Tommy Dorsey, Jimmy Dorsey, Glen Miller, and Artie Shaw. It was a great plan and it was cheap.

I never made any romantic liaison because of these dinners until my last semester at the University. However, I thoroughly enjoyed them because I evolved into an unofficial matchmaker on these occasions. I was the wholesome type, the sort of next-door-neighbor kind of girl, the guys could confide in me. Boys would often make a point of sitting at my table so they could ask, "Who is the blonde at the second table over? Does she have a steady boyfriend? Do you think I could get a date with her if I called?" I loved my role and several of the subsequent alliances ended up in marriage.

One evening fifteen of our girls walked across the river bridge to Whetstone House for the Wednesday dinner. The guys were in a real panic. The cooks had put granulated soap instead of flour on the pork chops in their big roaster and soap suds were pouring out of the oven and covering the entire kitchen floor. You wonder how in the world that could happen but it really was very understandable. We all had big tins, almost barrel size, lined up in our cellars. They contained such staples as flour, sugar, oatmeal, and granulated soap. Some poor cook who probably had never set foot in the kitchen until he came to college, didn't notice the difference between the flour and the soap. It was hilarious, but we were all vegetarians that night.

Silk stockings were one of our big challenges. They cost about a dollar, but that was terribly expensive. Nylons were not invented until during the war so the silk ones were our only choice if you wanted to get dressed up. They were very fragile and if one thread broke you got a run which would quickly spread from the top to the bottom. The runs looked terrible, but we had a small tool which would pick up the run row by row. It was meticulous, laborious work and you would think twice before you accepted an invitation for a date if you knew your only pair of stockings had a run in it.

Sometimes if we were all taking the same class we studied together. Once, seven of us were taking the same psychology class in a big lecture hall which seated about 150 students. The room was sloped, so we all looked down at the professor below. One night before a big test we got together and studied an old test which belonged to the house. Every house or dorm would have their file of old tests which had been collected through the years and they were used as study guides. This particular test seemed very comprehensive so we really studied it. It was a multiple choice test so it was not hard to memorize.

Imagine our amazement the next day when we opened our test and found that it was an exact duplicate of the one we had studied. We were seated alphabetically so we squirmed and twisted to see how everyone else was reacting. We were all at a loss as to how we should handle it. I decided I really wanted an A so I would only miss one or two of the questions. My friends were individually arriving at the same conclusion.

A week later the professor had the results on the blackboard when we arrived for class. He described them as very unusual because seven girls had made scores between 97 and 100 and the next highest score was 89. Some of us had babysat for his children and he probably figured out what had happened, but he didn't say a word and neither did we. It was the easiest A any of us ever made.

All of my grandchildren and my great-grandchildren will be amazed to know that we only had one telephone line and one telephone in all of Coast House. And we didn't see it as a hardship. The girls who went steady arranged a time when their boyfriends called and they didn't hang on the line forever. All of us knew better than to give our telephone number to everyone we met. It is so different now. I remember recently when one of my daughters remarked to her sixteen-year-old nephew, "I see you've had an operation."

He replied, "No I didn't, why do you say that?"

"Because you don't have a telephone on your ear."

Summertime

I stayed in Iowa City every summer until I graduated. Toward the end of my freshman year I was offered a half time job in the University Library for the summer. I needed the money but I couldn't afford to spend it on housing, and the co-ops were not open in the summer. A job in a boarding house down the street allowed me to work for my room, which I shared with another girl. After serving dinner, I could eat and then clean up, but for some reason, the breakfast servers were not allowed to eat anything.

The owner of that place was the meanest woman I have ever known. She would sit at the head of the table with her fourteen boarders at every meal. They were all women, mostly school teachers working on their degrees during the summer. Many of them were "twelve-week wonders" since they had attended Iowa State Teachers College for only one summer and then started teaching. We served them at one long table in the dining room. As soon as the meal was finished the owner would hurry out to the kitchen. At breakfast she would pour out the leftover coffee right in front of us and gather up every scrap of food because we weren't working for our breakfast.

Her selfish attitude was such a stark comparison to my mother's generosity. My mother fed every tramp who came to our door. During the Depression she shared our limited food with her brother and his son who had practically nothing. Gertrude would come home from college in Cedar Falls every weekend and Mama would send leftovers from Sunday dinner and garden vegetables back to school with her. She and her high school friend lived in a basement apartment and did their own cooking. Her willingness to share had seemed normal to me, until I saw this miserly woman pour coffee down the drain.

Subsequent summers were spent living at a professor's home. Dr. Herbert Spitzer and his wife Lois became lifelong friends. I had been a babysitter in their home and those summers turned out to be a wonderful experience. They were from Texas and talked with real cowboy twang, Even more strange was the kohlrabi they grew in their garden, but I actually liked it. And I loved their little daughter Martha who was about eight months old my first summer in their home. I still worked half time in the Library but when I was in their home I helped with Martha. It was a real joy after my experience at the boarding house.

Dr. Spitzer was a professor in the college of education and I had taken some interesting courses from him. He was developing a system of new math and he would test some of his theories on me. He would give me a problem and ask me to tell him exactly how I arrived at the answer. Later he became quite famous for his book on new math. He was also the principal of the University Elementary School where all education majors did their practice teaching.

Best of all, the Spitzer family enjoyed politics. It was like being at home to discuss FDR again. The three of us sat up late hanging on to every word coming from their little radio when Wendell Wilkie was nominated for President. Back then no one knew the convention outcome ahead of time and the decisions were real cliffhangers. Rumblings about Hitler in Germany were starting. We were really glad Wilkie was nominated because Robert Taft didn't seem to understand Hitler's potential.

Decisions

In the fall of my senior year Dr. Spitzer asked me to stop by his office one day after class. He offered me a Graduate Assistantship to be an Assistant Teacher in the second grade at the University Elementary School the next year. I knew it was a great opportunity, so even though I was sick and tired of studying, I didn't turn it down. Shortly after that the Dean of Women called and asked me if I was interested in being the Proctor (Housemother) at Coast House the next year. It didn't occur to me at the time but there was probably some collusion on these offers.

Then one night in November after I had accepted both offers I made another big decision. It was a very, very cold and snowy night. I left the Library at five o'clock and started up the long hill leading to Old Capitol. The sidewalk was so icy that I couldn't make any headway. I slipped back two steps for every one step I took forward. Finally I collapsed on the snow bank at the side of the walk. I needed to be at

Coast House by five thirty to work on the cooking detail. Laying half frozen in the snow bank was the low point of my entire career at Iowa. Tired to death, big tests looming, more broke than usual, for the first time I seriously worried about whether I would be able to make it. An even heavier class schedule would be required next semester to graduate next May.

With tears rolling down my freezing cheeks, I prayed hard and made a momentous decision. I would not graduate with my class. I would take fewer courses my last semester and make them up the next year even if it meant I couldn't get my Master's that year. Feeling suddenly relieved, I trudged back to Coast House. The next day I checked it out with Dr. Spitzer and the Dean and they agreed and their offers remained good. And that is the way it worked out. I chose not to graduate in December that next year but waited until May. By then I had all but six hours I needed for the advanced degree.

I really enjoyed being the Proctor of Coast House. All of my best friends had graduated the previous spring and there were about twelve of them so we had lots of new girls at the house. I realized that I would have to have a different relationship with them. No more talking them into quitting their studying to play bridge. I had never realized how many decisions the Proctor had to make and how much work it entailed but I learned in a hurry.

My teaching assignment was a joy. I had always loved children, but I never realized how quickly they learned and how smart they were. The school was on a hillside and the playground behind it sloped down to the Iowa River. Every child in school was constantly told never to leave the playground and never go down to the river. One morning I came out of the building for recess about a minute after the children had left. To my horror, five of my children were standing down on the river bank. Rushing down I quickly herded them back to my room. Inside I lectured them about the dangers of the river and how important it was for them to follow the rules. I announced that everyone would have to stay inside for the rest of recess. After a few seconds of silence, one little boy spoke up and said, "In other words, Miss Dresselhuis, you believe in the Mosaic rather than the Christian Law." When I realized what he was telling me, I was amazed. It taught me to never underestimate the brilliance of a seven-year-old.

During my last year, on December 7, 1941, Pearl Harbor was bombed. Since I was now the Proctor at Coast House I had a room by myself. Sitting at my small study table, the radio music was interrupted with an announcement from FDR – the famous "day in infamy" speech. Calling all of the girls together in the living room, we listened to the horrible reports on the radio about the ships that were sunk in the harbor. The next morning Congress declared War and our lives were changed forever.

The developments in Europe and the war against Hitler filled the newspapers and radio. The news reels at the movies showed Hitler screaming to the masses from his balcony. FDR was sending planes to England, the government was building up our Armed Forces and they were putting out huge contracts to build airplanes, ships, tanks, and ammunition. We had been getting ready but now we were suddenly in it.

Our campus was alive with war talk. We knew without a doubt what our future held, and we were sympathetic to the cause. We should have gotten involved before Pearl Harbor when stories about the killing of Jews, the concentration camps, and persecutions were widely known. Dad was terribly worried about his family in Holland. When Hitler marched into the Sudetanland we were convinced that he had to be stopped. All of the young men I knew were ready to go. A Navy pilot training program was started at the University, friends and relatives were being drafted or volunteered, and emotionally we were all at war.

Shortly after the Christmas break I met Charles at a co-op dinner at one of the men's dormitories. He told me that he had first noticed me at an earlier dinner, so he made it a point to sit at my table. A senior, Charles had planned to go to law school until the war came along. He was in ROTC so he knew he would automatically be in the service as soon as he graduated and he was ready to do that. We talked that night for hours, and then we started meeting at the library to study. When the library closed we would stop at a cafe at the top of the hill and each have a wonderful piece of chocolate cake for a total of twenty cents. If he had thirty cents we could have ice cream on the cake. In those days a girl would not have dreamed of contributing even a nickel but I probably didn't have it anyway.

We both worked, so we had very little time. We would take long walks along the Iowa River and talk. I told him all about our family and he talked about his. That spring Glenn Miller's Band came to Iowa City for a University Dance at the Union. It cost two dollars a couple but Charles saved the money, I borrowed a formal gown from a girl at the house and we went to the dance. It was the biggest thrill of my life. When we danced to *Moonlight Serenade* with my head on his shoulder I thought I had died and gone to heaven. Then we went outside behind the Union building and stood on the grass next to the River. He kissed me passionately and told me he loved me. I loved him madly and wished I could stay right there for the rest of my life.

Part of the graduation ceremony was his commission as First Lieutenant. In a few months he was shipped to Europe and fought with the Third Army. He wrote me whenever he could but I usually got the letters in batches every few weeks. He always told me he loved me and that he had something to tell me after the war. I was sure he was going to ask me to marry him.

In April I had a call from the University Placement Office. They told me about an opening for a first grade teacher in Monroe, Michigan and asked me to apply. I was happy to do that and shortly before I graduated I received a contract in the mail. The position paid fourteen hundred dollars a year and I was thrilled. Most of my friends who had graduated the year before me were making seven or eight hundred teaching in small towns around Iowa. (Incidentally, male teachers automatically got more money in those days and females had to quit teaching if they got married.)

In May of 1942, I graduated. The Spitzer's invited my whole family to have lunch on their yard that day. It was great that eight members of my family were there to celebrate with me. Dad was so proud that I was getting a Bachelor of Arts Degree. I probably didn't know half of what he thought I knew. But in spite of how smart he thought I was, I had a terrible lapse of memory that day.

I had to report for the graduation march an hour before the ceremony started so Dr. Spitzer took me down to the meeting place. It was a half hour drive from their home. We had almost reached our destination when I realized that I had left my Mortar Board with the fancy tassel back on their yard. I could not take part without it so we drove back to retrieve it. The big march had already reached the Field House and the Liberal Arts students had gone in first.

My family was all on the bleachers scanning the LA graduates with the white tassels when they saw me darting in and out between all of the colleges with blue, green and red tassels as I tried desperately to catch up with the white group. It was essential that I make it because the colleges were presented as units to march across the stage and receive their diplomas. I couldn't stand up amongst the greens and run down to catch up so I frantically worked my way forward until I caught up just in time to be seated.

On that same day, May 5, 1942, the Germans marched into Holland and took it over in five days. Two of my cousins in Rotterdam and one in Amsterdam were killed that day. I spent that summer at home in Parkersburg. I wanted to relax, see old friends and get my act together so I could take off for Monroe.

I was terribly disappointed when I got a letter from the Superintendent in Monroe saying that I was not eligible for a State Teaching Certificate in Michigan, since I needed two more hours of science. He suggested I attend summer school. I quickly enrolled in an Astronomy Class at the University which I could take by correspondence. It looked like the easiest course listed under Science. It turned out to be quite an experience.

I bought the book and faithfully completed the series of lesson assignments which came in the mail and returned them to Iowa City. Studying the sky as I was instructed, I recorded on the maps all of the stars I saw. It was more than a little disconcerting to receive the returned assignments with remarks in the margins like, "It is quite amazing that you observed this star. It usually takes one of the strongest telescopes in existence to see this." In spite of my unusually good eyesight I did manage to get a "C" in the course and the Teaching Certificate was awarded. And so I was all ready to be a bonafide teacher!

CHAPTER THREE
Teaching School in Monroe

And so I was off to Michigan on the bus. Monroe was a city of about 70,000 people, a paper mill town on the banks of Lake Erie between Detroit and Toledo, Ohio. A lot of poor people came up from Kentucky and Tennessee to work in the paper mills. The school had sent me a list of rooming houses so I took my bag and set out to find a place to live. I found a house not far from the school and rented a room. It was a lovely home and the people were very nice to me.

The first day I went to a meeting for new teachers in the Administration Building. At the beginning of the meeting the Superintendent read three names and mine was one of them. He asked us to stand if we were present and then asked each of us, "Where were you yesterday?" I was speechless. "Did you receive my letter informing you of the meetings?"

Nodding silently, I sat down and checked the letter in my purse – it stated the dates and times very clearly. To this day I don't know why I didn't read it correctly. How humiliating. It was one of those lapses and I was off to a terrible start. It didn't help when after the meeting the Superintendent told me that I was the only teacher he had ever hired without prior experience. I got the message. So much for first impressions!

Actually, my first year as a teacher turned out to be a very good experience for me and the children. It was a lot more work than I had planned on. I didn't fully comprehend what a big responsibility I had taken on until the door closed for the first time on that group of thirty-two children. My job was to teach all of them to read, write, add and subtract. How in the world was I supposed to do it? I thought about the pre-primers, the primers and the first reader books. That first reader had more than 150 pages and such hard words I wasn't sure if I could read it myself.

But together we learned. On that very first chaotic day we spent most of the time getting them all enrolled, and I tried hard to remember all of their names. Taking the class list home that night, I worked on it because I knew how important it would be to each child to know their name.

After I learned all the children's names I made it a point to get to know the parents. That took a little longer. One Saturday afternoon I went up to Detroit with some other teachers to go shopping. In Hudson's Department store I saw a man standing by the elevator who looked very familiar. Walking toward him I had a big smile on my face – now remember, I was a fresh-faced twenty-two-year-old at this time. He looked at me with an odd expression, but I just kept walking and smiling. When I got very close, I realized I didn't know him at all so I blurted, "Oh, I thought you were the father of one of my children."

His face dropped as the elevator door opened. He darted in and the elevator door closed. I looked all over the store for him but never found him. He was probably on his way to the suburbs. That poor man. I hope he didn't have too much cause to worry. He never learned the truth.

But not only did I have to learn the children's names, they had to learn mine. "Miss Dresselhuis" was not easy. To say it correctly there has to be a tiny break between the "Dressel" and the "huis" but the children didn't do it that way. I quickly became "Miss Dresseljuice" and it stayed that way. The spelling of my name was hilarious. At Christmas time I got presents with twenty-two different spellings – Dresseljuse, Dresseljuss, Dresseljuhs, Dresselhuse, Dresselhuss, Dresselhues, Dresselhughes, and more. At least most of them were more or less phonetic.

The First Day

Opening day was hectic. Each mother told the life history of her child. While filling out forms and collecting fees, I just smiled and nodded, realizing I couldn't possibly remember everything. But some first impressions were memorable.

Annabelle was a vivacious personality. This thin-faced, towhead with the freckles and pigtails captivated me on first sight. She was an independent soul and I wasn't surprised to learn that Annabelle was the youngest child and only girl in a family of eight children.

Paul peered at me from behind his mothers' skirts and when I asked his name, his mother answered. His eyes kept darting around but he seldom lifted them. He shuffled when he walked and from the first moment, it was obvious he was troubled.

Julie stood stiff and erect with her brown eyes flashing and her black curls swinging. Her mother explained that Julie was a "nonconformist" and she made it plain that she expected me to accept her as such. It amuses me now to remember how Julie surveyed this scene. While she was thinking that mama was getting me in line, I was already scheming about how I would change her. She and mama didn't know that I had already learned that "nonconformist" and "spoiled rotten" were synonymous.

Even that first day, Ronnie was swinging on the hooks in the hall and clambering up on the shelves. His mama didn't identify him when she registered him, but I mentally put them together when she told me that "she couldn't do a thing with him." She hoped I could make him behave. Heavens, two totally undisciplined ones!

David B. bade me goodbye very seriously that first day and said, "I'm glad to be in the first grade. My mother is glad to be rid of me and I'm glad to be rid of my mother." Fortunately, his mother had already left. Larry's mother stayed until eleven and Larry kept sniffling and turning around to see her. After several tries I finally convinced her that Larry would do better without her.

The rest of them were a maze of starched pinafores, stiff new jeans, missing teeth and wide grins. Today I love them all but looking back I can see that some of them entered my heart immediately, while others slipped in unawares along the way.

The mothers ran true to form that first day. When it came time for them to leave, they all got that same panicky expression in their eyes. I could almost see them trying to interpret my smile and manner. They all knew their own child's faults and shortcomings so well and they were so hopeful I'd be kind and understanding. I could almost see them thinking, "Please try to understand, please be good to him – he's so little and I love him so!" As I herded them toward the door they kept looking over their shoulders. I felt like an ogre standing between them and their beloveds. The thud of their collective hearts hitting the floor was almost audible when I shut the door. Only Larry's mother remained.

I turned around to face the children. Six-year-olds are always bursting with eagerness to love and please the teacher. That's an advantage no other teacher has. Their intelligence and curiosity are so obvious and they have so much to learn in the first grade that the challenge is almost tangible. Only little Paul disturbed me. His eyes were filled with distrust and fear.

The Second Day

The second day of school was more normal. Before the first recess bell rang, I carefully explained the whole procedure of lining up to go to the playground. When the bell actually rang, I asked them all to put their coloring away. Julie stood up and screamed, "No, I'm not ready." She plopped down and colored furiously. I explained we'd finish after recess, that we all went out together and that we must be ready when the bell rang. However, she got more and more excited and started stamping her feet and yelling so I told her to go out and stand in the hall until she wanted to be nice. That surprised her a little bit but she went, with the help of my hand on her shoulder.

Mr. James, the principal, had heard her screaming and he was coming down the hall toward us. I guess she knew who he was. She was duly impressed because she ducked back into the room just before he arrived. The other children were filing out the back door and she stalked by me very haughtily without a word. About five minutes before it was time to come in, she came over and put her hand in mine and grinned up at me so sweetly. Bless her, she always wanted to be good.

When I told her mother about the incident after school,

she acted a little put out. She made it clear that the teacher should do the conforming, but since she also had a four-year-old and was pregnant, I decided that she may as well learn now that the children do the conforming because the world won't.

After the ten o'clock recess I took the children on a dry run to the cafeteria. There's always so much confusion at the first group lunch that it's helpful if they could see where the silverware and dishes were, and if I could show them how to hold their plate and where to sit. During the whole process they kept looking at me so funny. I stood up there balancing the empty plate and glass in my hand and felt like a fool. They didn't say anything at the time but at the end of the day, Caroline told her mother, "Miss Dresseljuice took us to the cafeteria and we didn't get a thing to eat and then we went back again and that time we ate!"

We had the usual pandemonium when we actually had lunch. Annabelle was a big help. Although she was one of the first ones seated, she jumped up and helped shepherd half of the others to their table. Carrying a plate, a bottle of milk, silverware and napkin is quite a trick, but she was like an old mother hen hovering over her chicks.

Poor little Paul panicked. Mr. James came in about the time we were all seated and closed the big double doors. Obviously, claustrophobia is one of Paul's problems because he jumped up and screamed in terror. Taking my plate over I sat next to him, so he was quiet, but he never did relax. He didn't eat more than three bites of food.

Larry brought his own lunch and that complicated things. He said, "My mama wants me to eat just her cooking." That was alright except that the cafeteria was serving hot-dogs; he had a thermos of hot water with a wiener floating in it, plus little wax paper packets of mustard, catsup, relish and a bun. His instructions were for me to make the hot-dog because Mama said he might burn himself. Heavens, here I was sprinting around like a dogcatcher trying to direct the traffic, help carry the plates, mop up the spilled milk, prevent the tears, keep my eye on Paul's fears, and I had to mess with fixing his hot-dog when the cafeteria already had 500 of them made up.

Thankfully, his mother was coming in after school and I was optimistic enough to think I could teach her. Often a child who brings his own lunch will spread out a banquet of peanut butter jelly sandwiches, a cold chicken leg, a huge piece of chocolate cake, a candy bar, and pretzels while the other children sit in goggle-eyed rapture. Then their mothers will wonder why the children complain about the lettuce salad and green beans the cafeteria has to offer. Just a few of these culprits sprinkled throughout each of the public school cafeterias of our land can effectively louse up the hot lunch program for the whole country.

At recess after lunch Ronnie ran off the playground and took two other children with him. That's always a potential for a disaster, but fortunately I happened to see them. Racing about a half block, jumping shrubs in my high heels, and beating off dogs, I corralled them without any real problem.

From the beginning, Ronnie had a higher nuisance value than any other ten of them put together. He was the kind of child who would drive a teacher crazy and get terrible grades in conduct all through school. Yet, it was obvious from the first day that he had a wonderfully quick mind and he'd listen to anything that interested him. It's highly improbable that Ronnie will ever end up on a psychiatrist's couch and teachers will always consider him a problem. If he can be taught to discipline his imagination, he'll be a huge success in our capitalistic society because without a doubt, he'll be free-enterprising it up all over the place.

Larry's mother was at the door again when the last bell rang. We talked – really, she talked – for a good half hour and I could see immediately that she was going to be a problem. It was important that we come to some understandings and agreements. I needed a picture of what was going on in his life but she made it clear that she was there to tell me what I must do and when and how I should do it. For poor Larry's sake I tried to make her be a little realistic. She needed to learn more about how a first grade operates, but at the same time I wanted to get along with her.

She made it perfectly clear that she was out to protect this child to the nth degree. She had a valid reason for being somewhat fearful but she had let herself get to the point where her viewpoint was out of balance. Her daughter was in high school, and between the two children she had had four miscarriages. When Larry was three, he had pneumonia and she was scared to death that he might become ill again. So Larry was not to go out for any recesses; she would bring him in the morning and he was to stay in the room until she called for him every afternoon. That was ridiculous because they just lived on the other side of the block and he didn't even have to cross a street to get home.

Besides that, she wanted him to water color during recess periods because he enjoyed it. That's when I called a halt. For Larry's sake, I could go along at least temporarily with some of her demands but I had to make her face a little reality too. I reminded her that I had thirty-two youngsters in the room and that every six-year-old is crazy to dribble and smear with water colors and that I couldn't possibly work it out that one child would get three such chances a day.

She should have known my parents. With seven children, they taught us to that it was our business to get to school, behave ourselves and learn something. None of us had any problems with a teacher. If we ever complained about a teacher my father's constant mantra was, "Just listen to the teacher."

She also wanted Larry to remain in his seat and color during rest time because it might be too drafty on a mat on the floor. Surely, any intelligent person could see that if one stayed up and colored, they'd all want to. We compromised by picking out a place behind my desk where he would be out of any possible drafts. Lunch was never mentioned; I was afraid she'd just think I was too lazy to make hot-dogs and there were much larger issues at stake.

Trying to use humor, I pointed out that after all, children must play with other children in order to learn to get along. "After all, this is sometimes a hard, cruel world and we must prepare them." But she just looked daggers at me, as though she was going to see to it that nothing was ever "hard or cruel" for Larry. If it could only be that simple! We ended our conversation on good terms, understanding that we both wanted the best for Larry.

Poor little Larry. He was intelligent but far too serious for a six-year-old. He probably had as great a potential as any human being on this earth. What a shame that his mama wanted to limit him with her skinny, scrawny little worries when she could help him aim for the stars.

My parents were such an inspiration. As a Dutch immigrant Dad had the highest possible regard for education. He was a blacksmith and had no money to educate seven children, but he gave each of us a dream and a desire to learn which enabled us to go after our own. What a blessing, especially when compared to what this woman was giving to her son.

Show and Tell

As the days went by, I learned that first grade is a huge mixture of satisfaction, love, challenge, hilarity, frustration, enjoyment and exhaustion. Where else in this world could you be greeted with such sincerity? "My mama is coming down with the flu today and my aunt is coming down with a baby."

"My mama says, 'Isn't it a shame just when this family is finally getting rich that we have to be sick all the time?'"

It wasn't just their various mamas and states of health which were reported. I heard about the "new car that has push button windows instead of the curling kind" and the "two kinds of snakes that daddy found in the garden – one was a water 'mosicin' and the other just plain snake." All of this before roll call! Saner people with more sensible jobs and without thirty children to trip and trample over their feet all day, may have cleaner shoes, but I doubt that they can appreciate the reality of life as much as a first grade teacher.

Show and Tell sessions give you the opportunity to learn so much about the children. They also provide comic relief for the teacher and students. These times are highly recommended by the experts for a few minutes each day because the child learns to express his views publicly. And certainly it's good for the children to get rid of their worries and frustrations, and express their joys and hopes before going to work each day. Group therapy sessions which are so popular today are probably a spin-off of the original Show and Tell sessions. I wish I had recorded some of them. I would love to spend my old age listening to playbacks.

The stories they tell cover every imaginable subject. The majority of them deal with animals, health, their families, things they've done or places they've been. Their parents would be amazed to know how much a first grade teacher knows about them.

Annabelle's cat story was one of the best. It went, "We had a mama cat and a daddy cat and they had six kittens and then they had three kittens more and then four kittens and then a boxer killed the father cat and then one of the baby kittens got to be the daddy cat and then the mama cat had six more kittens but three died and they had four more kittens and then my mama didn't have any more friends to give the kittens to and we had too many cats but the mama cat had four more anyway and my mama got mad about all the cats and one day when I was in kindergarten my mama said we are going to quit having cats and she took all of them to a farm and now I'm in the first grade and we don't have any more cats at all anymore." She took a deep breath, laughed at her plight and took her seat.

Jan reported on her health one day. "Last week I had the chicken pops. I had big sore places all over me and they bleeded and blooded and itched and scratched and I had one great big one in my hair and it made a bloody hole in my head." She scratched tentatively at her head and came up triumphantly with a showing of blood on the end of her finger. Everyone's eyes followed her respectfully as the girl with the hole in her head took her seat.

One day Bobby told us about his trip to the theater. "Last night we went to see *Old Yeller*. I was glad to go because I hadn't been there since I was a little kid. The best part was where the little boy got to sit on the table and swing on the towel racks The other good part was that the dog was nice and Daddy bought all us kids some popcorn."

Anne told a mystery story one day. Very simply she stated, "I know a lady and she didn't have a heart attack and she's not dead." At every Show and Tell all the children are crazy to tell these yarns. Between "turns" they throw their hands into the air with such force that they propel their whole bodies several inches skyward.

Julie always made a dramatic performance. Her best one was about her dad's toe. "I've got some news to tell" she started. "It's bad news but it's real good bad news. My daddy got his toe cut off in the lawn mower." A gem like this doesn't happen very often, but it produced a wonderful effect. Everyone was spellbound. Julie folded her arms and with a pleased expression and a toothless grin she surveyed the reactions. She soaked up all of the emotion and then continued with the gory details. "When my daddy was going to the hospital, I found his toe by the lawnmower and I wanted to look for some more pieces but the neighbor lady made me go over to her house."

Paul never shared at Show and Tell. Even when he talked to me personally he was never able to tell a story. A few times when he looked calm I would call on him, but he'd hide his face in his hands and of course I'd quickly go on the next one.

Ronnie had a clever story one day. He had drawn a picture to tell about. He held up what looked like a perfectly clean piece of white paper and then proceeded to tell the tale it illustrated. "This is a picture of a snowstorm" he said. "It's a real bad snowstorm and everything is covered with snow. Right here…", he carefully designated a particular spot in the middle of the sheet, "is a rabbit going down his hole but he's almost in and all you can see is the end of his white tail." He held the sheet high and everyone looked with interest at his "picture."

Debbie carefully explained an incident. "After school yesterday, David's car, a brand new one, got hit against and tore up." She clapped her hands to illustrate. "A teenager came down the street driving like a fast teenager and when he got past, all the smooth parts on David's car were bumpy and the supposed to be bumpy parts were smoothened out."

Along in the fall Tommy told us, "The family next door is just like us – they aren't very rich and they aren't very poor, just medium. Last night they wanted to go to the live-stock show and my daddy said, 'Hazel,' that's what he calls my mother. 'Can we afford to go too?' and Hazel, that's my mother, said, 'Well, I guess we can if no dissure (disaster, I guess) hits us.' So we went and I saw chickens all folded up inside of eggshells and they worked so hard to get out they almost killed themselves. They'd peck and flop and rest, and peck and flop and rest, and peck and flop and rest. I got tired looking and then we went home."

One Monday morning Robert got up and said, "My dad wants to go fishing next Saturday and my mom says he can't go unless he paints the bathroom, but he says he won't do it." On Tuesday, again on Wednesday and on Thursday, Robert reported, "My dad still won't paint the bathroom and my mom still won't let him go fishing." But on Friday he got up and triumphantly announced, "Guess what! Last night my dad painted the bathroom and tomorrow he's going fishing." Everybody clapped.

Regardless of the money, time, effort and talent ex-pended on the newspapers and magazines published in this country, the hard, cold fact remains that nowhere will you ever get the fresh approach to news that you get during a first grade Show and Tell.

Comforting Paul

Practically everything about Paul worried me all year. From the beginning, he reminded me of a scared little rabbit, looking for a hole to dart into. Always tense and worried, he must remember the first few weeks of school as a real nightmare for him.

The first week, we had a film in our room. When I started to close the dark curtains, I noticed Paul getting pan-icky. I went over and explained to him all about the film – it was a particularly good one about animals. I also told him why we'd have to draw the curtains and close the door. He didn't make any comment so I went over and continued closing the curtains. When I turned around, that poor child was standing, clutching his desk in absolute terror. His face was as white as paper and his brown eyes looked twice their normal size.

At this point, the lights were still on and I was hesitant on whether or not to proceed. Knowing there would be many occasions when I'd need to use films during the year, I had to continue or he'd expect me to cancel every one. I asked him to sit by me next to the projector. Ronnie was to be the film monitor and I had wanted to start explaining his duties to him as we showed this first film. However, I limited him to simply turning off the lights so Paul could sit by me. I was careful to turn the film on a few seconds before the room lights went off.

For the first few minutes, Paul trembled. He whimpered but didn't scream. I kept my arm around his shoulders and kept calling his attention to the cute animals on the screen. Gradually, his terror disappeared although he never fully relaxed, as all the other children were ooh-ing and aah-ing about the film.

Paul was always restless. Frequently he'd get up and walk around the room. The other children understood. They knew without any explanation from me that Paul couldn't always stay in his seat. When he was in his seat, he'd keep putting his books and supplies away and then getting them all out again. His pencils were all chewed up and so were his fingernails. The only time he concentrated at all was when I'd pull up a little chair and sit right next to his desk to work with him. Even then he'd only stay with it for a few minutes before he'd start looking around to see if the other children were noticing. Or he'd start piling those supplies in and out, and it was time to quit.

He kept very much to himself all of the time. On the playground he would stand behind a tree and peek around at the others, or sit down against the fence off in a corner. If I started over toward him or sent a child to invite him to play he'd run like a deer.

Frequent conferences with his mother didn't provide the answer, although many of the reasons for his behavior were very apparent. He was an only child, born after his parents had been married for twelve years. According to his mother Paul was a terrible disappointment to his father and undoubtedly that was a big part of his problem. The father wanted a football playing, outgoing son. He was annoyed because his only child was a sensitive, shy, small boy. Paul undoubtedly knew this.

As a former teacher the mother had a very realistic attitude toward Paul. She loved Paul and knew he was unusually nervous. I suspected the parents argued a great deal about how he should be reared. In teacher's colleges and universities you are told how important it is that you understand a child's background to learn the reasons for their behavior. Great, but what does the poor first grade teacher do after she's figured out the reasons? You can't go in and rearrange homes and attitudes as you see fit. It was a hard lesson to learn but the best I could do was to help the child learn to cope with his reality.

Paul's father traveled from Monday morning until Friday night. Probably Paul and his mother lived very happily and too cozily in their little world all week long. She was so anxious to give him some happiness. With her background she knew how he should be treated, but she became overly protective of him. Knowing the tension and discord he would incur on the weekend, she compensated for it without even realizing it. It was difficult to help – she lived with the actual situation and I didn't.

His father never came to school. He probably didn't see any need for it and the fact was, he was only home weekends. In fact, the mother felt he would just "make it hard for Paul" so I didn't pursue that. We needed a school psychologist, but there was no help.

Paul did begin to trust me within days after school started. If something frightened him he'd move toward me instead of whimpering. On the playground, he began to stay in my general vicinity. If I moved, he'd move, although at first he maintained a respectable distance between us.

Surprisingly enough, he did a better than average job of learning to read right from the beginning. Being able to do it under such adverse circumstances proved he must have a lot more than average intelligence. He wouldn't volunteer in a group but when I would go by his desk, he knew the words and he could show me the correct answers in his workbook. However, his attempts to color and write were miserable. When I gave the standardized intelligence test to the whole room, he did so poorly that I couldn't even score enough of it to be able to figure an IQ. Once again, I wished we had a psychologist to advise me. I wanted so badly to help him.

A child like Paul is such a challenge. So many problems might be averted if we had the proper means to help children early on. I could only love him and worry about him.

The Cafeteria

In our school system we had what the administration referred to as, "self-contained classrooms." That was a nice polite phrase which meant, "We can't afford special teachers or assistants so you are stuck with your class from morning to night." Consequently, we went to recess, the cafeteria, the bathroom and everywhere else with our brood. We taught physical education – they jumped up and down in the aisles and acted out little poems like *The Itsy, Bitsy Spider*. For music class the teacher had a little pipe to toot the first note of a song, and then you all took off singing. If you were extremely fortunate some parent or the PTA provided a phonograph for marvelous sing-a-longs.

And then there was the cafeteria. When our appointed time approached each day we got ready by going to the restrooms to go potty and wash our hands. Then we stood in line, prepared to sally forth on the long, long walk to the cafeteria. To keep their attention I might start out by saying, "Today let's pretend our clothes are falling off and we have to hold them on." Obviously, this kept everyone's hands at their sides and while they looked a little odd walking down the hall with everyone clutching their sides and smirking foolishly, at least no one got bopped. We might even arrive in good order.

We slowed down to practically a halt to go through the line and this complicated things a little. The "holding onto the clothes" had gotten old and anyway the children have discovered that they could still push real good, even with their hands at their sides. One good pusher could start the whole line in motion so I reasoned, "Now let's not push in line. Everybody must wait your turn – everybody has to give in a little and be polite." This general theme carried us along the serving line.

One phrase caught David B.'s attention. "Yes, ma'am," he said. "Miss Dresseljuice wants us to be quiet all of the time but she has to give a little." This was the understatement of the century but it generated a little sympathetic cooperation. Sometimes in the "outside world" I hear someone say, "Don't just stand there – do something" and I listen in shocked wonderment. Don't they know that all through elementary school the teacher's constant battle cry is, "Don't do something – stand there."

We finally made our way through the line and got to

95

our appointed tables. There was a general stir of excitement about the time everyone was seated because they realized a great moment had arrived. Moving to each of the four tables, I appointed the "monister" of the day. Being the monitor was truly the most exalted position a first grader could attain. To be ruler supreme, the commander-in-chief, king of all for a few blissful moments was heaven itself. Almost every child from the shy to the aggressive, from the irresponsible to the responsible – all succumbed to the fatal charm of being the boss. As I approached the table each child declared, "I've never been it."

And after I make my choices the seven disappointed ones chorus, "He was it yesterday," but like the hand of fate I moved on relentlessly. Before I picked up my own lunch I covered the tables once more for necessary adjustments.

"I forgot my fork."

"Tommy stole my napkin."

"I forgot my straw," were common everyday ailments. Then there was that special brigade with their special problems – the group who would only eat their mamas cooking so they brought their lunches.

"I can't open my thermos."

"My mama put a hot dog in hot water but she wants you to make the sandwich."

"I've got pudding in a jar and I can't open it."

Settling the various and sundry problems I automatically repeated, "Now, everyone clean your plate." Going for my own lunch, I sadly noticed that we had rice – I hated rice but I had to file that away in my brain to deal with later. One more hand shot in the air.

"Please help me open my milk."

"That's easy, honey. You are in the first grade now and you should know how yourself. All you do is hold the bottle tightly with one hand and take the top off with the other. See?" My formula failed under fire and I spilled the milk all over my hand and the table. "Well, it usually works", I explain lamely. Her eyes meet mine sympathetically.

"Well, I'll usually try", she says soberly.

"Thank you, dear. Now will you please get off my foot and go get the kitchen lady?"

Again I started for my lunch and noticed that Ronnie's eyes were on the salt and that his open bottle of milk was on a direct path between his arm and the salt. As I opened my mouth to warn him, the milk spilled. "The kitchen lady is on her way." I stopped for the necessary threat to Ronnie and cautioned to the owners of the remaining bottles and went for a replacement and my lunch.

My lunch was a mountain of rice. How could I maneuver it into the garbage without being seen? I look up to see twenty pairs of eyes fastened on me and realized the rice must go – down the hatch. At the last minute Billy reprieved me by putting salt in his milk. Then I noticed Sharon slithering her salad off onto the floor. "Heavens, don't do that, honey. Try eating it. Someone will slip and fall." Tommy came up to ask if he could go to the bathroom. A second grader rushed by just then, and slipped on the salad. As I picked him up, I told Tommy, "We're not supposed to go the bathroom during cafeteria time." He looked desperate, so I said, "Well, hurry but don't run." I retrieved the salt and noticed Tommy back at my elbow.

"Should I hurry or don't run?" he asks.

"Oh, honey, walk fast and go on."

I picked lettuce and tomato off the second grader and returned to my rice. The school secretary arrived to tell me that Pam's mother had called and said Pam shouldn't drink her milk because her stomach was upset at breakfast.

I looked over in time to see Pam drinking the last swallow. Too late now, but the impending results may provide an exciting diversion for everyone but Pam during rest time.

I made considerable headway on the rice until David S. came up to report on Freddie who spilled Sandra's milk while pretending to be a space man.

"Don't put your fork in your eye."

"Put all four legs of your chair on the floor," I said on the way to the scene of the accident. Sandra was upset because the milk got on her dress, but a little sweet talk and a runner to get the kitchen lady with the mop and everything was under control again. It was time to review the tables one last time. The news items some wanted to report slowed me down a little.

"The cake I brought was that boy's mama baked whose dog got quashed by a car," says Tommy who likes his mama's cooking.

"Jack said something nasty – he said the cafeteria lady was fat!" reports Steve, a monister for the day. I glance over at the short, plump lady and note there is hardly room for argument.

"It's not nasty, but it's very impolite, Jack. Please get off my foot and sit down, John." Thus I continued my rounds.

A few more quick bites of rice and we were ready to clear. That meant each table made a pilgrimage to the scraping counter, where they pushed some of the leftovers into a trash container and some onto the floor, stacked most of the dishes and broke a few and then returned to their table to wait for the lineup. In an orderly line at the door, we pretended to be Indian hunters stalking thru the forest. It worked very well until we passed the Principal's office and Tommy shot Mr. James as he surveyed us from his doorway.

"Indians use quiet bows and arrows and the Principal

isn't a bear," I announced and Mr. James looked at me as if I had lost my mind. "Well, you are quiet," he commented and the children trudged on almost bursting with pride.

Just as we reached our doorway, we met the third graders heading for their turn in the Cafeteria. "What do we eat today?" the teacher asked me, but I couldn't remember. By the time I recalled the rice they had moved on. Well, she didn't expect me to know.

The Silent One

Carol didn't come to our class until early in October, but her story is the most beautiful, most poignant and most special of any child I ever taught. She started out in the fall in Alma Rice's first grade down the hall. The first week of school Alma mentioned that she had a little girl in her room who wouldn't talk. Jokingly I offered to trade her for two of my talkative ones, but Alma considered it serious even then. Carol had not said a single word to her or to any one of the children.

The next week Alma mentioned it again. She had called the mother, who had been surprised. She said Carol hadn't been terribly enthusiastic about school, but she had been telling them about various things that had happened. She hadn't seemed unhappy or unwilling to go. The parents hadn't realized that this silent business was going on. The only clue she could give Alma was that several older children in the neighborhood had told Carol during the summer that, "You have to be quiet at school. The teachers don't want you to talk. If you do, you'll get into trouble."

I had seen Carol on the playground and in the cafeteria. She was very pretty with big brown eyes, an olive skin and long, dark pigtails, but always very solemn. Later Alma mentioned that the mother was getting terribly upset. That was logical, but it wouldn't help if she pushed the panic button. Alma was trying everything – she changed her seat, she tried to enlist the help of other girls, she tried to trick her into speaking, but nothing worked.

On the playground one day, an upsetting incident occurred. Hearing a commotion, I noticed a group of children in a circle and assumed a fight had started. I rushed over and there was poor Carol. Several boys in her room were poking, pushing and pinching her. All the while they taunted her with, "Come on, talk, talk."

"Hurt her and she'll have to yell."

Forcing my way into the circle I shouted, "Stop, every single one of you" and from the tone of my voice they scattered in a hurry. I took Carol by the hand and the poor child was quivering all over. Her face was a dull red and her eyes were downcast. We sat down under a tree. I just smoothed her hair and kept saying, "Don't worry, honey. It's not so bad. We'll work it out." After awhile she leaned against me and I felt her relax just a little. Only once did she even glance up at me and of course she didn't say a word. As soon as the bell rang, she ran for the door.

Shortly after this, I had occasion to go into Alma's room. One little boy stood up and yelled, "Miss Dresseljuice, do you know we've got a girl who won't talk?" Immediately, half the children in the room were on their feet, pointing her out and talking about it. Poor Carol looked like she wished the earth would swallow her up. Alma hushed them but, of course, the damage was done.

Alma came to my room after school and suggested that maybe Carol should transfer to my room. I wasn't sure I could solve the dilemma, but maybe a change of environment would work. The children in her room were treating her like a side show in a circus and since Alma obviously hadn't been able to foresee a problem like this she hadn't been able to influence the attitudes of the other children early enough.

If she transferred now, I would have the benefit of knowing the whole situation and talk to my class in advance to enlist their sympathy and help. This would give Carol a chance for a fresh start. If we all really worked on this, surely she would relax and start to talk. We decided it was her best chance so we went to the principal's office together.

Much to our amazement, Mr. James didn't go along with our suggestion at first for good reason. He pointed out that I already had one more child than Alma did, but more important, this sort of thing would give parents all over the school ideas. He was right. Many of them would think they were justified in having their child transferred and usually their reasons weren't warranted. Then, too, this problem seemed like such a simple thing to him. We couldn't get a first grader to talk? But finally he understood.

Alma talked to the mother and they both talked to Carol who seemed relieved that there would be a change. I talked to my class and we discussed it very thoroughly. They ended up feeling very sympathetic, challenged and cooperative. They put themselves in her place and decided they wanted to help Carol so she wouldn't hurt anymore. We talked a long time. At first, we had a few holdouts. A few thought she was just being "ornery – why doesn't she talk?" but they changed their minds as we talked.

And so the next day as we had planned I intercepted Carol in the hall on her way to her room and said, "Carol, would you like to come and visit our room today?" She nodded her head and I took her by the hand and we went to our room. I gave her a seat and sent one of the boys down to Mrs. Rice's room to get her belongings. She didn't object. We went on with our usual day. Everybody was nice and at the end of the day she agreed to stay with us.

It wasn't easy. We followed our regular routine – our reading circles, phonics exercises, copying the simple words off the board, singing, and practicing our addition and sub-traction. The children all responded in their own way. Some just smiled, the girls stayed with her at recess time and all of them were kind. And this became our daily pattern. Once in a great while someone would get a little impatient but the rest of the children would immediately corral the offender. Carol began to relax and did all of her work very well but day after day she didn't say a word.

I tried vainly to think of what else I could do. She seemed to have formed a pattern with which she was content. But finally it happened! Just when I had hit bottom and decided it probably never would. But at eight minutes to ten, six weeks and two days after she came to us, Carol talked! I still get goose bumps just thinking about it.

We were in the reading circle as usual. Trying to look relaxed, I actually was feeling like a firecracker about to explode. I was beginning to think that this was hopeless and maybe Carol needed to go to a different school. As usual I called on the children to read in order from the beginning of the semicircle so I would spare her from being caught by surprise. She was the fourth one in the circle and while the third child was reading, I suddenly started to panic inwardly. "She won't read, I know she won't", I thought. "This is beginning to be ridiculous and I've had about all I can take," my mind raced on.

By then, it was her turn and as calmly as possible I said, "Carol?" In the next split second when she failed to respond, I had the awful thought that maybe she was enjoying all the attention she was getting, that she might purposely be dragging this on. I was so wrought up I simply couldn't continue, so I just suddenly announced, "Let's all go to recess."

My bombshell had no effect. The ten o'clock recess bell is such an established ritual that it's practically an institution. We always go through the little routine of getting ready and we never go before the bell rings, so they looked at me in stunned silence. From the looks on their faces they all sensed that something was wrong. I repeated, "Let's go to recess," and at that precise moment, Carol jumped to her feet and said, "I'll read!"

I had thought for weeks that when "it" happened, I would be very calm and that for her sake, I would act like it was nothing unusual. However, I hadn't figured on how strong our emotions would be. Wild horses couldn't have kept us calm. We were all so thrilled. I jumped up and hugged her and hugged her, half crying. Every child in the room jumped up and down in the aisles and hugged each other. Some of them ran and hugged her – even the boys. We were literally wild with joy. It was wonderful.

After a few minutes things calmed down so I had them sit down. All this time, Carol was smiling broadly. "Carol, would you like to read in the circle or in the front of the room?" She pointed to the front and my heart sank momentarily – maybe she wouldn't read. "Would you like to have a few other girls read with you?" She nodded. Everyone wanted to read with her but we decided on three girls and the four of them lined up in the front of the room. She was standing so that she would be third. I held my breath although none of the children seemed a bit worried.

The first child read. The second child read. And then, miracle of miracles, Carol read the third sentence of page twelve in our primer. She read as sweetly and calmly as if she had been doing it all of her life. I've never heard anything that sounded more beautiful. Everyone sat in hushed and reverent awe for just a moment and then they clapped and clapped. By now it was recess time and they all went out to the playground. I went across the street to buy suckers for all of us.

It was almost eleven o'clock before we settled down.

Carol's miracle happened in a way I had never anticipated. Her concern for me and her classmates caused her to forget her own feelings. She saw me becoming upset, something that hadn't happened before and she worried more about my feelings and those of her friends than she did about her own. And it had to happen when it did. It had to come after we had gained her confidence and love so she cared how we felt.

This whole endeavor was a beautiful experience for all of the children. Along with the reading, writing and arithmetic they had learned a lesson in love, understanding, patience and compassion, which no amount of talking could have gotten across to them.

And there was another wonderful angle to this. Paul was standing by his desk with a broad grin on his face looking genuinely happy. It was the only time all year that I saw him looking completely relaxed. He too, felt that he had made a contribution to Carol's breakthrough. It had been good for him to forget himself. That single moment of a feeling of accomplishment gave him a feeling of confidence that he never before had experienced. And Larry – he was deprived of normal social relationships, but he had a part in this. And Julie – she was thinking of someone outside of herself and she had really helped. And Ronnie – all of them, in fact, every single one of them.

On that day our first grade could have licked the world. We had met a terrific challenge, we had waged a long and hard battle, and we had won. And best of all, our goal had been of the highest and noblest order. There was no material gain in our victory, no glory or praise would come to us but together we had been able to help another human being by proving our compassion and concern for her welfare. And that's why we sat and licked our suckers in an atmosphere of complete happiness.

When Carol laid down on her mat after lunch that day,

she heaved a very long sigh of relief, smiled a little smile and then closed her eyes contentedly. For her the victory was the sweetest of all.

Good Morning

When adults walk into a typical first grade room most of them just see a bunch of cute, noisy children. But really, all of life is there – joy, happiness, laughter, learning, developing, kindness and unkindness as well as frustration, fear, sadness, heartbreak – everything but hate and prejudice. It takes our society a little more than six years to inflict those upon the heart of a child. In fact, you could observe all of these any day while I was taking up the lunch money if you looked carefully.

In our particular school system this task is a daily affair because the cafeteria ladies have to know exactly how many children are going to eat. We get it over with before our regular school day starts. Besides it helps the teacher get to know each child as an individual. You can't do that if you start saying, "Sit down, be quiet," the moment they step in the room so we always had a friendly conversation while I collected the lunch money. Every morning I would be sitting at my desk with pencil and record book ready for when the patrol boys would open the door and we'd be off! On a typical morning, the dialogue would go something like this:

"Miss Dresseljuice, did you know we got to eat out last night. I had a hamburger and fries."

"Miss Dresseljuice, I bought a crawdad to show."

"Good morning, children! May I have your lunch money, please Tommy? Put the crawdad on the sharing shelf, honey. Get off my foot, please Anne."

"Teacher, did you know I could spell encyclopedia?"

"Miss Dresseljuice, you know what? I'm not going to talk all day today."

"E-n-c-",

"Miss Dresseljuice, look at my new skin – I fell off the porch."

"Teacher, I got a new petticoat – with three rows."

"Can I fix the library books?"

"I'm glad you could eat out. I'll bet it was fun. My, that's a big skin! Don't call me teacher, honey. Annabelle, I'll be very glad if you stop talking so much. Yes, Jeanne, put the books on a nice quiet pile and say 'may.' Get off my foot, please, Mike E. Where's your lunch money, Jack?"

"Our new baby cried all night."

"Can I have some vanilla paper?"

"Miss Dresseljuice, I sawd Annabelle at the grocery store last night. She went by in a car and throwd me a kiss." Annabelle giggles and titters.

"I told my mama and daddy this morning, I'm gonna quit talking in school 'cause you don't want me to."

"c-y, c-y-, did you hear that part, Miss Dresseljuice?"

"My dad ate steak."

"Where's your other dime, Jan? Here's your nickel back, Annabelle. Your petticoat is beautiful – all those rows, honey. Ronnie, don't climb up on the shelf. Please get off my foot, Larry."

"I was just telling Larry, I'm not going to talk today. Not at all."

"Yeah, and I believe it, Miss Dresseljuice. Annabelle's looking real willing today."

"Miss Dresseljuice, the yellow paint's gone. How can I make a sun?"

"May I have your money, Debbie? Why don't you water the flowers, Ronnie? When your baby gets bigger, he won't cry at night."

"p-e – are you listening, teacher?"

"You didn't look at the new skin, that was the old stuff."

"No, you don't get a nickel back David B. You may have one piece of va – I mean manilla paper. Just make blue clouds, Larry. You're on my foot, Jan. Lisa, why do you have a Band-Aid on? Did you hurt your finger?"

"Bill pushed me and now I lost my nickel."

"d-i-a."

"I didn't hurt my finger, Miss Dresseljuice, but when I got home from school yesterday it was all pumped up."

"Can I paint?"

"Here's an apple mama said I should give you."

"Thank you, Nancy."

"Did I tell you when I was four a hornet stung me?"

"Here's a note – I gotta stay in for recess." The note reads, "Tommy has a post nasal drip."

"I'm gonna quit talking and I'm gonna be real quiet."

"Mike B. got my hook and I gotta put my sweater on it."

"Miss Dresseljuice did you know they had a fire in San Francisco?"

"Our dog had puppies."

"Daddy's never coming home, Miss Dresseljuice."

"Jeanne spilled the paint."

"Janet, your daddy will come and see you, I'm sure. Tommy, you may stay in for recess. Ronnie, get off the desk. Beth, get off my foot, please. Where is your lunch money, John? Caroline, please go after the mop. Be careful, your desk will tip over if you sit on the edge that way, Mike M. How many puppies did your dog have, Bruce?"

"Paul, come bring me your money, dear."

"Did you hear me spell encyclopedia? Huh,huh?"

"Mike kissed me!"

"No, John, you have to give me all four nickels."

"Thank you very much, Paul."

"Why do I have to give you four nickels when he only gave you two dimes and the nickels is the biggest?"

107

"I told you, you'd fall, Mike M. Everybody, get down and look for Doug's nickel. It's wonderful the way you can spell encyclopedia, Karen, but I believe you left the "l" out. Better start over. Are you hurt, Mike M? You didn't give me your lunch money, Bill. Let me do the mopping, please."

"Huh, teacher, huh?"

"I know nickels are bigger than dimes, honey – that's just the way it is." "EVERYBODY QUIET! I think Mr. James is talking on the intercom. Ronnie, if you watched where you were going, you wouldn't have knocked that chair over. Let Susan Lee have the hook, Mike E. Go help Mike E find his own hook, will you, Mike B? Kissing girls is silly, Mike M. Your new skin is real good! They put out the fire in San Francisco a long time ago, honey. Does anyone know what Mr. James said?"

"Teacher, my mama said we can't get a new baby."

"Miss Dresseljuice did I tell you what my brother ate?"

"Tommy, go to the shelf and get some Kleenex, honey. What did he eat, dear?"

The bell rang. A quick scurrying and scrambling like rabbits and miraculously, everyone was in their seat. Drawing a breath of deep contentment, I knew this would be a good day! No paper drive, no Red Cross money, no rain, no mud, no defense stamps, nobody broken out with measles, no Easter seals, no mad mamas, nobody sick to their stomach and at the moment, nobody on my feet.

"Stop talking, Annabelle. Let's all sing our good morning song!"

Yes, everything good about life can be found in the first grade.

Heartache

Without a doubt Janet was my saddest child this year. At first, I thought she was a daydreamer but later I realized she was worrying. Along in October she mentioned that maybe she would go to her grandmother's house to live, and that bothered me. Shortly after that, I was checking her writing when she suddenly said, "You know what, Miss Dresseljuice? My daddy and mama don't like each other." Her worries were understandable.

The next week her mother came to see me; she and her husband were getting a divorce. She was very attractive, in her early thirties, and I noticed on the record that they had two boys younger than Janet. What a tragedy. Sometimes a divorce is good for children, but often it devastates them. The children often feel responsible for it. I asked her if there was any chance for a reconciliation, and she said that it was too late because her husband definitely planned to marry his secretary. She looked so shaken so I told her I would try my best to help ease the effect this would have on Janet.

When I first started teaching I sometimes thought I had to take responsibility for trying to hold the family together, but I gave up on that. If I got so emotionally involved, I wouldn't be able to teach the rest of the children and besides, I don't suppose a first grade teacher has ever managed to save a marriage – she doesn't even know if it should be saved. You can only try and help the child get through it as best you can.

A few days later, Janet stayed behind when the children went to recess. With tears in her eyes she told me, "My daddy doesn't love me anymore."

"Oh, honey, I'm sure he does", I said.

"Well then, why is he going to move away and leave us behind?"

"Well, he loves you but he and your mama are cross at each other and they know that bothers you and your brothers."

"It doesn't bother me so much. I just put my head under the pillow when they fight. I don't want him to go away."

"He thinks it's best, honey."

"Well, then, why won't he take me along? I'm daddy's girl."

"Because you'd miss your mama and she'd miss you."

"Then he shouldn't go 'cause we'll all miss him."

Out of the mouths of babes.

What could I say? The "Janet's" in this world are more and more numerous. She spent most of her waking hours with me, but her father never came by, so I can't tell him that she isn't achieving up to her capacity, that her nails are bitten down to the quick, that she daydreams far too much and that she shares her worries with me almost daily. She needed some attention from him so much but he never came to school. I could only try and help her accept what was happening. I wasn't very good at it.

One day Janet fell and skinned her knee on the playground and I brought her in to apply a Band-Aid. She cried as if she'd broken her leg, but when I looked at the slight scratch and listened to her crying, I realized that she wasn't crying about the knee. She was crying about her daddy, crying about her lost security, crying because she was blaming her mother and her self, crying because her small world was going to pieces, and she couldn't prevent it, and crying because she was emotionally spent. Holding her closely, I fought my tears. I couldn't tell her it would be alright or that it wasn't so bad. I could only tell her that grownups have problems but they would get settled and things would get better.

That afternoon her mother said, "If we can just get through this I'll make it up to Janet later." Hopefully it would work, but, like Janet, I wasn't at all sure.

During the year, Janet changed. By spring she seldom

mentioned her daddy. Her defense mechanism was to become slightly harder and more brittle. She didn't interact with the other children as much, not even on the playground. She seemed to adopt an independent attitude and confided in me less and less. Because I hadn't helped her change anything she became slightly aloof toward me, too. We'd still talk, but it wasn't the same. Because of her thorough disillusionment with all of the primary adults in her life, it would probably be a long time before she would trust anyone again. It was heartbreaking.

The Basics

Teaching reading, writing and arithmetic is the only reason you have first grades. Beginning writing was probably the easiest to teach. It was called "Penmanship." They just had to learn how to make circles and straight lines and then conquer the challenge of getting them to sit on a line. Add a few connections here and there and it was just a matter of practice. They copied words, then sentences and then paragraphs off the board. Ninety-nine percent of them succeeded. They would all become good writers unless they became doctors.

First grade arithmetic at that time was also fairly simple. You were only dealing with two basic concepts at that level – to add and subtract. If you collected enough toothpicks, lollipop sticks or burned match sticks you had it made. Practically all of the children were able to handle it for numbers up to ten, which was all the curriculum required. A few could go higher and it was fun to help them with the "borrowing" bit. It was amazing how much they could learn, even though they were only six years old. You could spot future engineers even at that age.

Teaching reading was always the most fascinating for me. At the end of the year I looked at the whole class with so much pride. There were always one or two who weren't as good as I wished, but most of them were really good readers. It was amazing how it had all happened. What went on in their little heads to enable them to get it all together? Reading is really quite complex, but some children pick it up very rapidly and some really struggle.

No two children learn the same way. My philosophy was to present every way I knew and to latch on to what appeared to appeal to each of them. Sight reading and phonics both worked. A big argument developed over which system worked – I was a great believer in using both. I always taught the Scott, Foresman series – the *Dick and Jane* books, and I loved them. The first pre-primer had fourteen words in it and if they learned all of them by sight they had the basis for phonics. They had all the consonants – Dddd like Dick, Jjjj like Jane, Bababa like Baby, Ffff like Father and so on. And the pictures were great. Sally was the baby, Puff was the cat, Wag was the dog. They could hardly miss.

But sometimes they did. One little boy was having lots of trouble. He read, "Father is tall" and sure enough, there was the picture of the tall father. We turned the page and there was the picture of Sally and the obvious, phonetic "Sally is small" but he read "Sally ain't." You don't win them all.

Edwin was reading exceptionally well, and I said, "This is wonderful. How did you learn so much?"

"I look at the letters that stick up over the top and the ones that fall down under the line and I remember them." He had to do more than that, but whatever it was, it was working for him.

Jim could read very well when school started. I went to the school library and to other rooms to borrow books for him. His parents bought extra books for him to bring to school. He was especially interested in astronomy and we found everything we could for him on a level he would be able to understand. It was a challenge to keep him busy and interested.

One day I was sitting in the reading circle with the "Robins," the group having the most difficulty. From his desk Jim looked at me real funny and after awhile he got up and came over to me. "Miss Dresseljuice, why are you doing all that? Why don't you just let them read?"

When I first started teaching my goal was to teach every single child in my room to be able to read from the first reader by the end of the year. That meant they had gone through three pre-primers, one primer and the first reader. I was convinced that if I tried hard enough, they could all do it. It took me a couple of years of teaching before I realized that reaching my goal was not always possible.

We gave each child an IQ test the first week of school. It showed one ridiculous picture of a button-up shoe that must have dated back to the 1890s. No one ever chose it as the correct answer, so no one ever aced the test. It was surprising that the test did, however, have some validity. Unfortunately, each year there would be three or four children who scored in the high sixties or low seventies.

Usually they were children who had not been to kindergarten and had very little experience with books. But one or two of them would simply need more than one school year to get to the first reader level. It was part of my learning experience to realize that every child had to go at their own pace. You couldn't compensate by spending an unfair amount of time with them. Every teacher gradually learns that your goal should be to take every single child as far as they can go.

Motivating them was always the key to success. If you could get them really interested early on you couldn't keep them from learning. That is what really keeps the teacher going.

In the fall a state teachers meeting was held in Detroit. It was a two day affair, so I rode up with an older teacher who was a friend of mine. We went to the hotel, registered and attended a very nice reception. Later we went out to dinner with some other teachers from Monroe. The next morning my friend said, "Let's go shopping."

"Oh, my goodness! Aren't we supposed to go to the meetings?"

"Oh, I already don't teach as well as I know how to teach so why do I need to learn more?" It sounded good to me. We went shopping.

Discipline

Even children with special problems like Carol, Paul or Janet will generally succumb to the social order. Keeping a roomful of active six-year- olds under control every day for five days a week, every week all school year, is always a challenge. If the teacher can't do that she'd better quit the first day or she'll lose her mind.

There are many schools of thought when it comes to discipline – and it often comes to that in the first grade. Some teachers feel very strongly that better results will be obtained if the children suggest their own punishment. They like the "student council" idea and it may work fine with older children, but not with six-year-olds. They get so bloodthirsty.

When I completely ran out of ideas about how to punish Ronnie effectively, I said to the children on the spur of the moment, "What do you think we should do to Ronnie? He tripped Jeanne." Immediately everyone turned and glared suspiciously at Ronnie. Then they started recounting all the crimes he had committed all year and they came up with their ideas of a fitting punishment.

"No recess all year…plus a trip to Mr. James office for a good spanking…plus stand in the corner all day…plus stay after school every night till next summer." I ended up al-most defending poor Ronnie who, by this time had cringed down in his seat to about floor level. I didn't intend to use that system again.

There is another school of thought which is called "the strict" approach. It consists mostly of "don't," "sit down," and "be quiet" all administered in a very stern voice. It's the oldest theory going and it's based on the thought that if the class understands you are very strict they'll behave. It presupposes that the teacher is completely humorless, has no imagination and has a wide streak of dictatorship run-ning down her back.

I've tried this too. Not on purpose, exactly, but once in awhile I got up in the morning and with fire in my eye, de-cided that the whole trouble with this world is that nobody listened to a word I said. Marching to my class, I put a lot of long, hard writing on the blackboard and station myself at the doorway. As the children enter I inform them very sternly that they are to go right to their seats this morning and they are not to say a word. This is met with varying re-actions. Most of them look astounded – they can't figure out what hit me. Some look pleased – they think this a preamble to a field trip or something real exciting. Some look very philosophical – they, no doubt, have seen their mothers go through this sort of thing. Others want an explanation on the spot. They start out, "Why, but", but I stop them cold by demanding, "Get to your seat."

When I faced them one at a time, I could stand my ground. But when the bell rang and I stood in front of them, the full impact of their sad faces weaken me. I get a grip on myself by remembering the reason for this world's troubles, and I carry on. Everyone is quiet and we follow all of the "Rules." When I line them up later to go to the bathroom I say, "Walk, don't run in the hall." When a few run anyway I

say, "Walk! You are *going* to do as I say." I really tried hard
to be stern, but down underneath I knew all of the time that
it was a losing battle. By ten o'clock I conceded there is a
possibility that I was not destined to rule the world, and by
eleven o'clock I admitted that maybe someone else should
do it. Who cares?

It's such a relief to reach this stage. Then I could get
back to normal: that means that we all use our imaginations.
The point is that it's no fun at all for children to "sit down
and be quiet" but it's wonderfully exciting to be a jellyfish
draped across the seat. If you come into a room and everything is utter bedlam, it doesn't help a bit to yell at the obvious noise makers. They will stop only as long as the echo of
your voice remains in their ears. But come in and ferret out
the one who is acting the best and say in a very loud voice,
"Look at how good Beverly is being. Isn't it wonderful the
way she is doing just what she was asked to do?" Practically
everybody is interested in meriting such glowing praise.
They'll fall all over themselves in their rush to get into their
seats like the angelic Beverly, who has practically sprouted
wings by now.

Another angle to this approach is the out and out pretending business. "Let's all pretend we're on a desert island
and there's nobody around to talk to", or "Let's pretend we
are fairies being just light and pretty." When you hear a first
grade teacher carrying on like this, don't tell your neighbor
what an oddball she is. Just figure she's had lots of experience.

It would be nice to end right there and leave you with
the impression that the imagination approach is infallible,
but unfortunately, it has its weaknesses, too. Occasionally, a
docile child will come to school with fire in her eye. She too
will usually weaken by ten and conform by eleven. Or there
is the "all boy" who wants to be good and most of the time

he will be but every once in awhile he just can't resist the temptation to pull a braid or trip an unsuspecting teacher in spite of my "fairy" or "Indian hunter" routine.

The immature child is so concerned with his own little projects – like making bullets out of his clay when he should be writing, or sneaking licks off his sucker, that he doesn't care if everyone else sails off in an imaginary rocket. He'd rather make his bullets or get his licks in. Or there is the lazy child who doesn't want to make the effort to be an airplane, even in his imagination. A rugged individualist, like Julie, wants to make their own decisions about what they want to do and when they want to do it. But they realize before long that they are missing a lot of fun.

Then, unfortunately, there is the child like Ronnie, bless his heart, who liked to do his own thing most of the time. Occasionally, he would fly into the wild blue yonder with you but he has so much energy and so many ideas he wants to carry out that he's into something constantly. And though you try hard to avoid it, the truth of the matter is that he does get more than his share of attention. Children like this take patience, persistence, and understanding, as well as patience, persistence and understanding. Usually your note to the second grade teacher at the end of the year starts out, "This child is unusually active."

The pitfall the teacher must avoid in handling the ones who don't succumb to the "let's pretend" suggestions all of the time is the danger of excessive hollering and shouting. Every teacher needs a good shouting voice – I always feel that the mama or teacher who says she never raises her voice is either telling a lie or isn't doing a good job. But she must be very careful to save her shouting for only rare occasions and it is essential that it be a controlled shout which she can turn on in an emergency without having it really affect her own emotions. The child who is shouted at constantly shuns it as easily as a duck sheds water. But a sudden infrequent loud shout will get him or her every time.

By and large, I stuck with the imaginative approach supplemented by the emergency shout. Of course, sometimes in a noisy crowd downtown or at a ball game I find myself raising my hands and starting to say, "Let's all pretend," but usually I'm sane.

The Goat Play

Our school was poor, and the Parent-Teachers Association – PTA – was like a pack of rich relatives. They bought us records and record players, maps and globes, and countless gadgets the school board could never afford, so naturally we love them. But even better than the presents, occasionally, they ask a class to perform! We hit the jackpot because they invited us to put on a play at the March meeting. Any program put on by first graders probably represents more frustration for the teacher than anything that happens all year, but it is well worth it because the results are so sublimely ridiculous.

Three Little Goats was perfect for this performance. It had a big leading part for Ronnie, which would give him something to do. Several smaller parts could be cast easily from my group, and a speaking chorus allowed all the children to participate. The staging, properties, and costuming all looked very suitable and doable. Even the plot of the play was good, although it probably wouldn't matter particularly whether it did or didn't have a plot. By the time first graders have interpreted it, the audience never knows what was supposed to have happened – they'll just know it was funny.

The mamas started sewing costumes and teaching the solo parts, we all started chanting the chorus parts, and the play was successfully launched. About the time everyone had mastered their parts an epidemic of chickenpox hit us! We had to keep switching and rearranging in an effort to keep the parts filled. Fortunately, we started a couple of months in advance. After many practices and numerous changes the great day arrived and we had a full cast.

No one, under any circumstance, gets as nervous and excited as a six-year-old about to perform on stage before a real live audience. We didn't go on until four o'clock in the afternoon but, of course, the whole day was shot as far as learning anything was concerned. Every two minutes someone would ask, "Is it time?"

"How long until the play?"

"When will it start?"

"Does my hair still look good?"

Finally the day dragged by and the magic hour approached. Several mamas arrived early and we got the costumes on, we bathroomed, but didn't water them, slicked back the boys' hair, re-did the ponytails, straightened the braids, bows and ribbons, and retied the sashes. I checked to see that all those who were to take props had them in their little, hot hands. When all was in order they got in a line and we fluttered to the auditorium. No need for pretense today.

We arrived in time to separate the speaking cast from the chorus and got everyone stationed at their right entrances. The chorus looked really jittery so I went down the line and tried to reassure them. "You look so nice. Your mama will be so proud of you! Let's say the first line together, 'Over the hilltop – Over the hilltop'." I was saying it alone. No one even remembered what the play was about. I tried again and they came to life. Once they were started, I couldn't get them to hush. But the fateful moment was practically upon us, so I rushed back to check with Ronnie, my main character.

Even in the shadow of the stage curtains he looked

awfully suspicious to me. I hauled him out under better light. "Ronnie, you didn't have the chicken-pox when everyone else had them, did you?"

"No ma'am."

"Do you feel alright?"

"Yes ma'am." He didn't feel feverish – fifteen minutes more or less wouldn't hurt him – he could stay in bed fifteen minutes longer at the other end. I only hoped the audience wouldn't notice the speckles. I peeked through the curtains and got a quick glance of the packed house of smiling mama and grandma faces and got the cue from the principal to begin.

"Everybody think and do your best," I hissed loudly and nodded to the sixth grader to pull the curtain. It got stuck half way across and I stumbled over to give it a good yank. "Annabelle, you're first – go honey." They looked so cute with their flouncy skirts, slicked down hair and toothless grins I almost forgot myself what our play was about.

Beth was so engrossed in locating her mama that she ran right into Larry and set the first row into motion as they found their places and halted. Mike E. was deliberately pushing – that boy will push his way into heaven if he makes it – but finally the choristers were in their places. Their expressions amused me no end. Some were blushing, some were pale, some were tittering, some jostled their neighbors, many waved to their mamas and grandmas, and some stood aloof, probably pretending this was old stuff. Paul appeared to be mumbling a little. He was in the back row and this experience didn't seem to be upsetting him. That was very good.

The second grade teacher struck a loud chord on the piano and brought me back to reality. I crossed my fingers and prayed that all would go well. The piano got to the end of the introduction and there was dead silence. I peeked out and realized that my chorus was so entranced by the audience that they'd completely forgotten why they came. I waved frantically, the piano started over and this time they came through. They sang and chanted their way down through the first two pages of my copy and I began to breathe normally. Tears came to my eyes at the sight of Carol chanting away.

Ronnie, my spotted lead, was standing confidently by my side waiting for his entrance and everything seemed to be under control. "Talk loud," I said and Ronnie started for center stage. I looked at my script and waited for his "Billy Goats," but nothing was forthcoming. I looked out and saw his speckled face turn to a polka-dot green before my very eyes. His eyes were glued with horrible fascination upon the vast audience before him. Not Ronnie, I thought. Not confident, self-assured Ronnie. He knows his part cold. But yes, he was paralyzed with fear.

Frantically waving I sprinted backstage to the other side, jumping over old curtains and props as I went, and arrived breathless to carry on my waving. By now he looked like he might faint, but before he went down, I succeeded in attracting his attention. I smiled and nodded vigorously and hissed the words loudly trying desperately to ooze a little confidence out toward him. I caught his eye and gradually his face regained a little color, the terror left and he began to look closer to normal. Within seconds he was copying my "Billy Goats!" and by the time he got to the end of the second line his old confidence had returned. (This was really a good experience for him. He didn't forget it. It took him down a notch.)

I dashed back to get Brenda ready for her entrance. I stumbled over a rope and fell sprawling, my script flying all directions. Worse than that, I bumped against the back curtain and now the whole audience would wonder why it was waving but I grabbed the papers and hurtled on. I don't know why I worried.

Brenda looked at me coolly and asked, "Did you hurt yourself, teacher?" and then calmly marched out onto the stage.

I got back to my peek hole to see how things were progressing. One of the choristers had gotten warm and was fanning herself with the skirt of her pinafore but other than that things were going according to my carefully laid plans. My "bumblebee" came buzzing in now and stopped to deliver his lines.

"Mr. Goat," he started but what was this? Stevie, my well behaved, quiet little Stevie was taking over.

"You're not on your X," he told the bumblebee, who dutifully moved onto his chalk mark. "Judy, you're not standing in a straight line, and Mike, you don't talk loud enough." `

From here on it didn't matter that my script had gotten all mixed up. Stevie took over the stage direction and they did great without my help until he discovered that Julie didn't have her cane.

"Miss Dresseljuice," Stevie called out from the stage. "Julie didn't use her head and she left her cane down in the room." I rummaged around frantically and found it backstage. I pushed it out toward them and they carried on.

The audience was convulsed by now. First graders can steal any show. When they finally pranced off the stage they were carried away by their success.

"Wasn't we good?"

"Didn't Stevie do good?" they all clamored and I was forced to agree.

"You were wonderful!"

Resting
And every day all year we had the infamous "rest periods."

They are one of the great institutions and necessary evils of the first grade. Obviously, six-year-olds can't be expected to perform at top capacity from morning until mid-afternoon without rest, so a special period is scheduled for the children to prove that you are wrong.

In our room this contest came right after lunch. Yesterday was typical. An absolutely necessary part of rest period was to stop at the bathroom on the way back from the cafeteria. It is imperative that once they get on their rugs I am in a position to say, "No, you just went." As they came in I stood guarding the faucet, since it is equally imperative that no one gets such an ill-timed drink. I greet them with, "Have you gone? Spread out your rug and get on it." Everyone gets their rug from the shelf and goes to the place on the floor, which has been carefully prearranged by me.

The problems are always closest to me. The more I can trust them the further from me they are allowed to sprawl. Only the solid "A" in conduct students can be found in the far flung corners, while my desk is completely walled in with the noisemakers and paper wad throwers. Of course, that means that Ronnie is practically under my feet.

They always visit and dawdle, and would stretch this preparation time over the whole period if I let them so I have to use a gimmick to get them all in a prone position. "I'm going to count to ten", I say and for some odd reason this works. I don't know myself what would happen if I got to ten and they weren't all down. But of course that's only the beginning. The real tussle is to keep them there.

For the first few moments after getting settled they are fairly quiet but their little minds wander in all directions. They are not content long with quiet reverie though. They want to share their thoughts.

"Why isn't this Saturday? It looks like Saturday," observed Tommy.

"My daddy said our dog was the father of Jimmy's dogs' puppies but I don't know why he said that. Our dog doesn't live with them. He hardly even ever goes over to see them," Jeannie commented.

"Did you ever see pictures of skeletons, teacher?" asked Ronnie.

That's a good leading question but I was not going to fall for it, so I only answered, "Yes."

"Well, did you know that's all you are except for blood and bones?" I should have known I would get drawn into it.

"Well, we have hearts and souls and minds and a few other things too, honey."

"It's a good thing they are put on like they are because blood and skin isn't very pretty alone," he continued.

I won't pursue it any further. I could tell by the "gone" look on his face that he wanted to linger long and tenderly on the subject of skeletons, but at least he is quiet. I left him to his blood and gore and turned my attention to a few who have not entered the quiet reverie stage yet.

"Who is throwing crayons?" I asked.

Sixteen children answered, "David B. is. And he's getting them out of other kids deskus."

"Well, pretend you are a dishrag, David B. and lie still."

"Annabelle, what are you doing?"

"Just breathing, Miss Dresseljuice, just breathing."

"Well, stop crawling around while you breathe, honey and stay on your rug."

"Take your thumb out of your mouth, Stevie." Invariably in every batch of thirty there were one or two thumb suckers.

"Don't eat the chalk, Susan B."

"Teacher, my rug fell apart!"

"Well, Beth, I've been telling you for a week not to pull

the strings out of it." I hate people who say, I told you so, but after all!

"Jimmy D. stuck his tongue out at me!" shouted Tommy.

"Well, it won't hurt you, Tommy, but it makes Jimmy D. look awfully silly."

Isn't it strange, I mused, to have all these duplicate names in one class. The thirty-one of them probably have a total or fourteen names. One would think that hospitals or the government or someone gave parents a choice of only two or three names for each year's crop.

"Am I being good, teacher?"

"Yes, Annabelle. Very good, but please be quiet, too."

"Teacher, did you know that taxes are going higher and higher and wages are getting lower and lower?"

"David B. is pulling black stuff off the wall."

"David B., stop that immediately. That's the molding and it costs the taxpayers lots of money. I've already told you all about taxes." Obviously I must say more.

"Yes ma'am, I know. Yesterday when it was raining my mama came home in a taxes." Clearly I hadn't said enough.

"Oh David B., you didn't listen. Come and put your rug right next to me." He settled in very close to me and I looked down unbelievingly at him every few seconds, because he was being absolutely motionless. Every time I checked, he just stared up at me.

After two full minutes he said, "I'll bet you don't even know what to say when I'm so good like this, do you?"

I ruffled his hair and said, "Oh, David B., I'll think of something. You are so sweet."

"Ronnie kicked me."

"Somebody smushed my clay rocket!" The wiggling was getting quite general now, so I told a story.

"Let's all be dreamers," I said. "Let's pretend we are play-ing in a big, grassy meadow and a nice fairy comes along." I

125

go on and on and everything is peace and quiet until I run out of exciting adventures. When I retire I'll write daytime serials for kids because I'm so eminently qualified.

"Susan has to go to the bathroom."

"Karen B., be quiet. How do you know Susan has to go to the bathroom?"

"She told me."

"Well, you're not supposed to be talking during rest time," I hedge. It was an obvious stall. I was bound to hear more about it and I did.

"But Miss Dresseljuice, I do have to go."

"Are you sure?" Another stall. A vigorous affirmative shaking of the ponytail.

"Well, you know you are supposed to go on the way back from the cafeteria." Still stalling but weakening. Karen gets to her feet and by her stance, I know she is serious. "Alright, but go on the way next time," I tell her as she heads out the door.

"It feels like something is hanging in my throat."

"Judy is pushing me and she's hurting my bones and my tonsils."

That did it. The bathroom and health are the two hazardous subjects which are to be avoided during rest period. The complaints start coming in fast and furious. In moments half the room either feels sick or has to go to the bathroom or both. Suddenly I tower above it all and announce loudly and firmly, "Stop Miss Dresseljuiceing me! Everyone feels good and nobody has to go to the bathroom. Be quiet and rest!!!"

I take my seat amidst deafening silence. It was just the right amount of authoritative firmness and volume because it worked for maybe twenty seconds. I optimistically reach for some paperwork foolishly thinking I might have time to correct a few workbooks but another potentially dangerous subject is brought up. "Teacher, maybe we are going to move." Saved by the bell! I was so glad. I get so tired of resting!

Coping

Larry's mother continued her restrictions, and it broke my heart, but I had no choice. We had some beautiful weather in the fall and I wanted so much for Larry to go out and enjoy it, in spite of her ban against recesses. It was almost criminal for a six-year-old boy to have to stay almost completely inactive from eight-thirty in the morning until three-thirty in the afternoon five days week.

During recess he would stand by the window with his nose pressed against the glass, watching the other children. Of course, Ronnie and his followers were the most active ones on the playground and Larry would keep his eyes glued on their activities. I could have cried one day when he was watching them play baseball and he asked me, "Do you think I could hit a baseball?"

I tried my best to talk his mother into letting him go out for at least part of one recess each day and since she was at school so much I had ample opportunity to talk with her. She not only brought him in the morning and came for him in the afternoon, but sometimes during the day I would see her peeking at me through the little glass window in our door. However, I couldn't get her to agree to even a minute on the playground.

Then I resorted to trying to trick her into it. I told her that every other day I was on playground duty and that I wasn't supposed to leave unsupervised first graders in my room alone. I thought I could get her to consent to letting Larry just stand by my side during these recesses but she went to the principal before I had a chance to get to him and came back with a note of special dispensation. So that was out.

Then, during a cold snap, I told her that too many children were staying in. It was catching on like wild fire so I would have to require a note from each mother each day telling me whether or not she really did want her child to remain inside. However, this didn't work at all. I figured she would get tired of writing notes each day or would forget it sometimes. But after a few days I noticed that Larry had an undated note which he kept in his desk which he just showed me each day. Pursuing this course would only embarrass him so I gave up on that.

Then one day in December I did a horrible thing. The City Fire Department had a demonstration on the playground. This is about as exciting to a six-year-old as Santa Claus. When Larry asked if he could go I didn't answer him directly. I just said, "Everyone will go – just like fire drills." He was so thrilled he didn't ask twice.

It was a routine demonstration but, of course, all of the children were beside themselves with joy when they hoisted the extension ladders, swung them around, rang the bells and sirens, and flashed the lights. We had already gone five minutes into recess time when it was over so the children scattered for play. I deliberately waved my hand and looked away when I saw Larry start toward me. Although I wasn't on playground duty I didn't even go back into the building for fear he'd follow me. I just figured it was a beautiful day, he was already out there and he was going to have some fun for once. And he did.

Ronnie and his gang were playing their special brand of football; Larry ran up and down and jumped onto piles of players like a maniac. Once he even made a pitifully poor attempt at trying to kick the ball. He was almost hysterical with joy at his sudden unforeseen freedom. I prayed he wouldn't get hurt. But this brief incident brought on a major crisis and changed everything. His mother called me that night and told me, "something will be done about the fact that Larry was outside."

Late the next afternoon she came in with a note from a doctor saying that Larry was not to be allowed to go out for any more recesses for the balance of the year. I accepted it meekly but inwardly I was furious at the doctor. How could he be so foolish as to look only at the physical side of this? Was there something seriously wrong with Larry? Did he realize what he was doing to him? What possible motive could he have?

After school I went in to talk to the principal and he called the doctor. We learned that it was not Larry's' doctor who had written the note, but his mothers' psychiatrist. He said that Larry, his sister and his father would all suffer the most if the mother became so emotionally upset that she couldn't remain at home. And as we talked I realized that he was right. He felt that her condition would improve in time and mentioned that her husband was very cooperative.

I knew too that Larry loved his mother and that he felt no resentment about her demands. I could see that I would interfere with his acceptance of her if I tried to change the status quo so I quit trying. Many times it hurt me deeply to see him miss so much fun but I would remind myself that he was young, this probably wouldn't have a lasting effect on him and I should try and help him accept his life as it was.

And so my resolve earlier in the year to reform the mother went by the wayside. It was a learning experience for me. Once again it made me realize that under adverse circumstances the best a teacher can do is to try and help the child cope with the situation.

Progress for Paul

Paul continued to be a big concern for me. I wished his parents would consider taking him to a psychiatrist but I knew that was not going to happen because of the father's attitude. It would only cause more trouble if I suggested it.

A good thing was that it hadn't taken me very long to gain his confidence and love. In fact within a matter of weeks after school started he was clinging to me too closely. That's when I particularly felt I needed advice. If I let him make a second mother out of me I might just be exacerbating the problems he already had. I wanted him to adjust to his whole environment.

Sometimes I felt I ought to be stricter with him. In fact, I went to school one Monday morning determined to be firm, but fair. He had gotten into the habit of following me around almost constantly. If I ever took one step backward I stepped on him. And so I decided I'd start by requiring him to stay in his seat more and at least attempt to have him spend more time on the seat work the other children were doing. After all, I would be right there in the room, and surely he would see I wasn't exactly abandoning him.

However, I gave up the idea within fifteen minutes. The one bright spot in Paul's situation was that he continued to make good progress in learning to read and I knew that was terribly significant. Reading is the most complicated thing we learn in first grade. He also could do arithmetic orally. His writing, his written arithmetic, the coloring, in fact, anything he had to get down on paper was a miserable failure. Most of the time he'd look at a page for about thirty seconds and then grab a crayon or pencil and scribble through it even when I gave him the simplest work and sat down with him to do it. It was a mystery that he was learning to read but it gave him a measure of confidence which he needed so badly.

I guess I should have known that my efforts toward firmer discipline were doomed to failure but I had gotten myself quite enthused about it over the weekend. I was not getting results fast enough under my present regime. I reasoned that he had proven that he had sufficient intelligence and that if I would require more of him he might soon see that this was nothing drastic and maybe very soon he would learn to be comfortable.

He had gotten into the habit of coming over and standing by my side through all three reading circles and then I actually considered him a fourth group by himself because I read with him alone for a few minutes each day at his desk. I knew it was very good that he was so interested.

I started my brave new plan by telling him to stay in his seat until it was time for his circle to read. His dark eyes widened, his pale skin got even whiter and he looked as terrified as if I'd just told him I was going to push him off a mountain cliff. I started to weaken, Then Annabelle, who had started mothering him the first week of school, jumped up and reproached me with, "Miss Dresseljuice, you know Paul likes to stay with you." In fact, all of the children looked at me as if I were being terribly unfair, so I gave up. If they sensed his need so quickly then surely it was real. I didn't allow any of the rest of them to roam around at will and they didn't expect to. But they knew without any explanation that he needed that privilege.

Paul did make progress but not nearly as much as I hoped. There were times when a stranger could have come in for as long as an hour and they would not have noticed anything different about Paul except that he didn't stay in his seat all of the time. He got so that except on one of his bad days I could close the doors without any explanation to him. When we had a film he'd always get a library chair and sit next to me, but he learned to relax and enjoyed them. By the end of the year he didn't even put his hand on my knee, while the first month or two he'd clutch my leg unmercifully. Yes, he did make progress.

One peculiar thing about him was that he never seemed to be at all affected when I disciplined other children. He seemed to admire Ronnie. If I fussed at him Paul wouldn't seem to be bothered at all. Probably he shut himself away from it or maybe he saw that Ronnie had it coming to him.

Carol's problem was the only one that ever seemed to really take him out of himself. Sometimes when she would return to her seat after having failed to talk in the reading circle, he'd go over and stand by her desk. I never observed him saying anything but he looked sympathetic and she didn't resent him. Maybe she even appreciated it. To see the two of them together would be enough to move a heart of stone providing you knew the background. And when she finally talked, his joyful reaction was part of the reason I cried.

I promoted him with no qualms because he was a better than average reader. He read jerkily but he knew the words and comprehended the meaning. He was also good at oral arithmetic. His writing and art work were horrible but they aren't so complicated to learn and he'll pick them up later if he can just get straightened out emotionally. One good thing was that he learned to stay in his seat for longer periods of time. Failure was the last thing he needed. He needed the confidence he would get from being promoted and he needed to learn that his mama and I are not the only adults whom he can love and trust.

And so at the end of the year I pushed him out of our nest. Poor baby, he was not really ready but if he gets some understanding teachers and if his home life doesn't get any worse then maybe he'll be alright. It was the best I could do for my little Paul.

They All Pass

And so the year came to an end. It was a good thing because it was terrifically hot the last week. The children were cross and crabby and ready to fight at the drop of a hat. By two o'clock in the afternoon they were so listless that we really couldn't accomplish much. We just had stories and records and films. Even the Show and Tells weren't up to par. Ronnie's antics were particularly unfunny and I got cross, too. Tuesday Annabelle noticed, "Boy, teacher, you are hot and crabby, ain't you?" and I had to admit that I was. Her remark helped keep me in line the rest of the week.

The year had its trials and tribulations but like Nancy said about their family trip to California last summer, "I knew it would be good, but it was a lot more better than I expected."

I hoped Julie's mother won't spend the summer undoing everything we've accomplished this year; I wished Anne were a little better reader; I fantasized that Ronnie had learned to behave better, and I prayed that Paul felt more secure. But, that's the way it is in the first grade. You never turn out a finished product.

Carol never got to be a big talker. She'll always be rather quiet and reserved but she talked whenever there was a need to and I know she was comfortable. She always read in class and would volunteer in group discussions. She had friends on the playground and was happy. When she told me goodbye this morning I got shivers up and down my spine just visualizing how I would have felt if she had been unable to say it.

Jim did so well that it made my heart fill with pride,

although that's foolish because it certainly wasn't my doing. A child with an IQ and a personality like his can hardly miss, especially not one who is as interested as he is. Larry's mother was there, of course, and while I hate to lose Larry I must say I am not sorry to "pass" her. However, we had a very amicable parting. She even thanked me.

Annabelle hugged me so enthusiastically around the knees that she almost swept me off my feet. Later she brought her brother Wallace, then William – about four of them in all before she finally said the final goodbye. And Janet. Did I fail her? I'm afraid so. There is just so much you can do. But it is good that she learned to read, write and do her arithmetic better than average.

This teaching business is such a responsibility. In fact, the ideal teacher would have to be a miracle worker. You can't remake parents because of a Larry or Janet and you can't make a psychiatric ward out of the whole room because of a Paul. The children are all so different – some are too aggressive, some too shy, some can't learn easily, some are brilliant, some just average – yet you constantly must be aware of each child's needs and reactions.

And you learn that first graders are amazingly perceptive. One day a little boy named Ross arrived late for school. I asked him why and he said, "Well, my grandmother is sick today and I had to get my own breakfast."

I felt so badly for him because I knew his father was in the Army in Europe and his mother was a "Rosie Riveter" working in a nearby defense plant. I said, "Oh, honey, I'm so sorry. Will your grandmother be OK?"

"She'll be fine. She went uptown last night and drank too much beer."

Several times children experienced the death of a family member while they were in the first grade. In every case the family handled it very badly. Either they were so over-whelmed with their own grief that they didn't realize how their six-year-old was being affected or maybe they just didn't know how to explain it. I remember little Judy. She missed three or four days of school and as soon as she got back she told me, "I have a Show and Tell today" so I called on her first. She said, "My Grandpa died and they put him in a big, pretty box and he had a fancy suit on but he looked real funny. We all went to church and the preacher and we all sang songs and then we went out in the country and they put Grandpa in a big hole."

Everyone was stunned. I couldn't help myself. I said, "Oh honey, your Grandpa wasn't really in the box and that's why he looked so funny. He is really in heaven and that's a very good place." Judy and all of the rest of them looked very relieved. Fortunately, no one asked any questions.

A precious little girl named Jody experienced the death of her four-year-old sister. Annaliese died of leukemia after a ten day illness. When Jody returned to school I overheard another child talking to her on the playground. She said, "I know you kids never went to Sunday school so I know Annaliese went to hell." I rushed over and said, "That's not true. That's not true. Jesus loves all of the children, so Annaliese is in heaven." I knew teachers were supposed to separate church and state but I also knew I had to help my children with their grief.

Each child must know that you value him or her. Actually, it's more complicated than running a three ring circus. You can't do it perfectly. You have to settle for putting them in an atmosphere of love which must include contentment, motivation and challenge and then move ahead as best you can.

The only really sad day around a first grade is the last

day of school. Yesterday this place was like a morgue. The children just left with their "passed" report cards and I am so depressed I can hardly pull myself together to get at the dreary business of doing their final records and putting the books and supplies away for the summer. Of course, I need a rest and I certainly won't miss the constant chattering, the discipline problems, the sniffly noses, the fusses and quarrels, but I hate to lose them. I've learned to love them so much.

Only David B. failed to give me a wet smack on my cheek and a final hug around my knees. He is so dignified and serious and so intelligent. He gravely shook my hand and I wondered if maybe he didn't also realize that this was the end of our small, closely knit group. When the mothers came for their children at the end of the day they all looked funny because their mouths were so full of teeth.

Most of them hustled and bustled out into the summer thrilled to death at being second-graders and of course, that's a part of the wonderfulness of being a six-year-old. It's only the teacher who fully realizes that a chapter has closed forever. We've learned to work together and to depend on each other. Other adults, even school administrators, have no idea what a cozy, closed corporation a first grade room is.

I won't forget this bunch. When they come back, they'll be divided among the three second-grade rooms in this building. Some few will even move away but, as I told them this morning, they'll always be my friends. I'm grateful that I've had the opportunity to help them in a very meaningful way. It's what a first grade is all about.

And so, it's goodbye, my loves! There won't be another group like you. Each year will bring its heartaches for what I couldn't do and its glow for what I could accomplish. And that really is the story of being a teacher.

After School

There was more to life in Monroe than teaching school. For the first few months I was really lonesome. My small room didn't even have a chair in it. When I got home from school I'd sit on the edge of the bed and correct the workbooks. Then I'd walk down the street and eat dinner at a restaurant about four blocks away. A young high school teacher ate at the same place and we got to be friends. He liked me so I told him all about Charles. He was as lonesome as I was so we kept on eating together and he would walk me home afterwards.

When I got back to my room I would write letters to Charles, re-read his letters, and read books. I had a little radio but I was used to a big family and then a big dorm full of girls, so this was lonely for me. In late October an older teacher at school told me that she and another girl had rented a two bedroom apartment and asked me if I wanted to live with them. I jumped at the chance and it all turned out wonderfully well. They were great people and again I had a lifestyle I loved. They were both junior high teachers and had the same dedication to their kids.

Shortly after I moved I got a letter from my sister Alyce saying she had decided that she should leave Iowa. She just couldn't make enough money to pay next semester's tuition and was too frustrated to study. (Later in life she got a Bachelor's and a Master's degree.) If there were any jobs available in Monroe, Alyce wanted to move. The war had created many jobs in Michigan, so I assured her that employment would be no problem. My roommates were glad to have her be the fourth occupant of our apartment. She came back with me after our Christmas vacation in Parkersburg.

Dad took us to the night train in Parkersburg. We had a long layover in Chicago so we went to see a live production of *Summertime* in a big theater downtown. I remember how proud we were that the two of us managed to get on the "El," find the theater downtown and get back to the train station all by ourselves. It was pretty remarkable and took a lot of nerve for two young girls from Parkersburg.

Alyce got a job in less than a week as a social worker for the County. With all of the men off to War, jobs were plentiful. The only problem was that she needed a car. Vonda, one of our roommates, was from a small town in Michigan and she knew a man who had a car he would sell for seventy-five dollars. We were able to scrape up that much money so we met the owner at a filling station on Saturday afternoon. We said, "Is it a good car?" and he said, yes, so we gave him our money and drove off.

Neither one of us had a driver's license and neither of us really knew how to drive, but that did not deter us. Alyce decided that I should drive because I had more experience than she did. My only experience was when my high school friends Bob Bailey or Kay McDowell had let me drive their cars occasionally. Alyce had only one friend with a car, so I had twice the experience. But we took off anyway. Letting out the clutch and timing the shifting of gears was quite a feat but I managed with a minimum of lurching and had no real trouble until we got to the first stop sign. I put my foot on the brake and then realized that we didn't have any brakes – my foot was on the floorboard and we just kept going until we hit the car stopped in front of us.

There wasn't much damage. We hit the bumper pretty hard and gave the driver a jolt, but it wasn't too bad. Obviously, the man we hit disagreed. He jumped out of the car and was waving his arms madly so we got out too. We thought he couldn't talk straight because he was so angry, but we soon realized that he was totally deaf. We couldn't really communicate but we kept nodding our heads while he made his unhappiness evident. After awhile we got back in our cars and headed for our apartment going about five miles an hour.

We kept that car for several months until we could save $200 to buy a better one. But it was a constant headache. Alyce drove to see her welfare clients and they would have to use their cars to push her up the street until she could get the engine started.

Alyce had lots of crazy experiences with that car and on her job. One day she was visiting a woman who had four small children. The paperwork required information on the father(s) of the children including a physical description of their height, weight, eyes, and hair. Alyce was dutifully writing it all down until they got to the fourth child and then the mother said, "I really can't tell you much about him. He kept his hat on."

We had lots of good times in that apartment, entertaining friends and playing cards. All four of us went to the Presbyterian Church and three of us sang in the choir. We did a lot of ice-skating on Lake Erie and sometimes on weekends we would go to Detroit or Toledo to shop or go to plays or concerts.

One Saturday we all went to Detroit in Vonda's car and saw Helen Hayes in a matinee. We came out of the theater all excited about the great play and headed for the parking lot. Vonda tried to open the car door and the key wouldn't work. Then we all tried and became quite concerned because none of us could open it. We noticed a man across the street who was locking up his garage, so we ran across to get his help. He tried every way he knew and couldn't get it open. It was starting to get dark and we were all increasingly frustrated. He finally said, "Well, I could take the door off for you," and we encouraged him to do it.

When he turned to us with the car door in his hands we all exclaimed in a chorus, "This isn't our car!" I'll never forget the look on his face. He replaced it, we paid him and when he drove off he still had that "look" on his face.

We turned and walked over to Vonda's car, which by then was the only other car on the lot. The cars weren't even the same color. The owner of the other car never knew that the door had been off and on his car while it sat there. We drove over to Stouffer's Cafe with its blue checkered table-cloths and frilly curtains and never said a word until we had to order.

That spring we arranged for Mama to come for a visit. She loved it – we all did. I have a wonderful picture of her sitting by a tree on the shores of Lake Erie watching us ice skate. On Saturday we took the bus to Detroit and I remember the trip so well. We were sitting about half way back in the bus but as we got to the outskirts of Detroit Mama walked down to the driver. Soon he was slowing down and saying, "This is one of the Ford plants, and this is the road you take to cross the bridge into Windsor, Canada." No one seemed annoyed. All the passengers were looking out the windows learning things they had probably not even wondered about before.

Our apartment was a great situation for us. It was a du-plex and the owners lived downstairs. They were an older couple and we rarely saw them. We were subletting the upstairs from a Major and his wife stationed at Fort Sill in Oklahoma. We sent our rent money to them and the apart-ment was furnished with their furniture. Occasionally, we would hear from the wife who wanted us to send her spring hat from the top shelf of the closet or a favorite towel from a kitchen drawer, but we never met them.

We were shocked in the spring when the owners down-stairs told us that the couples' lease was up and they didn't want to rent to us after the school year ended. We asked why, they said that our card playing bothered them because we threw the cards down on the table so hard.

"And Mildred sings when she takes the laundry down the back stairs to the basement." I couldn't believe it. I immediately reverted to the thinking I had done when I got the D in Botany. Didn't these people understand? I always had the contralto lead in all of the high school operettas and I sang solos in church. Besides that, at Coast House we had weekly house meetings sitting on the floor in the big living room and the girls always asked me to sing at the end of the meetings. I had even sung "Oh, Holy Night" as a solo on the WSUI Radio Station in Iowa City and everyone in Parkersburg had heard it. They probably could even have heard it in parts of Illinois if they had tuned in. What was the matter with these people?

The next fall we did find another apartment, but it wasn't as nice as the first one and I never did understand those owners. So I had a new address for sending and receiving letters from Charles. The war was tough, he wrote, and he had some difficult experiences, but he always wrote how much he loved me and how much he missed me.

Sometime during that first year I saw a notice in the local paper that the hospital was looking for volunteer nurses aides. There was a critical shortage of nurses because of the war. I volunteered and two or three nights a week I would go over to the hospital after school and work from five o'clock to seven or eight. I was a sort of a go-fer. I served evening meals, filled water glasses, or just visited with lonesome patients. Walking down the hall one evening, I heard an elderly woman saying, "Dear God, I dropped my Kleenex. Please, dear God, help me get my Kleenex." I went into the room, picked up the Kleenex and put it on her bedside table for her. She thanked me profusely and I left. As I walked down the hall I heard her say, "Thank you, God." I thought that was nice.

In the spring of my second year in Monroe I saw another notice at the hospital which announced the formation of an Army Nurse's Aide Corps. It sounded interesting and thinking it might be a good summer job, I got an application. You could select a preferred location so I chose Wm. Beaumont General Hospital in El Paso Texas because my sister Etta and her husband Rollin were stationed in Sherman, Texas and I had never been there. I received an acceptance letter almost immediately by return mail and signed up for just three months. The contract stated that I would be paid on the basis of "$1320 per annum less $156 for Quarters per annum less $270 for sustenance per annum."

When the school year ended I spent a weekend in Parkersburg and then took the bus to Sherman, Texas. I stayed there three days for a great visit with Etta and Rollin, and then got on the bus to El Paso. I couldn't believe the barren landscape on that ride across west Texas. It was as different from Iowa and Michigan as it possibly could be. It scared me. Could I exist in such a barren land? And could I be a full time Nurse's Aide in the Army? What in the world was I getting myself into? I wished I were a little kid back in Parkersburg again. And then I worried about whether letters from Charles would reach me. It felt as though I was leaving him behind; mail was uncertain at best.

CHAPTER FOUR
An Army Nurse's Aide in Texas

William Beaumont General Hospital was about twenty
miles out of El Paso, Texas. Biggs Airfield was a half mile
down the road, and Fort Bliss, originally a calvary base,
about two miles away. The barren desert land hemmed in
by craggy mountains in the background looked like a popu-
lated Mars. My first impression was that Beaumont wasn't
a hospital at all – just a big bunch of barracks connected by
covered wooden walkways.

When I reported in I was assigned to a room of my own
in a barracks where about thirty nurses lived. I was "issued"
a supply of uniforms which consisted of blue and white
striped pinafores, white blouses and little blue and white
hats. Most of the nurses were on duty when I arrived about
five o'clock, but I soon met two other new girls who were
also in the Nurse's Aides Corps. Everyone was very friendly.
They were as apprehensive as I was. The few real nurses who
were there assured us that we would do fine. They were all
First Lieutenants but they welcomed us, since they were
desperate for help. I felt much better as we headed for the

mess hall. The whole thing was an entirely different world for me but I soon found my niche.

We spent the first week in a very concentrated training class. There were a dozen of us and we were a new experience for the instructors, too. They were hoping that we were willing workers because they were so short of personnel. The class was taught by a wonderful older nurse (I thought she was old but she probably was about fifty). I'll never forget that she started the class by saying, "I'm sure you are all worried about giving bed baths. Well let me tell you how you do it. You wash down as far as possible, then you wash up as far as possible and then you hand them a nice soapy washcloth and tell them to wash possible." There was an audible sigh of relief from all twelve of us. She was so right. That was exactly what we were all worried about. We relaxed and realized that maybe we could do this job.

Giving shots was another topic of study, but I became an expert at stabbing potatoes. We learned a lot of very practical things about feeding, casts, dressings, and wound care. Each of us would be in charge of an entire orthopedic ward during our shift. It was a very scary thought.

Ward 32 was my assignment. When I reported at seven o'clock the first morning a nurse told me, "I'm stationed in the next Ward and you can come and get me anytime you need me." She showed me all around and announced that I was their new nurse. One ward boy, a soldier, was also assigned to each ward and we were it! If anyone had a fever we had a number to call a doctor immediately, and the nurse was available nearby. Other than that we were on our own.

When I stood at the head of that barracks the first morning and looked down that long row with sixteen beds on each side, it was the same feeling as my first class of first graders, except that now their very lives could be at stake. It was an awesome responsibility. I was twenty-four years old and totally inexperienced. It was May of 1944 and World War II was raging.

My first impression was that everyone looked so sad. Seven of the patients on Ward 32 were ambulatory. They had arm or hand wounds which were in casts, but they could get around. A few had lost an arm. Some were healed and really didn't need to be in the hospital. Hopefully, they were going to get artificial limbs, but no one knew. Nobody had broken bones – if you are shot, the bones shatter. The rest of the twenty-five patients were bedridden with body or leg casts. The leg casts had big frames over their beds and a set of adjustable pulleys at the end of the bed. Most of the patients were Texans, since the Army tried to put them in hospitals nearest their homes. All of them spoke with decided drawls which amused me no end. Except for the Spitzer's, I had never really heard it before. After awhile, I started to talk that way.

Giving shots to potatoes had been so easy, but I failed miserably when it came to the real thing. The very first day on the ward, I was scheduled to give about ten shots. With firm determination, I started out. On my first attempt, I drew back, aimed and stabbed, but I couldn't bring myself to hurt this poor soldier, so at the last second I drew back just a bit. The needle penetrated the skin but didn't accomplish the injection.

But I couldn't quit at that point so I just wiggled and pushed until it went in further. When I tried to release the actual shot, half of it came back. It was awful. I was practically in tears by the third patient. It was unbearable to stab these perfectly innocent soldiers. Finally, the ward boy stepped forward and said, "Let me do it." I did, much to the relief of the poor patients who were beginning to look at me with horror as I approached them.

I soon realized that I could do this job because of the

way the hospital was organized. Patients arrived at Biggs Field by plane directly from the European battlefield. They were brought to Beaumont by ambulances and taken to an empty ward where doctors and nurses would assess their needs as quickly as possible. This triage looked a lot like *M*A*S*H*.

Some went directly to the operating room and others were assigned to wards according to their needs. None of them came to the wards where Nurses Aides were in charge. We got patients who had already received all of the professional help they needed and now they were just putting in time while their bones healed. It was a very good system. We didn't deal with any serious medications and professional help was readily available when we needed it.

Once a week a doctor and nurse team came by and checked on all of the patients. Sometimes they would arrange for a patient to go back to the operating room for more work. When bones are shattered, surgeons can't do all of the fixing at once, so many of our guys had experienced several operations. When the soldiers returned from surgery, they would often have pieces of shrapnel or bullets which they were given as souvenirs.

They would be gone for three or four weeks and sometimes they would come back with half casts and bandages which we changed every morning. We used lots of sulfa powder. When they were fully healed they would go back for full casts. Almost every day we were sending someone out for X-rays.

Every Saturday morning a very gruff Colonel and a crew of GI's came by for INSPECTION. The patients called the Colonel the "Plowman" because he walked rather bent over as if he were pushing a plow. His crew looked over every inch of our ward. One of them would get up on a stool and scrape his finger across the top of a set of lockers to see if he could find a speck of dust. Everybody watched! It was quite dramatic. They looked under every bed and into every corner. We usually "passed" but occasionally we would be cited because the pots and pans in the kitchen weren't stacked quite right or there was an overripe banana in the icebox. Everybody cheered when they left.

There was plenty of very necessary work to be done. A typical day for me was to get up before six and get to the mess hall for breakfast before reporting to my ward at seven. Breakfast for my GI's would just be arriving, so the ward boy and I would see that all of them were fed. It was not just a matter of putting out the trays. The pulleys for the leg casts had to be adjusted and patients helped to get into a sitting position, and the three in body casts and two in arm casts had to be fed by hand. The ambulatory patients would help with this as soon as they finished eating.

Once breakfast was cleared away the bed baths started and this took considerable time. The ward boy, "Kenny" was great – he did all of the "possibles" for the patients who couldn't manage it. He was a nineteen-year-old kid from Kentucky, a hard worker who really cared about helping. We got to be good buddies and he also improved my sex education. One day I was looking through the kitchen drawers for something and I opened a box full of foreign looking packages.

"What are these?" He came over and gave me a thorough 101 course in condoms (including pregnancies and syphilis). At twenty-four years old I never knew they existed. I looked at the ambulatories who had passes on the weekends from a whole new perspective, especially if I saw them stop in the kitchen on their way out.

After the baths, Kenny would sweep the entire ward and I would clean all of the bedside tables and get fresh water for everyone. Then I would take all of the temperatures and

respirations and record them. By then it would be time for
lunch and we would go through the entire feeding routine
again.

The long afternoons were the hardest for the poor patients. This was before TV's had been invented. A few had
small radios on their bedside tables but the reception was
horrible, probably because of the mountains and there were
few radio stations in the area. They would lay on their backs
and relive the horrible experiences which had brought them
here, or worry about their buddies still fighting in Europe,
or their families or their girlfriends or all of the above. Even
though they were all on the same ward, when they were
flat on their backs they couldn't see anything but the ceiling. We encouraged them to sit up and spent a lot of time
adjusting pulleys.

They never wanted to talk about their War experiences.
I know they thought about it a lot and sometimes I would
see two of them in adjoining beds talking very seriously. I
learned not to approach then because they would stop talking. I think they wanted to protect me. They knew I couldn't
really understand and they wanted me to stay happy, probably the best thing I could do for them. They were interested in what was happening, particularly in North Africa
and Europe. Most of them had been in the Third Army and
they wanted to know about General Patton, where he was
and what was he doing. I would keep them updated but
I never told them about the horrible casualties and they
never asked.

Then Kenny and I got creative. We bought fingernail
polish and painted everyone's fingernails and toenails. Later,
we collected money and bought yarn and I taught everyone, including Kenny, how to knit. We would get everyone in a sitting a position, sometimes put ribbons in their

hair and everyone would knit. Two of them had babies at home whom they had never seen and we must have knitted twenty-five blankets for each of them. Others had nieces or nephews or friends with babies, and they all received lots of hand-made blankets.

Reading was another good way to pass the time. Kenny rigged up a special holder for Roy. He was in a body cast, but he could use his hands, so the holder enabled him to spend hours reading. Our ambulatory patients would go to the hospital library or the PX for books and magazines for our readers. Most of our ambulatory patients would leave in the afternoons. They could go to the dayroom, the PX, the Library or walk around the grounds and watch the Italian POWs, who were our groundskeepers.

We had to work on Saturday mornings and very often we worked overtime so Sunday was really the only day we had to wash and iron our clothes. Our uniforms had to be starched and ironing them was a nightmare but it had to be done. I think the Good Lord understood.

My first summer there I had attended Chapel for a few Sundays. It was very poorly attended and I felt sorry for the well-intentioned chaplain because he obviously didn't know what to say to these poor soldiers. He usually sympathized with them and told them God would help them. I would have told them that I admired them for their courage and strength and maybe even the weakest, most scared ones would have assumed that maybe they had some. I would have told them to pray for even more courage and strength to bear whatever came their way instead of promising them that God would take care of all their problems. I was beginning to believe this myself.

One afternoon I was walking back to the barracks and I noticed Joe, one of our ambulatory patients, go into the

Chapel. Worried about him I went in to see if I could help. Much to my surprise I saw him trying to read words from a magazine

"Oh, Joe, I'm a first grade teacher, I can help you learn to read." At first he was embarrassed, but then grateful. I sent back to Monroe for some graded *Dick and Jane* first grade books and he learned very quickly. I would stop in the Chapel every day for just fifteen or twenty minutes and help him through the pre-primers and primer and teach him some phonics. Then we went through the first reader together and by the time I left at the end of the summer, he was reading independently with very little help.

At breakfast one morning Roy, one of the body cast patients, said he didn't feel good and didn't want to eat. His forehead felt warm so I took his temperature and it was over 102 degrees. I called for a doctor, who came almost immediately. They arranged to move him off the ward and a nurse later told me he had pneumonia. It scared all of us and we hated looking at his empty bed. Everyone cheered when he was brought back about three weeks later.

Another day I noticed that Arnold had two oranges under his pillow and several more in his bedside table drawer. He looked very embarrassed, but explained that when he was on the battlefield eating his rations, he would dream about good food, especially oranges.

"I wake up in the night and I know there are oranges in the kitchen so I go and get one." (He had casts on one foot and one arm and he walked with crutches.)

"I'll see to it that you always have two fresh oranges in your drawer and I'll peel one for you every single day."

"Oh, thanks, now I'll sleep better."

Mail arrived late in the afternoon and twice that summer patients got "Dear John" letters. Those were really bad times. To have the girlfriend you were dreaming about write and say, "I'm terribly sorry to tell you this but I have decided to marry..." Earl had lost one arm and both legs. He was devastated when the letter arrived. Word had spread from bed to bed and the whole ward was depressed when I came in the next morning

"Well, I should have known she wouldn't marry a freak," Earl lamented. It was like I was back in first grade. When something horrible happened you couldn't change it, but you could help them cope. One good thing was that he and the patient in the bed next to him became very close friends. I rolled their beds closer together so they could talk quietly. (More than 60 years later I still exchange Christmas cards with Earl and his wife. He is a retired Rural Mail Carrier in Texas.)

One morning I arrived on the ward and sensed immediately that something was terribly wrong. Usually I was greeted very enthusiastically but on this day everything was very quiet and you could almost feel the gloom in the air. Carl's bed was empty.

"What happened?" It was so sad. One of the ambulatories had a pass the previous evening and had gone across the river to Jaurez, Mexico. He had brought back a half pint of whisky for Carl, who promptly got drunk and fell out of bed. His right leg was in a cast, elevated by a set of pulleys, and so when he fell, his leg was broken again. More surgery was required and several weeks later he returned with a new cast. We were so happy to have him back. He took a lot of cheering up because after spending nearly a year in the cast, he was starting all over again.

The ambulatory patient who had bought the whiskey disappeared. We had a detention ward and he probably was put there. I hardly knew the night shift ward boy, but he too was gone and no one knew what happened to him.

My shift was from seven to three, but I often worked

longer hours. Sometimes Kenny would be called away to help with emergencies elsewhere and I would get a call asking me to stay until someone else reported for duty. I would never have left them all alone; someone had to be there to give them their evening meal! Everyone worked hard and long. The doctors and nurses worked unbelievable hours – I had nothing but admiration for all of them.

Leisure Time

After work I followed pretty much the same routine. I would go back to the barracks and visit with the other nurse's aides. It was also my letter writing time and time to go to the PX and take care of laundry, shopping and mail. Sometimes I would get batches of letters from Charles, which were forwarded to me from Monroe. He wrote about horrific experiences in the war. Details were scanty, but I knew that the fighting was intense. Writing to him almost every day, I tried to stay upbeat about our future.

At five-thirty we went to the mess hall. Since everyone ate together you got to know some of the other nurses and doctors, and hear about what was going on in other parts of the hospital. After dinner we usually walked across the street to the Officer's Club. Newspapers were available there so I knew what was going on in the world. It was mostly news about the war, in the South Pacific as well as in Europe.

The club was all very informal. We sat around tables and drank cokes and ate oyster crackers. A collection of doctors, nurses and ambulatory patients, who were officers, talked mostly about their lives before the war. About once a month we had a real Saturday night party and got dressed up and danced. Some romances developed there.

Usually on Saturday nights we would go in groups over to the big Officer's Club at Fort Bliss. Pilots and other officers from Biggs Field would also be there and everybody would really relax. A couple of nurses would get up on the table and dance. They weren't drunk, but they had enough to really forget their worries and have fun. They needed that – even though they were professionals they worried about these poor shot-up patients just as much as I did.

Early in August I began to realize that there was no way I could just walk off and leave at the end of the month. But I was in a real quandary because I couldn't just call the superintendent in Monroe and tell him to find another first grade teacher on such short notice. So I compromised. When I discussed the problem with our head nurse, a major, she readily agreed to let me leave and come back in January. She even told me I could return to Ward 32.

So in September I was back in my classroom with a fresh batch of first graders. I worked especially hard with them so they would all have a good start in reading. In December I told them I would leave after Christmas and explained why I had to go. When my replacement was hired I had her come in so they would know her and the transition would be easier.

In October of 1944 I stopped getting letters from Charles and was very concerned. He had written so regularly, I knew something must have happened. Finally, in early December I wrote a note to his parents. I had met them very briefly when we graduated. His mother replied in a short note: "Charles' wife was informed that he was killed in action on October 13th." I couldn't believe what she said, it was so heartbreaking.

I was confused and sad and angry all at once. I had dozens of unanswered questions. When did he get married? Was he married all of the time he knew me? Why did he tell me he loved me? Why did he write all those letters? What did he mean when he kept writing that he had something to tell me? What were his intentions when he did tell me? Did he maybe have a child? During our brief meeting, I remember Charles' mother had talked about the neighbor girl who missed him. To this day I don't know who he married, or when. I never got any answers. It haunted me for a very long time and obviously I have never forgotten, but life went on. It's no wonder that I hate war. But this book is not about my sorrow.

Alyce was intrigued with all of my stories about Ward 32 so she decided to apply to be an Army Nurse's Aide and requested an assignment to Wm. Beaumont. She was readily accepted so we started making our plans. We decided we needed a better car so we answered an ad in the paper and asked our usual question, "Is this a good car?"

Fortunately, we lucked out and it turned out to be a very trusty Chevy. We finished our work in Monroe, said goodbye to our many friends and drove to Iowa for Christmas. A week later we started our long drive to El Paso. My father and mother stood in the cold in the front yard waving goodbye. They must have been terribly worried about us, but they never discouraged us about anything we planned to do.

Early in January, 1945 I was back in my same barracks and working on Ward 32 again. Alyce had her own room in the same barracks. She got even less training than I had received and was assigned her own Orthopedic Ward. The general public had no idea how shorthanded the Army hospitals were. But we all worked hard and we managed.

The guys on Ward 32 were so happy to see me again. There had been surprisingly few changes. Some of the ambulatories were gone and we had three or four new "casts" but it was like old home week, and we were all glad to be together again. The meals, the bed baths, the temperature taking, and the rest went on as usual. We went back to our knitting, and some of them had advanced to knitting sweaters by now.

The "Dear John" letters, infections, new casts and operations were still part of the routine, but just like the war, life went on.

Soon after I got back I met a doctor at the mess hall and we became very good friends. He was a Captain and had gone into the Army immediately after he graduated from medical school. We would eat together whenever we weren't working and then we started meeting at the Officer's Club when we had time. Tom was from Georgia and had a charming Southern accent. I told him all about Charles and he told me his own tragic story. He had been engaged to Elizabeth, his high school sweetheart. He loved her dearly and they were scheduled to be married the previous September in a very big wedding in their hometown. The week before the wedding she got cold feet and called it all off. He had been heartbroken and we pooled our misery, consoling each other.

Trauma

We had a terrible incident at the hospital sometime in March. Two plane loads of patients arrived at Biggs Field on the same morning and there was a mix-up in our front offices. When the second plane was reported, someone apparently said, "Yes, we know," thinking they were talking about the first plane.

Thirty-two patients were unloaded into an empty ward and no one knew they were there. When I was walking home about four o'clock that afternoon I saw people running in and out of what I thought was an empty building. It was then that I learned that these patients had been alone and bedridden for several hours until a passerby had heard them screaming. Everyone felt horrible and we all worked hard until everything was under control.

When I have told that story occasionally through the

years, people look at me like they can't really believe it. War is so terrible, and unfortunately, most people still don't "get it." When will a civilized people learn that mass killing and maiming isn't a good answer?

In April 1944, Franklin Delano Roosevelt died. Everyone felt a tremendous sense of loss. I had admired and trusted him since I was a child. He was such a strong personality and what he said resonated with everyone. The soldiers could all quote what he had said in a fireside chat, "The only thing we have to fear is fear itself." It may have been a part of their training. No one knew much about Harry Truman except that he was from Missouri.

On May 8th the war ended in Europe. There was great rejoicing all over America, but no one was happier than our patients. Now they didn't have to worry about their buddies over there anymore. It didn't have much impact on our staffing. We assumed that the doctors and nurses in Europe would be going to the South Pacific. The wonderful part was that after a short time we stopped getting those plane loads of new patients.

In June I was transferred to a ward where all the patients were dying. It had been discovered while they were still on the battlefield that they had leukemia, cancer or some dreadful disease and they were sent back to the States to die. There were only eight or nine soldiers on this Ward and there was a real nurse on duty. There was a private room at the front of the ward. My job was to stay in this room with an eighteen-year-old Mexican boy who was near death. My instructions were to watch his breathing and call the nurse if there was a significant change.

The poor boy was beyond talking. All I could do was pat his hand or rearrange his pillow and watch. It was heartbreaking. His parents had been notified and after lunch his mother arrived. She had come by bus from some little town in Texas. She didn't speak any English so I really couldn't help her, although I don't know what I could have said to her. Jesse did seem to realize that she was there and that was very good. She just sat quietly by the bed, patted his head and cried softly. I couldn't sleep that night.

When I reported the next morning the Nurse told me, "He probably won't live through the day." I took up my watch again. His mother was already there. I mostly just stood at the end of the bed and suffered along with them. About eleven o'clock his breathing changed quite dramatically. I went for the nurse and she called for a doctor. When I got back to the room he was just taking his last breaths. It was the first time I had ever actually seen someone die.

The Ward Boy was very helpful. He, too, was Mexican (we didn't know the word 'Hispanic' in those days) so he took the mother out of the room and was able to help her. The doctor and the nurse filled the body cavities and tied his dog tags on his big toe, all Army protocol. Within a short time personnel arrived to remove his body. The nurse went back to the ward to talk to the other patients and I removed the sheets from the bed, emptied the water glass and just moved around in a state of shock. When I went back to the ward the nurse said, "In a few days we will have to move Sam up front."

I looked over at Sam and thought, "I can't do this."

At the end of the day I went to see the head nurse. I said, "I'll be glad to work two shifts a day on any regular ward but I'm a first grade teacher. I have to know I am helping and I can't help on a ward where everyone is dying. I don't know what to do. Please, please put me somewhere else!"

Immediately she said, "OK. We put you there because we know you're a very compassionate, person but I understand. Tomorrow morning go back to Ward 32." I was so grateful. I regretted it, but I knew my limitations.

Two weeks later I was called to the operating room to assist a nurse. She stood at the operating table and there was a small table behind her with various instruments and supplies. She identified everything for me and then had me stand between her and the table and hand her whatever she asked for. When they brought in the patient, I knew it would be a leg operation, but I didn't dream he was going to lose it. Tears flowed down my cheeks during the entire procedure. When it was over the doctor told me, "I never had a crying nurse before, but you did great." I was proud that I had done it, especially after my failure on the dying ward.

Alyce had her share of trauma that summer, too. She had a date on a Saturday night with Glen, a "fly boy" from Biggs Field. They decided to go over to Fort Bliss to dance and they took our car. On the way back they had an accident. Glen wasn't hurt, but I got a call that Alyce was in the hospital. I was frantic. I rushed over and when I saw her in bed with her head swathed in bandages, I almost fainted. She had a big cut on her head and other cuts and bruises but she wasn't seriously hurt.

Glen was there, worried half to death. He was a pilot about to go overseas, so had told the policeman that Alyce was driving. If his commanding officer found out that he was driving the car, he would be removed from his crew and probably demoted. We agreed not to tell. It seemed like the right thing to do for the war effort. I don't believe Alyce was ever asked. Maybe the policeman also realized what would happen. Later we collected insurance for our beloved Chevy which was wrecked beyond repair.

On a Saturday afternoon we went to El Paso and saw a car parked in front of a filling station with a sign, "For Sale – $295." It looked good to us so we asked our usual question, "Is this a good car?"

They said, "Yes," so we bought it. When we got back to

Wm. Beaumont we mentioned to two friends at the club that we had bought a car. In those days, every boy in the country grew up learning all about cars and they immediately wanted to see it. Within minutes they had determined that it was an old taxi cab that had already been driven into the ground. They insisted that we go back to the filling station. They were both officers and when they confronted the poor scared salesman he readily agreed to return our check and take the car back. He even agreed to take all four of us back to Beaumont. We didn't buy another car until after we went back to Iowa.

Tom and I continued to meet; we were good for each other. Both terribly busy, we would eat together or have drinks at the Officer's Club when we could. Sometimes we would go into El Paso or across to Juarez on Saturday afternoons, but it didn't happen often because Tom was usually on call and couldn't leave the area. On Saturday nights we would sometimes go to the big club at Fort Bliss. We began to grow very fond of each other and our conversations were no longer just about Charles and Elizabeth.

We were both in a quandary. And no, in case you are wondering, we weren't having a sexual relationship. In those days, nice girls didn't have sex before marriage and decent men respected women. In this century that doesn't seem possible, but it was then. By June he wanted us to get engaged and I was seriously thinking about it. We realized that we really cared about each other.

Moving On

Early in August there was a strange happening in the ward. Suddenly, a very bright, strange light lasted about five seconds. There wasn't any sound. Everyone in the mess hall and at the club was talking about it that night and we all decided that something must have happened at White Sands, not far away in New Mexico. We knew they were doing a lot of experimenting with rockets.

Then on August 6, 1945 an Atomic Bomb was dropped on Hiroshima in Japan. On August 9 a second bomb was dropped on Nagasaki. The newspapers were full of it and the radio talked about nothing else. We couldn't believe President Truman would do such a thing. The strange light we had seen earlier was really the very first A-Bomb being exploded near White Sands. We learned that 140,000 people had been killed outright in Hiroshima and Nagasaki and unknown numbers were suffering the effects. And then on August 15, Japan signed an unconditional surrender. We were so relieved. The war was over! There would be no more dead or wounded. But it was hard to reconcile our joy with the horror of the killing in Japan. There was lots of debate about whether or not it was justified. We had very mixed feelings but of course we were thrilled that it was over.

Everything changed. In June, when the war in Europe had ended everyone expected the troops, including the doctors and nurses would all be going to the South Pacific. We expected that war to last another ten years because of the way we were taking one island at a time. Now it was really over. We wouldn't be getting more plane loads of patients and the doctors and nurses could return Stateside. On September first we were given notice that the Army Nurse's Aide Corps would be disbanded effective September 30.

First, I had to make a decision about my relationship with Tom. I was seriously considering staying in the area. Then early in September that changed drastically, too. Very unexpectedly Elizabeth called him one night to tell him that now she was ready to marry him. She wanted him to come back home and get married as soon as he could arrange to be there.

We talked and talked and really agonized over it. In the

end I encouraged him to go back to Georgia and marry Elizabeth. He had known her for so long and had loved her for years. Since he was a very conscientious person, I was afraid he would feel guilty for the rest of his life if he didn't go. I also knew that everyone in his family loved Elizabeth and the two families were close friends. They probably never would have accepted me. He had always planned to practice medicine in his hometown when the war ended. He had prayed and prayed about Elizabeth and now it looked like his prayers were answered.

I convinced him that his attraction for me was based on the fact that I was a good listener and a good friend when we both were confused and lonesome. We had helped each other tremendously. I could look at the whole Charles chapter in a better way. Tom still had some misgivings but he decided to go back. And I agonized over whether or not I should have encouraged him to do it.

Alyce and I started making plans about what we would do next. We were proud to have been members of the Army Nurse's Aide Corps and we were proud of what we had done. Nursing is truly a noble profession and we admired every single one of the nurses and doctors we had come to know. However, neither of us wanted nursing to be our lifetime career. Neither of us had ever seen an ocean, so we decided to go to either California or Florida. Alyce always asked me what to do. It was a lifelong habit from when we were kids. I never wanted to tell her because I knew that if it didn't work out, it would be my fault. It was a game we played to the end of her life. Finally, I said, "Florida," so Florida it was.

It was hard to leave Beaumont. We left our wards in very good hands but we were going to miss our guys and they were very sorry to see us go. It was a good feeling to know we had done our part for the war effort. We had both grown up a lot because of all our experiences. We had made a lot of close friends. It was a chapter in our lives we would always cherish. Memories of Tom lingered.

We took a train to Denver and spent the night there. When I look back I am amazed that we had the nerve to do the things we did. We spent a day there and then got on the Illinois Central to go to Parkersburg. Dad met us at the train at midnight and carried our two big bags up the long hill home. Mama had hot chocolate and cookies waiting and as we sat around the table we told them about our plan to go to Florida. As usual, they supported us.

We stayed about a week and during that time we bought a car with our insurance money from Veron Shuck. Born and raised in P'burg, he and his brothers had businesses there and all of them were highly respected. This time when we said, "Is this a good car?" Veron gave us the complete history of it from the day he bought it brand new. It was another Chevy and it was a great car.

Just before we left Parkersburg I got a very surprising letter from Tom. He had written to me in their hotel room a few hours after their wedding, while Elizabeth dressed for dinner!

"All I can think about is you." A telephone number was noted if I wanted to reach him. It was devastating. At first, I just wanted to jump on the train and go back to Beaumont. I was tempted but I didn't. Our lives had gone their separate ways. I still think about him occasionally and I hope he has had a happy life. Like Charles, Tom became a cherished memory and I pressed on.

We had saved practically all of our salaries while we were at Beaumont because we had neither the time or the need to spend it. So we started out for Miami feeling financially secure and confident that it was going to be a great adventure. Mom and Dad were standing in the front yard waving goodbye as we drove away.

CHAPTER FIVE
The Miami Adventure

*F*ree road maps were available at filling stations in those days, so we had no qualms about finding Miami. We had a great trip with only one mishap. After several days, we arrived in the Cumberland Mountains – lush, green, beautiful scenery on endless winding roads. Late in the afternoon we found a small motel and restaurant and decided to stop for the night since accommodations were few and far between. Everyone was very friendly; they had local crafts for sale at the restaurant and we enjoyed picking out a few. After a good home-cooked dinner, we slept very well, ate a big breakfast and started out bright and early the next morning. Again we drove through beautiful forests and curving roads hour after hour.

About noon we started looking for a small town so we could stop for lunch. Alyce was driving and I checked the map to see if I could figure out where the next town was. I was having a hard time and then I noticed a very odd thing. The roadside signs looked very familiar. We had seen the names of those towns before. The horrible truth dawned on us. We had turned right instead of left, north instead of south when we left the motel that morning. Alyce had been driving but I had been a lousy navigator!

That night we were back at the same motel where we had spent the previous night. When we walked in the desk clerk said, "I thought you girls were going to Florida." We didn't want to talk about it. Other than that we had a great trip. The Cumberlands are beautiful and we got a good look from the north and the south sides.

We arrived in Miami late in the afternoon and found a motel for eighteen dollars a night. Quite a shock for small-town girls, since we had been paying seven or eight. Exploring the city we drove around. Unfortunately, we drove down Flagler Street – the wrong way. This time I was driving and just didn't notice it was a one-way street. We didn't have such things in Parkersburg. When a policeman drove up beside us on his motorcycle to stop us, we just froze.

"You're going the wrong way!" I was scared to death, mainly because of his uniform. Mr. Lumley was our only "peace officer" in Parkersburg and he didn't wear a uniform.

"What are you going to do to us?"

"Do you see that big building down there?" he said, pointing to the tall Dade County Courthouse down the street. "We usually take girls like you and hang them from the top of it!" He drove off without giving us a ticket. Our Iowa license plate probably had a lot to do with it. We got off Flagler Street in a hurry.

Before we went to bed that night we had to see the ocean. It was easy to find. We took off our shoes and socks and chased the waves out and then ran back with the ocean at our heels screaming and hollering at each other in sheer delight. We stopped to rest and we heard a voice coming out of the darkness.

"Mildred Dresselhuis, is that you?" We turned to see

a girl running toward us excitedly. It was Mary Cook, my good friend from the University of Iowa. We had spent many hours working together in the Library. Her husband, Don, was in the Navy in the South Pacific and she was visiting her brother and sister-in-law in Miami. It was a great reunion and we continued seeing her while we were in Miami. (In fact, we remained friends until she died when she was 82 years old. Her only son, Dwight, was killed in Vietnam.)

The next morning we got up bright and early to go job hunting. Our plan was to get a newspaper, check the "Help-Wanted" columns and go from there. After breakfast we drove to a newsstand, where I actually parallel parked without hitting anyone. I thought that was a good sign and it was. We had parked in front of a USO (United Service Organization), and across the street was the Dade County School District Administration Building. Alyce went to the USO Building and I went to the school district.

When I walked in, several girls were working behind a long counter. None of them even looked up, so I just said, "Do you need a first grade teacher?" They all jumped up at once and said, "Yes, do you have a certificate?" One of their first grade teachers had a serious operation on the first day of school and was not able to return for the whole year. This was the middle of October and a series of substitutes had not lasted more than a day because the children were getting wild. Within twenty minutes I had signed a contract and had agreed to start the next morning. As I rushed back to the car I saw Alyce emerging from the USO building.

I called out, "I have a job and I start tomorrow!"

"I have a job and I start tonight!" We immediately set out to find an apartment.

The school people had given me a list and we found a small but adequate apartment in an elderly woman's house. Mrs. Close was a dear widow and her son came by every afternoon to check on her. Her house had been converted into two small apartments and living quarters for her. Two teachers lived in the front apartment and we had the back one. Actually, it was just a bedroom with a small sitting area and two chairs on one end, a closet and a very small bathroom. All four of us had access to her living room where we spent a lot of time playing bridge and listening to the radio. There was a large papaya tree in the back. At first, I thought that was neat but the soft fruit kept falling down and getting squashed. Then the ants would come crawling all over them. To this day I don't care much for papayas.

Alyce came back from her first shift at work and reported that she had met this really neat sailor from Kansas – Don Harper. I had never seen her quite so excited about a boyfriend.

The next morning I set out for school and the first thing I learned was that they raised the bridges in Miami to let the tall ships go by. As I waited for the bridge I remembered my faux paux the first day of school in Monroe and thought, "Oh, no, it's going to happen again!" Fortunately, I made it in time.

The principal gave me a very brief orientation which ended when the bell rang. He took me down to the room and it was utter chaos. The class had several long, narrow windows to the floor and the children were running in and out of all of them like a dance line and screaming at the top of their voices. I reached out to grab one and my hand accidentally hit a little girl right in the face as she flew by.

She screamed and hopped around holding her face as if I had half killed her – everyone stopped dead in their tracks. I knew instinctively that this was my moment to get control and I made the most of it. I ordered them into their seats in a voice that scared even me, but I got their attention and we moved on to a great relationship.

On Sunday we found a big Presbyterian Church and within weeks I joined the choir. (As I look back now I realize that I have sung in the Choir in every place I have ever lived except at Wm. Beaumont General Hospital.)

I met two men who were as different as day and night but I didn't really like either one of them. My principal introduced me to the first one. One day when I was taking my children to the cafeteria, the principal and another fellow were standing by the office watching me. Later I learned that the principal had invited him over to "take a look at me" and decide whether or not he was interested. I passed the test and Fred called me. He was thirty-eight years old which, I thought was ancient, and he collected black onyx pieces. After about our fourth date he wanted to give me a black onyx ring. I thought he was boring, rather weird and much too old so that was the end of it, except he kept hanging around and I had a hard time convincing him I wasn't interested.

Phil was entirely different. The mother of one of my students introduced us and he was pretty exciting. He had been the youngest full Colonel in the Air Force, according to his story. He had flown "the hump" with Jimmie Doolittle delivering supplies during the war. From a very wealthy family in New York, I had never known anyone like Phil and I was pretty carried away for awhile. He took me to several fancy restaurants in Miami. But he began pressuring me and I was a little scared, since I had never been treated like that before.

Then one Sunday afternoon he took me to meet his mother at her winter home on Biscayne Island. It was quite an impressive place. She was very nice and her maid served us tea. Then she asked me about my "background," so I told her about my family in Parkersburg. When I mentioned that my father was a blacksmith, she visibly blanched and

I suddenly felt sorry for her. I thought, "This is not for me." She would never understand anything about me or what is important to me. I have nothing in common with this nice lady or her handsome son. That was the end of that. I never went out with him again. His lifestyle didn't appeal to me at all. Never, ever would I be embarrassed about my father. To the end of my days I will be forever proud of him and how he lived his life. To my credit, I think I also realized that Phil didn't care about me. He just thought that I would be so impressed with his family's wealth that we could "go all the way." (That's what you called having sex in those days). Wrong!

My first grade was unusual. When I started in October, I only had nineteen students. It gradually increased in December and by January I was deluged with children, mainly from New York who arrived for the winter.

For the next four months I had fifty-five children! Fortunately, all of them were very smart, but many of them were also spoiled so some days it was like a zoo. The principal helped by bringing in practice teachers from the University of Miami, but I usually didn't know who or how many would be there or when they would show up, so it was impossible to make any plans. By the first of May most of the children started to disappear and I ended the year with only twenty. It wasn't easy. I regretted that many of them had not received the individual attention they needed. I hardly got to know some of them. It was frustrating.

Alyce enjoyed her work. The USO was a military club, open to all of our American soldiers, as well as Allied forces. Often she would organize big dances on Friday and Saturday nights and would enlist me and our other two house-mates to help entertain. She particularly needed us for the Russian dances when her usual crowd of girls wouldn't show up. We were told to act like typical American girls, which was pretty difficult to do when your dance partners couldn't speak a word of English. You just smiled and nodded your head and danced until you hurt!

By December Alyce and Don's relationship was getting very serious so we decided to drive home together for Christmas vacation. We saved our money and came up with a budget for food, gas and motels. At the time gas cost twenty-nine cents a gallon and you could buy a big sandwich for ten cents.

Leaving right after school on a Friday afternoon, we drove up the coast and about dinner time we found a nice restaurant on the ocean front. When they handed us a wine list and Menu with no prices listed, we should have known we were out of our league, but we ordered as if we knew what we were doing. We enjoyed our meal, but when Don got the bill we almost fainted. Our first dinner cost ninety percent of what we had budgeted for food the entire trip! We ate mostly potato chips and popcorn all the way home.

I left them in St. Louis and took the bus to Des Moines while they continued on to Kansas to meet Don's family. They joined us for Christmas in Parkersburg and announced that they were engaged and planned to be married in May when Don would be out of the Navy. And that is the way it happened.

One day in late February I came home after a particularly trying day at school and Myrtice, from the front apartment met me at the door. She had just read a notice in the newspaper that the U.S. government was seeking applications to fill clerical positions working for the American occupied forces in Germany. She was all excited and suggested that we apply. I thought it would be exciting and I could go to Holland and meet my Dutch relatives. It wouldn't hurt to make a phone call and get more details. Typing and short-hand tests would be given the next Saturday morning at a downtown hotel.

Nervously I sat down in front of the typewriter in a cavernous hotel room with about fifty other applicants. I hadn't typed or taken any dictation for four years and I had no idea whether or not I could pass. Myrtice was literally shaking all over. It was about three weeks later that we learned through the mail that we both passed both tests. Probably the fact that we both had college degrees had a lot to do with our meeting their qualifications.

But that was just the beginning. We started a long process of filling out paperwork. At the end of April we were finally accepted and told that we would be given one week's notice to report to New York. We were given a long list outlining what we could bring with us. Then it dawned on us that we could be called before school was out. Myrtice also taught first grade and you don't just leave your children the last month of school. But we made it through the year.

I went home right after school was out to sing, *Because* and *I Love You Truly* at Alyce and Don's wedding on May twenty-sixth. It was a great time with all the family except I still worried that we would get called to go to Germany before I got back. But again, it didn't happen and I returned to Miami.

It was a hot and humid summer in Miami (before air conditioning). I had sold my half of the car to Don, so we had no transportation. Almost every day we would get on the bus and go to the beach. We were exhausted by the time we returned and disappointed day after day when no notice from the War Department arrived. Finally, we got the letter telling us we would sail from New York on August eighteenth. Flying into high gear we packed everything on the list and made arrangements to get to New York.

We took the train and arrived at Grand Central Station in New York the night before we were to leave. Finding a phone to call my parents one last time, I became terribly homesick. Had I lost my mind to go across the ocean to a war-torn country I knew nothing about? I even considered going back to Iowa and to find a nice first grade to teach.

As I left the phone booth almost in tears I looked up at Grand Central's sweeping marble staircase and was shocked to see Norris Pritchard from Parkersburg walking down the steps. We had gone through high school together and were good buddies. Neither of us could believe that we would meet in New York City! We had a great visit and he convinced me that going to Germany at this time would be a fabulous experience.

The next morning Myrtice and I got up at dawn to be sure we would have ample time to find the correct pier at which the *Henry Gibbons* was docked. She was from a small town in Georgia, but she had spent a lot of time in Atlanta, so she knew more about getting around than I did. Influenced by Ginger Rogers' movies, we knew they had big dances on ocean cruises, so we had packed evening gowns. We were so naïve. Then came the rude awakening!

As we boarded the ship we were given a slip that said "C-5" and a soldier told us where it was. Well, where it was was in the very bottom of the ship! The *Henry Gibbons* had been a troop ship during the war and so our accommodations were nothing like a luxury liner. We had to laugh about our evening gowns. The bunks were in tiers of four high and very close together. Each of us had one-fourth of the space under the bottom bed for our bag and one hook on the wall for our clothes.

We shared a shower which was just a big room with about twenty shower heads coming out of the walls. Two or three inches of water always covered the floor. Drainage was obviously a problem when you were below the water line. We were overwhelmed and excited at the same time. None of us had expected this but we sensed it was going to be a real adventure.

The dining room was nicer: tablecloths, cloth napkins and excellent food. Two nice men at our table loved to play bridge, so we played cards with them nearly every day for the nine-day trip to Bremerhaven. They were older than us, traveling to be judges at the Nuremberg Trials. One was from Virginia and the other from Illinois. They were very proper and we all shared stories about our families and friends. Both of them were expecting to have their families join them in Nuremberg within a month. It was a great way to spend the long days.

In the evenings we would see movies or visit but always we would spend time out on the deck. Seeing the wake of the water behind us and the bright stars in the sky gave us a sense of the magnitude of the earth we had never experienced before. It was absolutely beautiful. The funny bunk beds were like cradles at night and we really had a very enjoyable and smooth trip all across the Atlantic. So we arrived in Germany full of anticipation of what was before us. It would be the most memorable, significant journey of my life.

CHAPTER SIX
In Occupied Germany

*W*e docked at Bremerhaven sometime in the night. At breakfast the next morning we were given our "orders" to go by train to Frankfurt, where we would be given our work assignments. We would get our luggage when we arrived in Frankfurt. On the crowded train the countryside through Germany was very picturesque – hills, fields, rivers and small villages. We made a stop in Cologne and saw the Dom, an ancient cathedral which had been partially bombed – half of the magnificent steeple was missing. Miles of grape vines grew on terraced hillsides along the Rhine River, interrupted only by postcard castles. When we got to Frankfurt, it was entirely different.

The reality of war confronted us. The smell of dead bodies still remained, although the war had been over for fifteen months. We rode through the streets on the way to the hotel and it was unbelievable. The streets had been cleared but there were piles and piles of rubble on both sides of every street. Hand painted signs stuck in the rubble gave mute testimony: "453 died here," or "247 died here" or smaller signs saying, "Wife and three children here."

173

The piles were only broken by a few side streets which had been cleared. Plumbing pipes loomed up from the rubble two to ten or more stories high with bathtubs still attached at twenty or thirty foot intervals. It was incredible. You immediately thought, surely human beings could have devised a better way to get rid of Hitler. How could so much destruction have happened? How many innocent children were under those piles? It was a very sobering introduction to Occupied Germany.

The next morning we reported to the American Headquarters in the I.G. Farben Building and learned that we were working for the U.S. War Department but assigned to USFET – the United States Forces in Europe. A nice Lieutenant gave me orders – I would work in the Personnel Department at Heidelberg Post and reside at the Nesbit Hotel. Myrtice was assigned to a job in Nuremberg, so we had to part ways but we stayed in touch for the rest of our lives and saw each other occasionally. She stayed in Nuremberg about five years and married an Army Major who was stationed there.

At lunch I was relieved to see a familiar face. Marti and I had become friends on the *Henry Gibbons* and she was also assigned to the Personnel Department and the Nesbit Hotel in Heidelberg. She became another life-long friend. We shared all kinds of joys and sorrows together. On the train trip from Frankfurt to Heidelberg she told me she had come to Germany because her husband was here. They had been married for ten years and had lived and worked in Washington, D.C. until he was drafted into the Army.

He had become a "90 day wonder," what we called the soldiers who were sent to Officer's Training School, and now he was a Colonel. He had been in Europe for three and a half years.

"Two months ago he wrote me a letter and said he

wanted a divorce so he could marry a German girl. I cannot believe he really wants that, so I got the job so we could work this out."

Marti and I only spent three months at the Nesbit Hotel and then we were invited to share a German home with an American woman who was head of I & E (Intelligence and Education) for USFET. Her job as a civilian employee equaled the rank of a one-star General, so she was entitled to housing on that level. Houses for the high ranking officers were all "liberated" from the richest Germans in the area. This large, beautiful house was high on the mountainside. Heidelberg had a marvelous, medieval Castle which overlooked the City, with its famous University below. We passed the Castle on our way up the mountain to our home. From our dining room balcony you could see the Neckar River and a monastery across the river. Every night about sunset long rows of monks walked slowly across the horizon.

The next three years that I spent in Heidelberg were amazing. I started out as Receptionist in the Personnel Department at the USFET Compound. After about three months I was promoted to be a Personnel Assistant responsible for Recruitment. We filled all of the vacancies in the Heidelberg Post and they were occurring very frequently because soldiers were being returned to the States and were not replaced. We filled jobs with other civilians or Allied personnel who were already in Germany. Next in line for jobs were displaced personnel (DPs were often former prisoners or slave laborers from other countries who were unable to get home). Indigenous personnel – Germans – were then recruited for jobs. If no qualified applicants were found, we recruited from the Zone of the Interior (ZI), that's what we called the United States.

Schools for the many American children who were now living in the "Zone" were opened, and most of the teachers

175

and administrators had to be recruited from the ZI. Since I knew a little of the language, I was also responsible for recruiting the German workers from the local Arbeitsamt (Labor Office). I may not have been the best qualified person for the job, but I was there and willing to work. I had to be a fast learner in order to become a personnel professional practically overnight.

Early in my first year I learned more about the sex life of the American military than I wanted to know. We learned in our orientation class that there were rules against fraternization with the Germans and I accepted that without much thought. Then I was in Frankfurt attending a class and we left the I.G. Farben Headquarters for lunch. As we were coming out of the building a Staff Car with big flags was just arriving. The woman I was with asked if I would like to see General Eisenhower. Well, of course. He had been the war hero and we considered him responsible for our victory.

We waited and very soon the General appeared and he had a girl literally hanging on his arm. I said, "Who in the world is that?"

"That's Kay Summersby – she was his driver and now she lives with him." That was more than a little disillusioning for a girl from Iowa, but it was the beginning of my awareness that almost everybody did it. Many of these officers and soldiers had been in Europe for years so I guess I should not have been surprised. In any case, Eisenhower set the tone and these affairs were commonplace. The rules against fraternizing were totally ignored.

One of the people I worked with was the Finance Officer, Jack, who was a Captain. He talked openly about the German girl he lived with. In fact they had a daughter and during the time we worked together they had twin sons. Those boys were about three months old when the Captain got orders to return to the States. For months after that the

German girl would come to our office begging for information – at least his GI Dog Tag numbers but we were not allowed to give her any information.

(Years later I was working in the state personnel office in Little Rock and I saw a notice in the newsletter saying that Jack was a new employee in the finance office. I was actually sitting there wondering if it could be the same person when he walked in the door. We greeted each other and talked about Heidelberg, but never mentioned his personal life there. He told me all about his wife and two grown children. I knew he was begging me not to say anything about his former life and I never did. It was all just another reason to know that wars are bad.)

From a cultural standpoint, everything was in utter chaos when we arrived – the economy, politics, government, finance, even religion – nothing was normal. The cities had been virtually destroyed. You could ride for miles and miles in Berlin, or Munich or Frankfurt and see practically nothing standing. Heidelberg had been saved from the bombing because of its history which was so closely connected to education and the arts.

Many of the renowned German poets, artists, musicians and philosophers had attended Heidelberg University. You could sit on a bench just above the city and look down on the University. The bench was covered with names, such as Goethe and Strauss, carved into the wood when they had attended the University. Only the bridge in central Heidelberg had been destroyed and it was blown up by the Germans themselves because they thought it would keep the Allies from advancing through the city. The first week we were there Marti and I took a long walk through the streets and down to the Neckar River. When we came back we remarked to the man at the desk of the Nesbit, "It is such a beautiful city."

"You should have seen it before the fire," he replied. We asked when the fire had occurred. "Oh, the French burned it in 1066."

The first year I was there Americans used the German currency, marks. You could buy a carton of cigarettes at the PX for the equivalent of three dollars in American money and walk out of the building where there would be Germans willing and eager to buy the carton for the equivalent of $800! Americans were sending home more money than they earned by dealing on this black market. Cigarettes and coffee were the primary basis for buying and selling. German stores were open for only a few hours in the morning and you would see women with a basket of marks to buy bread and flour.

When I lived at the Nesbit Hotel we had practically no heat. Each resident had a small room with a radiator in it and we all used the bathroom at the end of the hall on our floor. You could put your hand on the radiator and it was barely warm, and the bathroom was downright cold. Tepid water made showers miserable. After work we would go right to the Reichspost Hotel a block away. All of the American civilians ate their breakfasts and dinners there. The dining and sitting rooms were warm and the food was good. We would linger as long as we could and we became a very close-knit group. When you went back to the hotel you had to go to bed immediately to keep warm and if you wanted to read you had to sit up in bed and wear gloves. I was only there until November, but the weather is very cold and damp all fall in Heidelberg.

Of course, the Germans were far worse off. They had no fuel and the hills around Heidelberg were always full of people picking up sticks to burn. They had little food and had electricity only a few hours a day. The children were so pathetic. Most of them had no shoes. They would have pieces of cardboard or wood tied to the bottom of their feet. Some of them had raggedy jackets or sweaters when it was freezing in the winter. Some didn't even have those. Many of them would stand by the PX but you learned in a hurry that you couldn't throw them candy bars. You might start a real brawl. Later, after I was married and we lived in a house in the city down below the children would eat out of our garbage can. I would put canned food and staples out on top of it and it would disappear almost immediately. The people who start wars certainly do not consider the innocent children!

My job was very interesting from day one. My immediate boss was a Captain who was still living the horrors of the war. He had helped liberate the Dachau Concentration Camp and he described the horrors of finding the skeletons and half dead people. When the Americans arrived, the Colonel in charge sent to the village below for the Burghermeister (mayor). He wanted the Germans to be aware of the exact conditions that existed before anything was changed. The Burghermeister was given a tour and was visibly shaken. He insisted that the German townspeople didn't know what was happening at the camp. The Colonel instructed him to return the next morning with all of the burghers (city council). When they didn't appear he learned that the Burghermeister and his wife had hung themselves.

The Captain was really on top of our recruitment goals and he organized and supervised us fairly and efficiently. However, I was shocked at the caste system that existed in the Army. At Beaumont we had worked and lived with Nurse Lieutenants and Captains, and we all got along fine. In the hospital the only people we looked up to were Surgeons, who were greatly admired by all of us. Here it was entirely different. Rank was everything. Generals were like Gods even if they acted like fools.

Everyone had an equivalency rating; I started out as a CAF-3 which was lower than any 1st Class Private and ended up as a CAF-9, which was between a Captain and a Major. We had uniforms we could wear if we chose, but usually we just wore them when we traveled, when it was important to be recognized as Americans. They just had patches on the sleeves which designated us as War Department Civilians. We were always being asked by Army personnel, "What are you?" I never felt like a "what."

Some of the civilians felt so ostracized that they decided to organize a social group. We really had no beef to fight for, and I personally was not offended but a lot of them felt like they were being looked down on. Civilians from all over the Heidelberg Post were invited and that meant most of the area south, east and west of Heidelberg. I was elected Secretary and immediately committed a faux paux (again) which soon led to our demise.

As Secretary I sent out a letter announcing our second meeting. One of the first things I had learned on my job was that all of the correspondence going within the Heidelberg Post was to have the signature line, "By Order of the Commanding Officer." If it went outside our Post, it carried the line, "By Order of the Commanding General." Since we had decided to include civilians up in Frankfurt, I used the broader term to include everyone. Man! All hell broke loose.

I had committed a grievous sin since I was a mere civilian writing to other mere civilians. Imagine the nerve I had to use a reference to the Commanding General! It was sheer innocence on my part, but I was ordered to go to Berlin and report to General Lucius D. Clay's Headquarters to explain my actions. I didn't know if I should laugh or cry. I asked my Colonel boss if they would send me home and he said, "No, you'll probably get a reprimand in your personnel file."

So I set off to Berlin more in wonderment than fear. It turned out to be an unexpectedly great experience. When I walked into Headquarters the next morning I really was scared. It was like the time the Policeman stopped us in Miami; I felt like a criminal. The Major sternly asked me to explain my actions, but I think he felt a little sorry for me and he asked much more quietly where I was from back home.

"Iowa," I murmured.

"Oh, my goodness, I'm from Iowa too." We started chatting and it was amazing. He had also graduated from the University of Iowa and even more startling, his wife had lived at Coast House my freshman year. She was a senior, and made the Iowa swim team. She and their son were on shipboard coming to Berlin as we spoke.

I did get the reprimand – he said "Don't do it again," but he added, "I don't see any need to put it in your file – verbal is enough. There's a party at the General's house tonight because he is being awarded another star. I have to stop by to see if the General needs anything. Do you want to go along?" Of course I did. I only had my uniform with me but he said, "That's fine, we aren't real guests."

The party was great. It was in a beautiful old mansion where General Clay lived. I didn't meet the General, but I talked to a nice Colonel while my new friend talked to the General. We had a drink and then the Major said we should leave. I went into the bedroom where I had left my coat and made another faux paux. Before I left I decided to go to the adjoining bathroom. When I opened the door, a General, who had entered from a door on the opposite side, was doing you know what. I retreated in a hurry, grabbed my coat and ran to tell the Major, "Let's go right now."

When I told him what happened he laughed and said, "Are you snake bit or something?"

The next day the Major took off from work and showed

me all over Berlin. This was prior to the blockade of Berlin and long before the Berlin Wall was built. We walked right through the Brandenburg Gate and saw the pile of rubble over the "Fuehrerbunker" where Hitler, Eva Braun and Josef Goebel and his family were thought to have committed suicide just before the Germans surrendered. We were told it had twenty rooms on two levels and two exits, but all you could see was a pile of bricks. It was in front of the building with the famous balcony where Hitler made the speeches we had been hearing on the radio since 1939. The building had been partially bombed but the balcony was still intact.

The city had been virtually destroyed. It was easy to imagine the hundreds of B-29's flying over dropping bombs night after night after night. Practically all of my friends from Biggs Field and many other places had been a part of it. Now you could ride for miles and miles through Berlin and not see a single building standing. Many of the Germans had cleaned out corners of partially destroyed buildings. They had piled up loose bricks and used canvas tarps for roofs and doorways; whole families were living in these makeshift shelters. The early spring of 1947 was cold and bleak. As usual, I worried about the poor, innocent children. They certainly were not Nazis, but they were victims.

After lunch we went out to Templehof Air Field and I got on an Army plane for the flight back to Rhein Main in Frankfurt. My faux paux had turned into a memorable adventure and I thanked my new Major friend profusely. Later I called his wife and had a nice chat with her.

Actually, flying in and out of the Berlin airfield was an experience in itself. In those days landing and taking off from Templehof was terrifying. When you banked and approached it, you saw a narrow corridor between tall buildings. My heart almost stopped when I realized we had to go through that corridor to get to the ground. Taking off was the same thing. You could actually look into apartments and see people a few yards away as you went up. You just prayed the pilots knew what they were doing.

My one-year contract ended in August 1947, and then I was offered a promotion to go downtown and take charge of the Arbeitsamt. I would be the only American there. More American families were coming to Germany, and they all needed maids, cooks, yardmen, and nannies for their homes. Also, many of the soldiers had earned their points and were going back to the zi, the states.

These soldiers had held clerical or a variety of maintenance jobs after the fighting ended. All of them had to be replaced. We followed the same pecking order that was used at the Heidelberg Post – Allies, Displaced Persons, the Indigenous (Germans), and last American civilians recruited from the zi.

As the American population grew it became apparent that it would be much more efficient for the higher ranking officers to be able to go directly to the Arbeitsamt to get their household help. Also, the Americans needed to know more about the Germans who were working for them. For all of these reasons the "brass" had made the decision to put an American in charge of the Arbeitsamt.

I was also greatly influenced to sign a new contract and take the job since I had met Rufus Norman, a soldier from Alabama. He had wanted to marry me the day I met him, and early in August we got engaged. I signed the contract, went home to Iowa for two weeks and then came back to take the job at the Arbeitsamt.

I met Norman (I never called him "Rufus") in March of 1947 when I was still working out at the Command Post. One day I got a call from a Colonel in Frankfurt who said he had a soldier who was scheduled to return to the zi but he wanted to keep him as a civilian worker in Heidelberg if that could be arranged. It was possible and we started talking about the paperwork which would be necessary – he would have to be honorably discharged by the Military and then we could go through the routine of turning him into a civilian employee. All of this took a couple of months, just to get him properly discharged.

Then Norman came to Heidelberg to take care of the civilian end of the paperwork. When he walked through the door, I thought he was the most handsome man I had ever seen – tall, black curly hair, dimples – he had it all. I already had his application on my desk but I had not looked at it very carefully. In those days "Single" or "Married" were still on the application and I quickly looked down and was so happy to see a check by the "Single."

The Arbeitsamt

My new job made me a part of the actual occupation at a critically important time. Before I started I was sent to Frankfurt for two weeks training in how to be a Personnel Officer. It was pretty overwhelming to learn what they expected me to do, but I hung in there. It was a good thing, because the number of Germans working for Americans in the Heidelberg Post would swell during the Berlin Airlift to 25,000!

In late September of 1947 I started my job as Director of the Arbeitsamt. I was told to report to the Burghermeister at City Hall, because he had controlled it for years. He had been told that I would be in charge and he was to take me to the site which was a former post office building. It was a beautiful day and I walked into the imposing Stathuis (City Hall) with great expectations. A receptionist was sitting in the middle of a huge lobby and she told me to take a chair against the wall. I sat down and almost immediately heard very loud voices coming from the Burghermeister's office. It seemed like there were at least six or seven angry men and they were arguing about something, probably me. I sat there for about ten minutes and then I realized that this was one of those take charge, do or die moments for me.

As I started toward the door, the receptionist jumped up and started hollering, "Nein, nein Gnadege Frau" (No, no, gracious lady), but I just kept going. I opened the door and there sat the Burghermeister behind a massive wooden desk and eight Burghers sitting in big chairs facing him. Immediately, there was dead silence. They stared in disbelief at this twenty-seven-year-old American girl, who thought she was going to run the Arbeitsamt.

Instinctively, I knew that I had to take charge – just like when I walked into that rowdy first grade room in Miami. Marching right up to the Burghermeisters desk I started pounding on it with my closed fist. In a mixture of broken German and English I told them in no uncertain terms that I was very unhappy that they had made me wait for ten minutes and I expected to be taken immediately to my new position where they would introduce me as the new Director.

It worked. They sat in stunned silence for about two seconds and then the Burghermeister stood up and said, "Yes, yes, I will take you now." And he did. (When I left that job this same group hosted a reception and dinner for me in the famous castle and gave me a large, pewter Key to the City of Heidelberg which I still have on my coffee table.)

My introduction to the Arbeitsamt was equally interesting. When we went into the front door we entered an enormous room with about fifty desks. Each desk had a chair next to it and the workers were interviewing people for jobs. Back in one corner was a large glassed-in office. There we met Hans, who was until now, the Director. He politely acknowledged our introduction and even bowed slightly, but I could tell by the look in his eye that he didn't like me and he didn't plan on surrendering any authority. Again, I knew instinctively that he had to understand who was boss. He had moved a second desk into his office which was to be mine.

I made my point immediately by telling him that this would be *my* office. We went out into the big room and started rearranging desks so that there was an area just outside my office, which would become his office. I let him have the very beautiful area rug from my office and it outlined his office space. I also let him take his chair, but I kept his desk and made him take mine. He took his plants, but I told him we would deal with the filing cabinets later. Even the Burghermeister helped with the moving. Hans got the message. I'm sure he was furious. Over time we managed to have a good working relationship, although we never really trusted each other. We did learn to respect each other because both of us wanted the Arbeitsamt to be successful, and it was.

I spent the first few weeks just learning how they operated and who did what. I was at a distinct disadvantage because my German was very poor. I could understand it better than I could speak it. All of them could speak English, but I was very aware that Hans especially could sabotage me. After the first week I chose Han's secretary, Ursula, to be my secretary. I sensed that she was sympathetic to my cause and she didn't like Hans. It was the smartest move I made. She wasn't a tattletale, but she gave me honest answers and she knew the whole operation.

During my two weeks in Frankfurt, the military trainers said to start by classifying all of the jobs, but there was no real need for it. The sole purpose of classification is to insure equal pay for equal work. We were in a highly unusual position. The German marks were so worthless that the finance office couldn't even get the employees to pick up their checks. They never even asked about the salary when they were interviewed.

American jobs provided a warm place and a free lunch. Many of them wanted access to the black market – they would have opportunities to get cigarettes and coffee. Most of the girls who applied wanted to know American men. Their goal was very often to be able to live with one or even better they might become a war bride and get out of Germany. And their system was working.

Hans had been fully cooperating with these girls. He personally had interviewed all of the clerk-typists going out to the compound and he didn't care whether or not they were qualified. I wasn't sure just how he made his decisions but I was highly suspicious. And unfortunately, many of the American men who got all of these pretty blond girls on their staff didn't care either.

Concentrating on the employment area, I made it my main goal to get the best person in every job opening. All of the requisitions for openings at the Compound came to me first and I determined the qualifications for them. This meant reorganizing the interviewers and training them to be specialists in different areas.

I set up a Training Section in an upstairs room and put an older German woman in charge. She highly disapproved of the current system, and I mandated that every girl who went out to the Compound as a clerk-typist or secretary had to pass typing and shorthand tests. Hans was removed from the process. After a few weeks the poor German woman came down and said the girls were all very angry and she couldn't control them. They didn't like the new system and they wanted to rebel.

By then I knew just what to do. Marching upstairs I laid down the law to them. I told them I knew exactly what their intentions were and they had better get with the new program. They were going to be able to type and take dictation before they would have that chance for a ticket to America. They too, got the message. It was probably the biggest single change I made in the employment process.

As the weeks went by I earned the confidence of the workers. They realized that I was not what they had feared the most – an ugly American who hated the "Krauts." They learned that I was fair, but tough. Even Hans got on board; he probably worried that Ursula knew where the bodies were buried, and he never knew how much she told me.

Ursula became my rock. I could trust her completely. She knew when Hans was about to hire a former Nazi for a position out at the Quartermaster where he would be in a position to steal us blind. People like that lied on their applications of course and I didn't see most of them. I really relied on her and she was one of the few workers whose background I got to know. She was married, but her husband was still a prisoner of War somewhere in Russia. She had heard nothing from him for two years. When he was drafted into the Army they had a little three-year-old girl and she was pregnant with Heidi. Her husband had never seen Heidi, now five years old.

When the war was over and the Americans were moving into Heidelberg her older daughter had acute appendicitis. Everything was in utter chaos. Ursula had to get on the crowded street cars and make several changes before she could get to the Hospital. When she got there the Americans were just taking it over and all of the German patients were being moved out. She did find her doctor. He was moving out, but he took time to examine the child and determined she needed an operation immediately. She had a ruptured appendix. He said, "Come to my house and I will operate on her on my kitchen table." He did but the little girl died two days later.

Almost every afternoon Heidi would come about five o'clock and stand by a tree outside our window waiting for her mother. I would motion for her to come in. Every day I would bring an apple or orange or a candy bar for her. I kept it in a desk drawer and she knew just where to look for her surprise. I remember the first time I put a banana in the drawer. She picked it up and bit into it without knowing you had to peel it. She had never seen one before.

Sometime in November Heidi failed to appear for two days in a row. I asked Ursula, "Is she alright?"

"No, she is sick." Two more days went by and she was still sick. Ursula said, "We have no medicine," and I thought, tomorrow I'll bring her some aspirin.

That night I was at the Officer's Club with a group of friends; Norman was out of town. As we chatted a German waiter came up and said, "There is a German man outside who wants to see you about a sick child."

I went out and it was Heidi's grandfather. "Heidi is very sick with pneumonia and the doctor says that only Penicillin can save her. Can you get some for us?" My heart sank. Penicillin was still quite new and probably it was not available for the Germans.

I got the address and said, "Go home and I will bring some if I possibly can." I went back into the club and called the Station Hospital – the very one where Heidi's sister had been taken.

When I spoke with the officer in charge he said, "No, I'm not authorized to do that." I begged him to call his Commanding Officer to get a waiver, but he insisted that it wasn't possible.

"I understand."

I went back to my table and explained my dilemma. A good friend who was a Captain said, "The soldiers in the barracks black market in everything imaginable. Let's try."

And so we talked to dozens of soldiers until one o'clock in the morning, to no avail. I knew I could get my friend into big trouble and it wasn't working. We drove to the address of Ursula's home.

We climbed up to the third floor of this cold, dark apartment building and knocked on the door. The moment the door opened I knew – Heidi was dead. The room was full of people, all crying. Nobody said a word to me. I saw Ursula across the room and went to her but I couldn't say anything. They thought that because I was an American I could have helped if I really cared. I didn't even try to explain. We just left. I never recovered. Because of Heidi I am still driven to help children whenever, wherever and however I can. And I still hate war.

The next morning when I entered the Arbeitsamt no one greeted me. I walked from the front door through the big room and back to my office and no one said a word. But they were very used to death and dying and they didn't expect an American to care. Why should they? Fifty million people had died in the war. One more child couldn't make that much difference. And so we carried on.

After a week Ursula came back to work. Neither of us ever mentioned Heidi. Sometimes late in the afternoon I would look out of the window at the tree where Heidi always stood. I glanced at Ursula, and tears would be flowing down our cheeks, but we didn't talk about it. I never knew how much she did or did not understand. Even now, my tears fall on the page.

One child I was able to help. An interviewer from out front came to my office and said, "There is a little German boy here who wants a job. He heard there was an American here and he said, 'My mother told me the Americans would help me'. He says he is fifteen years old, but he looks like ten or eleven." Will strode confidently into my office –

he had quite a story. From a little village near the Austrian border, most of his family had been killed. Before she died, his mother had told him, "Go find some Americans, they will help you." He had apparently walked or hitched rides for several hundred kilometers to get to Heidelberg. He had begged for food or taken it from the fields. He had a wonderful spirit about him. He looked at me with complete faith and trust that now he had found the answer to his mother's plea.

I called a friend who arranged for Will to go out and live with some soldiers in their barracks. I never saw him again but I checked on him occasionally and he was doing great. The soldiers treated him like their younger brother. He was shining their shoes and doing all kinds of errands – probably jobs they were supposed to do, and everyone was happy. He probably grew up in those barracks.

One day a Colonel came into my office to arrange for household help. This was not at all unusual since wives and families were regularly arriving from the States. As I took down the information, his name sounded familiar. Unbelievably, this was the family from whom we had sublet our apartment in Monroe, Michigan! We had never seen them because they were in Oklahoma at the time. He could hardly believe it either. When they got settled his wife called and she invited me to lunch at their home. You can imagine my amazement when I walked in and there was the furniture we had in the Monroe upstairs apartment! We ate lunch at the very table where Alyce and I had played cards with our roommates, and thrown them down so hard that the owners downstairs had thrown us out. What a small world!

Rules and regulations were everywhere. A young Lieutenant was newly married, but he couldn't get his wife on the eligibility list to come to Germany. Families came first. When he realized it was hopeless, he paid for her to come to Paris where he picked her up and brought her to Heidelberg. Later he got a letter from the Housing Officer, "It has come to the attention of this office that you are living illegally with your wife." So ironic when most of the military were living with German girls.

If a single, American civilian worker got pregnant, she was sent home in disgrace and had to repay the government $700 for her transportation. However, many German laws were still in existence, so if a German worker got pregnant (probably by an American) she received a substantial bonus and three months leave with pay.

From time to time we had special projects at the Arbeitsamt which were very interesting. One day I got a call that fourteen German scientists would be going to the States and we were to process them and arrange German housing for two nights. According to War Department regulations they were not allowed to be housed in any American facilities. This seemed rather ridiculous since they were going to the States but we followed instructions. They would be leaving from Frankfurt but there was no housing for them there. Years later when Werner Van Braun became famous I wondered if he was one of that group.

Finding the housing turned into an almost impossible mission. At first I sent some German employees to locate rooms. When they returned empty handed I decided to go with them because we were under time pressures. I was amazed at the living conditions I encountered. We went first to hotels and rooming houses, then to apartment houses and finally to private homes before we were successful.

Everywhere we saw eight or nine people sharing single rooms and fifteen or twenty sharing small apartments. The halls were full of mats and cots, and bathrooms were shared by maybe fifty people or more. I asked, "Where do all of these people come from? Heidelberg wasn't bombed." They reminded me that Berlin, Frankfurt, Munich, Stuttgart and all the major cities in Germany were destroyed. Survivors from all over Germany flocked to Heidelberg. All of these people, especially the children, were still suffering consequences of the war.

One day I called the Quartermaster and had them bring me an extra filing cabinet. When I opened a drawer I found it was full of documents marked "Top Secret." I called the OSS agency (they preceded the CIA) and they panicked. They said, "Don't leave it. Keep your eyes on it until we get there." So I sat and sipped my coffee and stared at the file until four very serious men in uniform arrived. The soldiers really scared the poor Germans in the outer office. They had a huge lock box on wheels and removed those files as if they were bombs. I hope they contained something worth their trouble. We never heard from them again.

The Marshall Plan

I was only at the Arbeitsamt a matter of months before the Marshall Plan was introduced. It took time, but the results were astounding. We had heard rumors about it and it had been discussed in the *Stars and Stripes* (our only newspaper), but I didn't know much about it until I went out to the Compound one day. My Colonel boss told me about the experience of our Commanding General. He had been called up to Frankfurt along with twenty-seven others of the top "Brass" and they had met a full day at the I.G. Farben Headquarters with General George Marshall, the Secretary of State.

Our General had reported that after all twenty-eight of them were seated around a huge conference table, George Marshall entered. He introduced himself and then asked each member to introduce themselves. As they went around the table he looked at each one very intently and the rest of the day he called them all by name and amazingly, never made a mistake.

All of the attendees were very impressed with what he had to say. He talked about after World War I, when Europe was pretty much left to recover on its own. It took a long time and many of the punishments inflicted on Germany had resulted in resentment and Hitler's later success. Marshall described an economic plan which would be implemented – financial reforms would be the first step. He had timetables for when, how and who would implement the plan. All of the attendees were very excited by the end of the day.

When the financial changes took place in Heidelberg, the Germans lined up at City Hall on a Sunday and turned in all of their old Marks. The single file line stretched out for blocks. Each person was given 250 new Marks plus a schedule as to when and where they could later redeem certificates they were given for other assets they could prove they had.

Our landlord, Mr. Koinecke was so excited. He and his wife, their two daughters and their son lived in the basement of their lovely home which the Americans had "liberated" and I now lived in. We were never down there so I have no idea what their living arrangements were.

We four American women lived all over the house. Mrs. Koinecke was our cook, the two girls were our maids and Mr. Koinecke who had been the City Architect was our yardman. We seldom saw him. If we came home and he was working in the yard he wouldn't even look up. I can see him yet leaning on the rake and looking away when we approached. We never knew if he was embarrassed by the situation or very angry or what, but we thought it best to leave him alone.

On this Sunday when we gathered for supper we could hear him singing in the basement. When Mrs. Koinecke served us she excused him by saying, "Oh, he is so happy. He says this plan will save us, we will live to see better days." He was right; things started improving almost immediately.

At the same time the Germans got new Marks, Americans were issued a new Script and we were no longer allowed to use Marks or American currency. It had a huge effect on the Black Market almost instantaneously. Americans were no longer allowed to buy anything on the German market. We were not to give Germans any of the new Script and they were not allowed to give us their new Marks. It didn't work perfectly. The Black Market continued, but on a much, much smaller scale.

It also changed our financial situation at the Arbeitsamt. The Germans were paid in the new Marks but now they had value. Classification of jobs became an issue and we had to really make adjustments because now "equal pay for equal work" had meaning. Our Finance Office had to arrange to deliver the paychecks to the offices where people worked, because now the employees wanted them and the checks couldn't be dispensed from one office.

The whole Marshall Plan was pretty phenomenal. It will go down in history as the best reconstruction plan ever devised. (It is so sad that now Bush doesn't have a plan in Iraq; in 2006 those people don't have their electricity and water fully restored and civil war is erupting.)

I was so fortunate to have been assigned to the Arbeitsamt. Many Americans, especially the dependent families came to Germany, lived in a compound with other Americans and never met any Germans except for their few household employees. They took a lot of trips but very few of them had the opportunity to know the people. I had the rare chance to get to know a lot of them.

Sometimes after work we would stay late and talk about the war, the Marshall Plan, and the future of Germany. At first I was more than a little annoyed that every single German I ever knew always said, "I was not a Nazi." I wondered, "Who were all those screaming people below the balcony at Hitler's speeches?" I learned a lot about making assumptions.

Taking advantage of the repression after World War I, and the global economic depression, Hitler had been a brilliant psychologist. Early in his career he did all kinds of things which really drew the people to him. He built the Autobahn, a state of the art highway. He arranged a coupon system for ordinary people to be able to purchase a brand new Volkswagen. The small villages had radios in their Burghermeister's offices and all of the homes had receivers. This was an astounding innovation. The entire village could all hear the radio, but only the station the Burghermeister chose, so it was quite a propaganda machine.

Hitler would come to Heidelberg and tell the people about the horrible things the Jews were doing in Munich. Then he would go to Munich and tell them about the horrible things the Jews were doing in Heidelberg. And early on he started the Hitler Youth Movement. It was a mandatory program which met on Sunday morning during the Sunday School hour. Parents were held accountable if the children did not attend. Slowly his Dictatorship evolved but it was not until he marched troops into the Sudetanland that the ordinary Germans realized what was happening. That was what I heard from my employees. They also predicted that America was going to have real trouble with Russia and the day would come when America and Germany would fight together against Russia. It was all very interesting.

It was becoming very apparent by the fall of 1948 that the plan for the four zones which Roosevelt, Churchill and Stalin had devised was not working. The biggest mistake was the way Berlin was divided into four zones which isolated it from the rest of the American Zone. In October the Russians started the blockade of Berlin which meant no food, fuel or other supplies would be able to reach Berlin. In a very short time the people would be starving and freezing.

The Americans came up with a very ingenious, ambitious plan. They would fly everything needed into Berlin to insure the survival of the millions of people living there. It was called the Berlin Airlift and it worked. Thousands of people were involved. Planes took off from Rhein Main in Frankfurt every two minutes, were unloaded immediately when they landed at Berlin's Templehof, and sent back to Frankfurt as soon as possible. It took an incredible amount of planning and execution to make this work.

Our Heidelberg Office received requisitions almost daily for truck drivers who transported goods to Frankfurt and participated in the loading. Applicants didn't even have to know how to speak English. They just had to learn "load" and "unload." They picked up their loads from all over the Zone and then headed for Frankfurt.

On every flight the American airmen would see German children standing on the hillsides on the route to Templehof. They started dropping candy bars with little parachutes attached to them. They dropped thousands of them. American and Allied military wives in Berlin published a cookbook entitled, *Operation Vittles*, which featured recipes and anecdotes about their experiences with their German cooks. Their experiences were familiar to me.

I asked our cook, Geneva, one day if she could make an apple pie and she said, "Of course," and she made a fairly good one. Later I asked her if she could make a lemon pie and again she said, "Of course." It was not fairly good – it was sliced lemons between two crusts! The *Operation Vittles* cookbook was a great success – I still have my copy. It has several pictures of the German children getting their candy bars on the hillsides.

We realized later that the blockade and the Berlin Airlift were probably the beginning of the Cold War.

After Work

During all this time I was having a very happy and significant personal life. One of the first things I did after I arrived in August 1946 was to make arrangements to visit my relatives in Holland. We were allowed to ride trains and street cars anywhere in Germany by just showing our passport, but we had to get visas and pay for transportation if we left Germany. I had been there about two months when I made my first trip to Holland. It was so wonderful. I met so many aunts and uncles and cousins and they were all such good people. Dad's three brothers looked remarkably like him. His sister acted like him. All the in-laws and the many cousins were delightful.

On my first visit I went to Winschoten in the northeastern part of Holland near the German border. One of my uncles rented a huge moving van and about forty relatives sat on benches and chairs in the back of the van for the trip to Drieborg, where my father was born and raised. I was introduced all over the village as the granddaughter of "the tall one" – it was the first time I knew that my grandfather, Eddo, was almost seven feet tall! I saw Dad's birthplace and the blacksmith shop where he learned his trade from his father, who was a "Meister" blacksmith. (Years later a distant relative researched the Dresselhuis family tree and discovered seven generations of blacksmiths!)

It was incredible. We went to the home of a cousin in nearby Nieweschans who made tea for all of us. We sat in a park across the street from her home and had a delightful tea party.

I asked how my father ever made the decision to go to America and how could he afford it? I was told that the government encouraged young men to leave because they had so few opportunities in Holland and the government paid their fare. Their original plan was that the whole family would follow my father once he got settled but actually only two sisters made it to America. The brothers got interested in girls who did not want to go and all three of them started a bicycle factory in Winschoten. The sister who remained also got married and didn't want to leave.

I walked along the railroad in Nieweschans where Dad had taken the train to go to Rotterdam where he sailed for America. He had extra clothing in a bundle he carried on a stick on his shoulder and that is all he took with him. He knew very little English. He did know a former villager, Henry Mulder, who had preceded him in his journey. Henry and his family had settled in Parkersburg, Iowa and that was my father's destination.

I also visited Oldeboorn, a village in northern Holland where my dad's youngest brother Frank lived. He was a minister in a Reformed Church, he was married to Agatha and they had four children. Uncle Frank told me that he was nine years old when my father left for America. "Your father told me he would come back and bring me some peanuts." I determined right then that I would save some money and buy Dad a ticket to come back. It had been forty years since he had left Holland.

Everywhere I went in Holland I heard stories about their horrific war experiences. Under the brutal Nazi occupation, the Netherlands had endured bombings and widespread hunger. My first night in Holland I stayed with my

Aunt Schauk in Winschoten and shared a bedroom with my cousin, Ettje, who was about twenty. Their home was the top two floors of an elegant, old building that housed the "Dresselhuys" children's store.

From the window of her bedroom we could see a bombed out church on the corner. Ettje said, "I was standing right here when the bombs dropped and I just prayed that one would drop on us. Everything was so bad." Her father was Willem and his story, like many Dutchmen, was tragic, yet heroic.

From the earliest part of the war Willem was a part of the underground movement. They started by helping young Jewish boys escape to the South Pacific. At that time part of their home was an apartment where a Jewish family lived. Willem tried to help them leave but the father and mother refused to go. The daughter did not want to leave her parents so only the son left. He was twenty years old and Willem helped him escape to the South Pacific. He left home in a wheelbarrow covered with wood. Willem wheeled him to a farmhouse which was their secret headquarters. It had to be a very complicated operation. After the war the boy returned, but his parents and sister had died in a concentration camp in Germany.

Ettje told me her father would sometimes put a note in her mitten when she left for school. She was instructed to stop by the bakery and give it to the owner. Her mother, Schauk often objected to his work.

"Willem, you have to think of your wife and children," she would admonish, knowing the risks if he was caught.

"I have to think of all wives and all children," he would soberly reply. His work continued into the second year after the Five Day War. The Nazis who always patrolled the streets came into their home late one night when all of the family were sleeping. They broke down the door of the store and tramped up the stairs. Uncle Willem went out of the window and hung between their building and the one next to it. The Nazi soldiers ransacked the entire house and kept inquiring about Uncle Willem's whereabouts. The three children and Aunt Schauk were terrified.

Finally, they left and tramped down the stairs. They got to the street and one of the young Nazi's said, "You know, that bedroom window was open. I'm going to go back and check it." He returned and found that Uncle Willem had just pulled himself back up into the bedroom so they took him. The next morning Aunt Schauk went to the Stathuis (City Hall) to try and find out what happened to him. She saw a huge truck being loaded with underground workers including Uncle Willem and the Mayor of Winschoten. They were prodded with bayonets, forced to board the open truck. Schauk said that as they drove off, Uncle Willem stood at the back of the truck and saluted! They were taken to Bergen-Belsen. My aunt was deeply depressed and hardly spoke to anyone. She would spend her days sitting in a rocker by a second floor window looking up the street waiting for him to return.

At the end of the war the Mayor was among those who were liberated and he returned to Winschoten. He said they had all been slave laborers and had spent most of their time digging ditches. They slept in two tiered cages with two men in each cage. Every morning they had to line up for roll call. If someone did not appear the man sharing his cage would have to go back and look. If he was sick or maybe dead, his cell mate would have to drag him to the line up. If he was not there dogs would be sent to find him. It was just a few months before they were liberated that Uncle Willem's dead body was dragged to the lineup.

All four families of my father's siblings had horror stories about the war. The Five Day War when the Nazi's invaded Holland had started on May 5, 1942, the very day I had graduated from college. At that time two cousins were serving their time in the Army. They were in the Netherlands Motorcycle Corps which approached a German troop train arriving in Rotterdam. All of the German soldiers were leaning out of the windows holding white flags so the motorcycle troops continued toward the train. As they got close, the Germans shot them all down.

The family learned rather quickly that one cousin was dead. They could not learn anything about Uncle Sikko's son. He had been working in the family's bicycle factory along with his father and two uncles before his Army service. He and Uncle Willem had become very close because they did the marketing and public relations for the company. Uncle Willem decided to drive down to Rotterdam in his pickup truck to find out what had happened. When he arrived the whole city was in turmoil after a devastating bombing.

Uncle Willem went from hospital to hospital trying to find him. Finally he found a nurse who said, "He sounds like one who was here yesterday but he was near death. We could not help him." She gave him the name of a morgue where Uncle Willem found him. His body was badly mutilated but Uncle Willem cut two locks of his hair for his mother and his girlfriend before they put him into a sealed casket. Uncle Willem returned to Winschoten with his body where they buried him.

Another girl cousin was killed that first day of the war. She was sitting by the canal painting the scene when a bomb dropped nearby. Another cousin, Uncle Frank and Aunt Agatha's seven-year-old daughter died later during the war. She had measles and probably pneumonia and they could get no medicine for her.

Ettje and I rode bicycles all over Winschoten. We went to one area which was completely deserted. She told me that this was the area where 800 Jews had lived and they had all been taken away. She said, "We don't touch anything. We are waiting to see if some of them come back." I remember we looked into store windows – even in a jewelry store with diamonds on display, nothing had been touched.

I stayed for several days in the small village of Oldeboorn where Uncle Frank and Aunt Agatha lived. They had four children – Ettye, Agatha, Jon Eddo and Francisca, only four years old. (The oldest daughter of every Dresselhuys family was named Ettje or Ettye.) At breakfast the first day they served the regular bread and cheese and tea but they also put a fried egg on a plate in front of me. Aunt Agatha said that a few of the villagers had chickens and one had brought her this egg for the American relative who was coming to visit. Francisca was looking at it very longingly so I pushed it over in front of her. She shared it with her brother and sisters.

They had to hide Jon Eddo all during the war to keep him from being taken as a slave laborer. He was twelve years old when the war started and the Nazi soldiers patrolled the streets constantly. They never knew when they might come by or enter the house, so they kept Jon Eddo under the stairs for almost four years. By removing one board he could slip in and out. If he came out someone had to be out front watching for the soldiers. He never went outside during those years. He slept under the stairs even though he grew so much that he couldn't stretch out under there.

A crippled American plane had crashed on the edge of Oldeboorn. The five American soldiers aboard had all died. Uncle Frank had conducted a funeral service for them on site and the villagers dug graves for them. The Nazi's didn't interfere. At the end of the war Uncle Frank notified American authorities, but when I visited the graves were still there.

Ettye enjoyed wearing one of my uniforms and we walked all over the village. She was about sixteen at the time and she loved it. I had a camera and many of the villagers had their pictures taken with me and Ettye in our uniforms.

Uncle Frank said that a Nazi soldier would always come to their church services to be sure his sermons were "in order."

"I found I could preach without disturbing them." Some of the relatives didn't approve of that and felt he should have done more. In spite of the fact that the Dutch people remained resolute and so many of them helped with the underground they felt that Holland did not do enough.

My cousin Sikko said, "In Denmark the King wore a Star of David on his sleeve and all of his countrymen followed his example. Our Queen went to Canada. That was not right." I couldn't agree with him, since I had heard too many stories of incredible bravery. I could fill books with examples of their bravery and sacrifice. Americans had no idea of the reality of War in your own country.

The next year I saved money and sent Dad a ticket to come to Holland. It was a memorable visit. His sister, Ada, came with him. Her husband, Ole, was a wealthy farmer and she could well afford this trip. I flew to Amsterdam and met two uncles and a cousin and together we waited for their plane to arrive. Such a reunion it was! My Uncle Frank got his peanuts! We took the train down to Roermond where he was now Pastor. About twenty relatives were there to greet us and we sat in a large circle and talked, laughed and ate into the wee hours of the morning.

I asked my Dad whether they had any trouble on the trip. He laughed and said, "You're just like your brother and sisters. They all came home to tell me how to get to Chicago and New York. They had so many concerns that I finally had to remind them that I had made it to Iowa from Holland before they were born, and I was sure I could get back." And he did! They visited all of the relatives all over Holland. He wrote letters back to the *Parkersburg Eclipse* which were absolutely delightful.[1]

When it came time for he and Aunt Ada to leave, the pilots on his airline were on strike so their trip was delayed for several days. I had flown to Amsterdam to tell them goodbye, but we just visited instead. We did walk down to the terminal to inquire about a possible departure and we had an experience which was typical of Dad. We were sitting drinking coffee when we overheard a young woman talking to the ticket agent. She was terribly agitated and was practically shouting, "We are having a big showing in New York tomorrow and I have to be there with all of the clothes." She went on and on.

After a bit my Dad got up and went over to her. He tapped her on the shoulder and said, "You know, this young man cannot help you. He doesn't fly the plane. Why don't you come over and have a cup of coffee with us." She looked very startled but she picked up her purse and came over to our table.

Dad got her some coffee and spoke very gently. Before long she was telling us her whole life story. We talked – mainly she talked – for at least an hour. When she left she thanked Dad profusely and said she was going to look at things from a whole new perspective.

But I didn't just go to Holland. My friends and I made frequent trips all over Europe. Lots of my friends had Volkswagens – you could buy them for $800. Often on the weekends we would go skiing in southern Germany. It was

1. I have copies of all of those letters but I'm not including them in my book – I'll never finish this if I try to describe his life as well as mine.

easy to cross over into Salzburg, Austria. We made trips all over Europe and some of the best adventures were with my friend, Marti. Our friendship grew from the day we made the train trip from Frankfurt to Heidelberg and lasted until she died in 1989.

Marti and I shared the master bedroom at the Koinecke's house high up on the mountain. At night she would tell me about her colonel husband who wanted a divorce and we would make plans about how she could see him. She did not just want to call him on the phone. He was stationed in Darmstadt which was about forty-five minutes from Heidelberg. At least three times on Sunday afternoons we drove over to Darmstadt. We were able to find the house where he was living and we would park across the street, but she could not bring herself to go knock on the door. It would be too traumatic if his German girlfriend answered the door.

Then we heard that the troops from Darmstadt were in a big parade in Heidelberg. Our compound had been a German Army facility and consisted of a rectangle of buildings around the big parade grounds. I went to the parade but Marti stayed in her second floor office to watch from there. Our plan was that I would speak to her husband personally if I could possibly get to him and tell him that Marti was there. Then he would have the option of seeing her.

As I made my way to the parade, our boss, the Captain, stopped me. He wanted a picture of General Clay who was present for the occasion. Since the Captain was in the parade, I volunteered to do it. I took the Captain's camera and maneuvered myself right up to the stage, focusing the camera on the General. An instant before I snapped the picture, an elderly German man on the stage suddenly stepped forward. He realized what he had done and apologized profusely, "Bitte, bitte, Gnadige Frau", he said. I got a very good picture of him which I still have. I am so glad I have it because the man was Konrad Adenauer who later became the very beloved "Die Alte," the first Chancellor of the reborn Germany. Unfortunately, I did not get to talk to Marti's husband.

One day at lunch in the mess hall Marti unexpectedly met a mutual friend she and her husband had known when they all worked in Washington, D.C. He assumed she was there as a dependent and was flabbergasted when he learned the truth. He offered to go and see her husband, which he did. He reported back that her husband had been terribly surprised, but he refused to talk about it. Marti had high expectations that he would contact her but he never did.

We had been there almost a year when we saw Orders going through Headquarters that her husband had been transferred to the Zone of the Interior (the U.S.). Marti was crushed. She had gotten the job and had come all the way to Germany to see him and now he was gone. He had known she was there, but had never contacted her.

When her husband had left Washington to go into active service, Marti had put their furniture into storage and had paid the storage bill for the ensuing years. But the bills stopped coming after he returned to the States. Marti wrote to the storage company and got back a letter saying that "the Colonel and his wife" had picked up the furniture. She was stunned.

A friend who was a lawyer in the Attorney General's office investigated and found that her husband had gotten a divorce in his home town on the grounds that she had abandoned him! The divorce had been finalized a few months after she had arrived in Germany.

But that is not the end of the story. Marti stayed on in Heidelberg for six years. When she finally returned to the States, she was met at the airport by her former husband! He had divorced the German wife and wanted her to remarry him and forget everything that had happened. She found that to be impossible, but they did continue to have a relationship.

Marti returned to Washington and found a very good job. Her ex-husband was retired and lived in the Midwest, but he would come out once a year and they would vacation together. This went on for about twenty-five years. Then one year he told her that he had very advanced cancer. They spent one last vacation together. Several months later she received a note from a friend of his that he had died. They too, were victims of the war. She lived in Arizona for the last ten years of her life and we remained very good friends until she died.

More Trips

Our Heidelberg group made lots of trips together. Three times the Personnel Department requisitioned Hitler's Yacht, which was available to sections or departments at the Compound. You just had to sign up for it. It was anchored on the Rhine River and we loved the scenic tours. These were great, relaxing times, but always somewhat sobering when we remembered its previous owner. The yacht had a permanent crew and it accommodated about ten or twelve of us at a time.

In southern Germany there were several famous ski resorts;

Garmisch-Berchtesgarden was our favorite place to go. It was so picturesque – go and see for yourself. On my first ski trip, I was terribly excited. We put the skis on in the Skihaus and shuffled our way over to the slopes. I was headed for the beginner's slope but the trail passed the more advanced slopes. I was shuffling along with great difficulty when one of my friends behind me called out to me.

There were some other people between us so I stepped

off the path to let them go by. With long, ungainly boards strapped to my feet, I started slipping until suddenly, I was hurtling down the steep slope!

Instead of bending slightly forward over the skis to balance, I was leaning back almost perpendicular to the skis. I was in a trance as I flew down the mountain, utterly helpless to do anything. All I could see was the blue sky above me and I had no idea how this would end. I was conscious that some other skiers were along side of me – I guess they were going to pick up the pieces. I just kept going faster and faster. Somewhere along the way I lost track of my ski poles but they wouldn't have mattered.

Finally, the slope veered off slightly to the left at the bottom of the first big hill, but I didn't. I ended up in a soft snow bank which finally stopped me. Other skiers dug me out immediately and miraculously I wasn't hurt at all. I was returned to the Skihaus on a sled and revived with hot cocoa. Other skiers kept coming by asking, "Are you the girl who almost got killed today?" At least I had my fifteen minutes of fame but I never became an enthusiast of skiing. We made many more trips, but I enjoyed sipping my cocoa more than the limited skiing I did!

And there were lots of other interesting things to do at Garmisch. Hitler's Eagle's Nest was located there high up a mountain. It was a large compound with quarters for SOS and the Gestapo arranged in neat rows on the mountain slope in front of the house. An elevator went up through the mountain to get to the "Nest." The house had been partially bombed but was mostly intact. I have a piece of brown marble which I "liberated" from Hitler's bathroom on the second floor which is on my coffee table. A white marble piece from Eva Braun's bathroom was inadvertently thrown out one time when I moved.

We also made memorable trips to Salzburg and Vienna

in Austria, to cities in France, Switzerland, Italy, Czechoslovakia and Luxembourg. Some of my friends went on longer
trips but I couldn't afford them all. I preferred going back
up to Holland to see my relatives and the plane fare wasn't
very expensive. I hope everyone who reads this will make
all of those trips for themselves.

On the way back from a trip to Paris, I visited the American Cemetery in Luxembourg and found Charles' grave. I
stood by it for a long time and then started looking around.
Very close by I saw the grave for Don, his roommate and best
friend at Iowa. I will never forget Charles, but our whole relationship will always be a mystery to me. It is small wonder
that I hate war. But this book is not about my sorrow.

One very hard trip we made was to Dachau Concentration Camp, on the northern outskirts of Munich. It was
unreal. We drove back in the mountains alongside a railroad track to get there. The trains on those tracks had carried thousands of people, mainly women and children, to
their deaths in the gas chambers at Dachau. We were there
on a nice winter day, fairly cold but there was snow on the
ground and the sun was shining.

The details of the buildings are blurred, but more than
fifty years later I distinctly remember my feelings. A long
gray building right next to the railroad track looked clean,
cold and bare inside. But you immediately saw what looked
like shower heads about five feet apart around all four walls.
On the far side a conveyer belt disappeared into the wall –
something like the baggage carousels at the airports. This
belt was about eighteen inches off the floor and about thirty
inches wide. There were two small windows near the top at
the far end of the building, and an adjoining room.

New arrivals at Dachau were herded into the building
when they disembarked from the trains. They had to disrobe
and then the gas shower heads were turned on. The Gestapo

watched from the windows, and after the prisoners were dead they were loaded unto the conveyor belts. Or maybe they had to get on the conveyor belts before they died. As the guides were describing these procedures, I got very sick to my stomach and rushed outside.

I thought about the children especially. Most of them were Jewish; hopefully, they didn't realize what was happening. The mothers and grandmothers must have felt absolutely helpless. They surely cried out to God to help them or did they think God had truly forsaken them? The horror of it was unimaginable. I will never, ever forget it.

When I went back inside they were talking about how they took the gold out of the teeth and retrieved jewelry. They called that "processing" before the bodies were burned in the furnaces. Sometimes they made lamps out of skulls. The huge furnaces were spotlessly clean now. I closed my eyes and tried not to listen when the guide talked about the thousands in this furnace and the thousands in that one. Those images are imbedded in my mind forever. It seemed surreal. We were talking about human beings in the twentieth century. How could it be?

This experience has influenced my thinking to this day. I'm a political wonk, a peacenik and I pray differently than I used to. As I write this Wars are still going on but most people live in their own little sphere and concentrate on being happy. It is frighteningly reminiscent of the apathy the Germans described – they didn't pay attention to what was going on either. Will we ever learn?

One weekend Marti and I and two other girls at our office took the Orient Express to Prague in what was then Czechoslovakia. The train was the top-of-the-line, state-of-the-art train in Europe at that time. But it wasn't very fancy on that trip. It was so crowded we had to stand up most of the way for hundreds of miles. And it was just dimly lit.

We went hurtling through the night and if it hadn't been so crowded you probably would not have been able to remain in an upright position. You stood with your feet well apart to keep your balance.

This went on for a couple of hours when suddenly the air was split with the sound of gun shots and the train started screeching to a halt. The gun shots were coming from the adjoining car and I'm not sure whether any bullets came whizzing through our car. We were all petrified. When the train finally stopped some ruffians were removed from the car ahead of us. We heard lots of loud voices and could see flashlights, but it was pitch dark outside so you couldn't really tell what was going on. After a bit everything quieted down and we resumed our trip. Apparently, the shooters were abandoned out in the middle of nowhere. And this was wintertime in the mountains!

We arrived in Prague just after dark. We rode to the hotel in a sleigh drawn by two white horses. We were all tucked in with blankets, it was snowing softly and the stars were shining. It was about as picturesque as it could get and we loved it. We rode around for a long time and it cost us a lot when we finally got to our destination. The next morning we could see the railroad station just below the hill from us about two blocks away. But we had a great ride. It was worth what we paid.

This was a very old, elegant hotel but, as in Germany, the bathroom was at the end of the hall. I realized that I couldn't read Polish and didn't know the Men's from the Women's, so I went back to ask Lizbeth, one of our traveling companions. Her father was a Polish immigrant and she knew the language. She translated for me so I returned and opened the bathroom door. There were four or five men in there so I rushed back to the room.

"Lizbeth, you've forgotten Polish!" She disagreed ve-

212

hemently and we marched back down the hall. As we approached we saw a group of GI's leaving the bathroom. They were the ones who didn't know the language!

The shower head was mounted on the wall about eight feet high; I couldn't reach to adjust it and it was pointed directly at the wall. The water ran down the wall so the only way you could even get wet was to skootch up against the wall and squirm around. Rather difficult way to get clean.

After my bathroom experience, we went down to dinner. The dining room was lovely – typically European – and from our table we could see the lights of the city. It was still snowing and we were enchanted with the view. Every table had a very ornate, old fashioned telephone on it. We barely got seated when it started ringing. Lizbeth answered it and we soon learned that everyone in the room had a telephone. It was great fun. You would answer the phone, listen to some jabbering and then a grinning young man would appear and you would dance with him on the small floor at the end of the room. I was good at this because of all the times I had danced with those Russians at the USO in Miami.

I was dancing with a tall, handsome man and he slowly started dancing me away from the dance floor, across a hall and up a large open staircase. I started to panic, but I figured that before we got out of sight of my friends, I would just start to scream. After all, I knew all about sex by now. Just before I opened my mouth, I saw a large dance hall on the second floor filled with dancing couples. We both laughed and laughed. We danced and danced all evening. When my friends and I decided to go back to our room he jabbered and jabbered and I laughed and kept shaking my head "no." I never saw him again, but it was great fun.

Married

Norman went on a few of the trips with my friends, but he

213

loved to hunt and fish, so our courtship consisted primarily of outdoor activities. I had finally accepted his proposal, so we would be married nine months after we met. On week nights I was busy getting ready for the wedding. It took weeks for me to make all the preparations. I had bought white velvet in the States when I was back home in the summer and a German woman had made my dress. Marti had arranged for the flowers. A cake was special-ordered from the Reichspost – the downtown German hotel where we first had our meals before we moved up on the mountain. Frau Koinecke had prepared everything else for the reception. About forty friends had been invited and one of them was going to sing *Because* and *I Love You Truly*.

We had to go to the City Hall the day before to be legally married. (This was the same City Hall where I had confronted the Burghermeister and the Burghers.) Uncle Frank's ceremony would have nothing to do with the legality of the marriage. Two friends went along as witnesses. We were ushered into a large room and told to sit on four big wooden blocks in the middle of the room. A German man dressed very elegantly stood before us and read questions about their Laws which another German man translated for us.

"Are you presently married to anyone else?"

"Do you have any children?"

"Is Germany your land of birth? Name your birthplace." Afterwards, we signed all kinds of papers and were then given a "Certificate of Marriage." Norman was shocked that I wouldn't go back to our new home with him.

"I don't feel married until Uncle Frank does it."

We were married at four o'clock in the afternoon on Thanksgiving Day 1947. Our friends came to the Koinecke's house up on the mountain where I had lived for more than a year. Uncle Frank and my cousin Jon Eddo arrived from Holland the day before the wedding.

Everything went off without a hitch on our wedding day except that by two o'clock the cake had not yet arrived. I called down to the hotel and they said, "Oh my goodness, we didn't know today was Thanksgiving, but we will get you a cake." And they did, but it hadn't arrived by the time the ceremony started. When we were taking our vows we heard men's voices hollering and shouting. I was so nervous I hardly heard a word Uncle Frank said. I must have said "Yes" at the right time and I remember the kiss but that is about all.

Immediately after the ceremony I went out into the kitchen and poor Frau Koinecke was almost in tears. The men had had trouble getting up the mountain because of the ice and snow. They had had to get out and push their vehicle – that was when we heard the shouting. Worse than that, they had baked and frosted the cake after my telephone call so it was still hot from the oven. By the time they arrived all of the red roses and green leaves plus most of the white frosting had slipped off the cake and were surrounding it in puddles. I just took a knife and scooped it up and deposited it back on the cake. It turned out to be sort of striped – pink and red and all shades of green plus some white. I carried it out myself and we all laughed about it.

We didn't go on our honeymoon for two days because I did not want to leave Uncle Frank and Jon Eddo alone. So they stayed with us on our wedding night. The next day we drove Uncle Frank down to Stuttgart to see a pastor friend of his. Before the war they had been working on a translation of the *Heidelberg Catechism* into a Ukrainian dialect; it had never been printed in that language. They arranged to resume their work. Uncle Frank was thrilled to see his old friend again. Wars are so insane.

After we put Uncle Frank and Jon Eddo on the plane we drove down to a resort on a beautiful lake in southern Germany. It was surrounded by snowy mountains. I was deliriously happy – being married was absolutely fantastic.

We lived in a duplex for about two months waiting for better quarters to become available. Then we moved to a luxurious apartment in a large building on the Neckar River. When we lived in the duplex we had a cook who was really something. I guess the people at the Arbeitsamt thought I would be very impressed because of her background, but I wasn't. She was from a very wealthy family in Berlin and had been a prominent socialite during the Hitler days, at least that is what she told me and it probably was true.

She really was pathetic, wearing party gowns, high heels and lots of expensive jewelry even in the kitchen. She said those were the only clothes she had. I could have lived with that but it was the stories she told that turned me off. She would drop names like Hitler, Eichman, and Goebels and describe the fancy parties they all attended. I informed her in a hurry that I was not the least bit interested in hearing stories about her criminal friends so then she went around with her nose in the air. We did not take her along when we moved. Besides everything else she was a lousy cook.

Our new apartment had spacious rooms, high ceilings and beautiful furnishings. I had visited it once while our predecessors, a Colonel and his wife, were still living in it. She told me that she owned the drapes but she would sell them to me for $100. That was a very good deal because they were lovely and there were lots of them at the high windows which went from floor to ceiling. After we moved in soldiers from the Quartermaster came to inventory all of the furniture. I told them that I had bought the drapes and they said, "No you didn't, they belong to the Quartermaster." I was so disillusioned. I thought she was so nice.

We had been married for about a month when we made a trip to Paris with some friends. On the way Norman told me he had a big surprise for me. He had arranged to buy a beautiful, almost new, maroon Buick from the Mayor of Paris. I was thrilled until we got back to Heidelberg and he told me that he had borrowed the money from a friend and we were going to be paying huge monthly payments to him. We both were making very good salaries but Norman never learned how to manage money. Dad used to say, "It doesn't matter how much money you make. The trick is to always spend less than you make." His financial irresponsibility was an increasingly big problem throughout our marriage.

Heidelberg has mild winters and on nice weekends we would go hunting with another couple who were good friends. The Koineckes had a cabin up high in the mountains which they let us use. Herr Koinecke wasn't allowed to carry a gun, but he would come with us.

In Germany hunting is a complicated procedure. Groups of people would precede the hunters into the woods, hitting on the trees with big sticks, scuffling the leaves, and shouting to drive the animals into a particular area. They were called "beaters." We were told that when Hitler had gone hunting large groups of beaters would actually corner one or more animals in a rather small area. Hitler would emerge from his parked limousine, walk a few yards into the woods and start shooting like a crazy man. If he didn't hit anything one of the men in the group would kill a boar or deer and let Hitler think he had done it.

Early in our marriage Norman and I went on a hunting trip by ourselves. We walked single file through the woods. Norman kept turning around and glaring at me because I was making too much noise stepping on twigs and leaves. All of a sudden he stopped dead in his tracks and I looked up to see a magnificent deer about ten yards off to the side of us. He was looking around sniffing the air obviously enjoying himself. Suddenly there was a blast from the gun and the deer fell over. He didn't die instantly, he kicked for awhile and then became very still. I sobbed uncontrollably. I just wasn't prepared for this. It was my last hunting trip. I was never invited again and I wouldn't have gone anyway. I did continue to go up to the cabin once in awhile but one or more couples would go with us and only the men would go hunting.

Once a general from Frankfurt came down to join them (I am almost positive it was General Omar Bradley). They all had breakfast at our house but Norman fixed it. I didn't get up.

One Saturday night the men came home with a large boar. We had a groundskeeper named Fritz who always hung around until the hunters returned. He was quite elderly, a very nice man and a good worker. The hunters would only keep the choice parts of the meat and then Fritz could take the rest of it home in a burlap sack he would carry on his shoulders. This meat was probably priceless for his family. He would go home on the streetcar. We knew he had to change streetcars in the middle of town but he always managed.

In the morning Fritz's wife called. When he had changed streetcars the night before, a group of drunk GI's had emerged from the GI Club across the tracks. They saw Fritz and started crying out, "Oh look, there's a Kraut and he has been out stealing stuff." They jumped on him, kicked him and beat him. We went to the hospital to see him and it was horrible. He was half conscious and unrecognizable. The worst part of it was that there was really nothing we could do. It was illegal to give them money and they could have gotten into trouble if they had tried to use it. It was unbelievable and I just couldn't understand it.

I said to Norman, "How could those young, American boys possibly have done something like that?"

"It was easy. When those boys went through basic training one of the most important things they had to learn was to hate the 'Krauts.' If they didn't hate them they wouldn't be able to kill them. And they couldn't just turn off their hatred when the war was over and they were occupying the land." Just think what a terrible thing we did to millions of our young men. No wonder that so many of them who survived never wanted to talk about the war. We never saw Fritz again. Such experiences were just part of the scene.

One night when we were still in the duplex I woke up and realized that there was a light coming from the hall. I got up and followed it to the kitchen. When I walked in a man with a big burlap sack was standing in front of the refrigerator putting food into the sack. I realized he probably had a starving family, so I walked to the cupboard and put canned goods into the sack. When the sack was full I walked over and unlocked the door. He kept repeating "Danke, danke," (thank you, thank you) as I let him out into the dark cold night.

Norman woke up when I got back into bed. He couldn't believe what I had done. "You could have gotten killed!" He bought me a small pistol but I put it in the bedside table drawer and never touched it.

At Christmas time I went to a wonderful party the Red Cross was giving for German children. Their office was in a large, old hotel on Hauptstrasse. When I walked into the darkened ballroom there were about three hundred children quietly seated on the floor. Suddenly a huge Christmas tree at the front of the room was lit up. The colored lights glistened on the silver tinsel and a golden star shone at the top. The children were awestruck. They had never seen anything like this. It was sheer magic. There was not a sound in the room. Tears were streaming down many faces, including mine.

After we had been married for five months I learned I was pregnant. I was deliriously happy and so relieved. I was beginning to worry about how awful it would be if I never had a baby! I sent telegrams to all of my family and started knitting immediately. Since I felt fine, I kept working at the Arbeitsamt for about four months. When I began to be noticeably pregnant, I had to quit. It was not proper for pregnant women to work in those days. The Burghermeister, the Burghers and the Arbeitsamt staff had the big party for me at the Castle. It was a very memorable occasion, and already I missed my job.

Although our apartment was beautiful, to this day I don't like big, dark, heavy furniture. We had no closets in the bedrooms so besides the big four-poster beds we also had huge, dark dressers, commodes, and a massive armoire. The cook and the maid ran the place; I felt like a visitor.

A group of American women organized "Kinder Kare." There was a very real need because there were so many orphaned children in the Heidelberg area. We worked with an existing German Orphanage which concentrated on taking care of babies. Many of them were the illegitimate children of U.S. soldiers. This was before the Army was integrated and there was a very large contingent of black soldiers stationed at Mannheim, very close to Heidelberg. At least half of the orphaned children were black. They were desperately in need of everything – milk, baby food, supplies, clothes, and furniture.

The Buster Brown Company sent us five hundred pairs of children's shoes and Eli Lilly sent boxes and boxes of baby formula. I know that many other companies responded, but those two impressed me the most. Later as I raised my own children back in the states, I always bought Buster Brown shoes and Eli Lilly pharmaceuticals if I could because those companies responded so generously to our cries for help.

Our beautiful eight-pound baby girl was born at the 120th Station Hospital in Heidelberg on February 13th, 1949. We named her Nancy Alyce. I had an uneventful pregnancy, but she came two weeks later than we had expected. Labor pains finally started early on Sunday morning. I woke Norman and he said, "It's too early to go hunting."

It was snowing lightly as we drove to the hospital. Getting her born took most of the day and when it finally happened, she came feet first. Fortunately, there was an experienced German woman doctor present. She knew just what to do. I doubt that the American lieutenant doctor had ever delivered a baby but he was nice and very reassuring. Fathers were not allowed to be present in those days and that was a good thing because Norman was outside throwing up.

Little baby Nancy was precious. I had a "spinal" for the birth and was told to lie flat on my back for twenty-four hours or I would get a terrible headache. I couldn't possibly do that. Motherhood was so exciting, I kept getting up to care for the baby, not caring if I got a headache. They kept me in the hospital for a full week. It wasn't necessary but that was the routine in 1949.

When we went home our cook and maid insisted they needed help with the baby. I had every intention of taking care of her myself, but I relented because they were both good workers and I didn't want to lose them. I had purchased an electric washing machine from a family who was returning to the states – and it wasn't owned by the Quartermaster. Washing machines were practically nonexistent in Germany then. When Americans brought them over they had to be rebuilt because the electricity was on different currents. When they left they were anxious to sell them

The new nanny was about forty-five years old and she was convinced she knew absolutely everything about babies. She was equally convinced that I knew nothing about babies. If the baby had not been breast fed I may not have been allowed to ever hold her. The Nanny looked at the washing machine with utter disdain. "We don't do that in Germany," she said. "We have facilities in the basement. I will sanitize them," she informed me.

One day I went down to the basement to see the "facility" and I couldn't believe it. There was a huge black pot up on a metal stand and it had a gas burner under it. The nanny was standing on a chair with a pole in both hands which she used to stir the diapers in the steaming hot, soapy water. Then she used the pole to lower the diapers into a tub of cold water on the floor and repeated the operation to get them into a second rinse tub. She wrung each one out by hand. It was even worse than my mother's operation. At least Mama didn't have to burn her hands wringing out diapers. It's a wonder the diapers withstood the ordeal. But they were ultra clean.

Norman's job was quite unique. When the war had ended equipment was scattered all over the German territory. Tanks, jeeps, trucks, munitions carriers, and fuel tanks were just some of the machinery that had been disabled, broken or just abandoned as the war progressed. Each piece had to be evaluated and decisions made whether it would be sent to existing American bases in the Zone, junked, returned to the States or sold to foreign countries. Some vehicles had simply run out of gas, or the drivers had been killed. Sometimes they would find fields full of airplane motors or replacement parts for jeeps, which were all brand new. Turkey bought a lot of that equipment and arrangements had to be made to ship it by rail or transport them on the rivers.

The work was always interesting and different; he was good at it and seemed to really enjoy his job.

We made a trip to Paris when Nancy was about three months old. We went to the Folies Bergere and Nancy went with us in her ever-handy basket. She couldn't see from her vantage point, but I was amazed that the naked women were so beautiful with the colored lighting and swirling scarves.

On the way back to Heidelberg, Nancy was sleeping in her tied-down basket (the forerunner of car seats) and Norman was dozing in the passenger seat. When I approached the Border Station I slowed down and prepared to stop. However, the guard waved me on so I just waved back and proceeded on down the road. I got about fifty feet and the guard shot at our back tire. What a commotion! Norman jumped so high he almost hit the ceiling of the car. He thought the war had started again and let loose with some very colorful language. Nancy was crying and we were almost instantly surrounded with guards who pointed guns at us.

The first guard had intended to wave me to a space at the end of the Guard Station where I was supposed to stop, so they could inspect the car. I should have known that because it always happened. I just thought they recognized that we were Americans and allowed us through! Wrong! After a brief search, they sternly allowed us to leave.

Sometime in May of 1949 Norman's boss was transferred back to Washington, D.C. where he was to have a desk job. The colonel had moved to Heidelberg from Frankfurt and we had become very good friends with him, his wife and their three adorable children. Norman's contract was going to expire in August and we had to make a decision whether or not he would renew it. The Colonel told us he wanted us to come to Washington and he would have a job for Norman, so this sounded very appealing to us. It would be fascinating to live in our nation's Capitol and Norman enjoyed working with the Colonel, so we started making our plans.

Going Home

And so in August, 1949 we left Germany. Nancy was six months old.

We shipped everything we owned except the washer, amazed at how much stuff we had accumulated. Even the red Buick was shipped – the Army paid for all of it. We sent all of it, except the car, to a storage place in Washington. We drove up to Frankfurt expecting to leave from Rhine-Main the next day. But, of course, this being the Army we had to "hurry and wait." I don't know what the snafu was but we had to wait for about ten long days. I had minimal supplies and no equipment for Nancy and we had nothing to do except sit out in front of the barracks with other families who were also waiting.

We made friends with some of these people, but others were so angry you couldn't get near them. We were given cloth diapers for the babies and those who needed it were supplied with milk. We all ate in a mess hall. Finally, on the tenth day an officer came bursting into the mess hall when we were eating breakfast and announced that everyone with children under four years old would be leaving "TODAY." Later we learned that a baby had contracted measles and they wanted all of the children out of there as quickly as possible. Three hours later we were boarding the plane.

The trip was uneventful because, thankfully, Nancy was so good sleeping in her basket most of the way. At the time, I didn't reflect on my stay in Germany. However, my experiences there resulted in my lifelong concern for children and my participation as an activist in politics.

When we landed in New York, nausea overtook me. The

customs forms were weaving as I tried to describe what we were bringing into the States. The Customs Officer was pretty upset when he opened the first bag and saw all of the trinkets and gifts I had brought for my family, but had failed to declare. He started to really read me the riot act but I feebly informed him, "I'm sick." When he looked up and saw my green face he realized I might throw up all over the place at any moment. He quickly closed the bag and let us through.

We stayed overnight in New York City where I saw television for the first time. As I carried baby Nancy into the hotel, I glanced in the bar and saw the TV mounted on the wall. I walked right toward it and stood there mesmerized. Even little Nancy was fascinated. It was something like when I saw *Rebecca of Sunnybrook Farm* back in P'Burg – a monumental moment.

The next morning we went down to the pier to retrieve our car. It was quite a sight! We stood on the dock and watched as five cars were unloaded before our maroon Buick appeared. It was something to see them pick it up from the bowels of the ship with huge tongs, swing it out over the water and deposit it very gently within fifty feet of where we were waiting. A dock worker drove it over to the edge of the dock and verified our paperwork, so we climbed in and drove off.

Norman saw the drive through New York City as an exciting challenge. He thought he was as good as any experienced taxi driver although I was far from certain. After about ten seconds of sheer terror I decided to play with the baby and pretend everything was going to be just fine. We made it but I didn't breathe normally until we were finally out in the country.

The Colonel and his wife had invited us to stay with them in Washington, D.C. and we arrived at their lovely suburban home in the late afternoon. When we sat down to dinner, I was excited to learn about the job, so we could concentrate on finding a place to live. We were not prepared for the shock in store for us. The Colonel regretfully told us that he could not get a job for Norman because he had been on "limited" status as a civilian employee overseas, and as such, he did not have any rights for transfer or promotion within the permanent Civil Service.

We stayed another day and enjoyed the sightseeing tour the Colonel's wife gave us and then we headed for Iowa. We were terribly disappointed but we decided to visit my family and then make a decision about what we would do next. We were confident that Norman could find a good job so we weren't scared.

We had a great family reunion in Waterloo, Iowa. None of them knew Norman or baby Nancy, and we met new nieces and nephews who had been born during the 1946–49 period. Everybody loved everybody. Then we made the rounds to visit individual homes. The last visit was to my brother George and Thelma's home in Odebolt, in the northwestern part of Iowa. George made a proposal which we accepted after just a few days.

My brother had been a lawyer in Odebolt for sixteen years at that time and he knew the territory. The area was growing and there was a demand for another farm equipment business. George was willing to put money into getting us started if we were interested. He and Norman began surveying the possibilities the next day and within a week decided that George would build a commercial building on the outskirts of Lake View, a town ten miles from Odebolt. George was able to get a franchise with the New Holland Farm Equipment Company and we were off and running. We rented a house in Lake View and arranged for our household goods to be shipped from Washington. We were all very excited.

CHAPTER SEVEN
My Midwest Journeys

Lake View, Iowa

Lake View is a typical, small Midwest town, a great place to live when you have young children. It had a population of about 2,000 and was built on a picturesque lake. We lived there for five years and during that time we had two more children – Mary Patrice was born on August 18, 1950, and two years later, our son, Jon Rufus, was born on September 3, 1952. They were adorable, healthy, wonderful children.

Lake View was different from many small towns since it had a large group of young, progressive businessmen who had talented, active wives. Together they made Lake View an unusually interesting, vital town in which to live. Every year they designated a special weekend during the summer and had a big parade, ball games, bazaars and special events. This festival was a big deal in a rural area because you quickly got to know a lot of people and it was fun working with them.

Norman added to their efforts by suggesting they have their parade on the lake. This was an idea he brought from Heidelberg where they had a huge celebration on the fourth of July every year, the anniversary of when the French burned the Castle centuries ago. The Germans put red lights inside the Castle, so it appeared to be on fire as it loomed far above the city and the Neckar River. They decorated floats on sail boats which paraded on the river below. Norman helped the Lake View crowd adopt the idea of a parade on the lake and it became very popular; thousands of people from all over the area came.

During the winter seasons they put on some spectacular operettas in Lake View; it was surprising how much local talent existed. The plumber had a beautiful tenor voice and the high school music teacher was a marvelous soprano. After a few seasons they got married. It was like a Nelson Eddy -Jeannette McDonald thing, but unfortunately, it didn't work out very well in real life and they later divorced.

It was very easy to get involved in Lake View. We joined the Methodist Church because all of our new friends went there. It was by far the most active and they didn't have a Presbyterian Church locally. Norman joined the American Legion and I joined their Auxiliary, The Women's Club, which had a national affiliation, and The Garden Club.

Before long I was asked to join a bridge club. It had just eight members and we met once a month in our homes. About every three months we would have a party at night and invite our husbands. The Christmas parties were really special. We drew names and gave each other ridiculous gifts. Norman had brought a huge boar head from Germany. It was the largest he had killed and was such a prize, that we had a taxidermist preserve it. He hung it over the doorway in our farm equipment business and it was quite a marketing tool. Farmers from all over the county came to see it. After a few years the boar's head began to deteriorate so we took it down and used it as a gift at one of our Christmas parties.

For years after that it was passed around and every Christmas seven couples would worry that they would receive it.

But the best thing about living in Lake View was that all of our friends also had young children. Babysitters were very limited. There were only two older women available and a group of young girls. All of us young mothers would arrange with each other as to who got the older ones especially if we had longer daytime needs. Sometimes we pooled the children but we always worked it out amicably.

After renting for the first year we bought a house on a hill in a really great neighborhood. Everyone had children and we all watched out for all of them. The couple next door had three who were older – about nine to thirteen – but they were very good to my little ones. On the other side of them was a wonderful Catholic couple who had seven children. The mother was a super friendly, easy-going soul who took everything in stride. She was a marvelous cook and always had freshly baked cookies on hand. They had a huge sandbox where my little ones were likely to be found.

The couple across the street from us had three boys and a girl and they too, were a little older than ours. They had lost their first child, a little girl who had died of pneumonia on Christmas several years earlier when she was just three years old. The mother really latched onto Nancy. If she was missing I knew right where to find her.

Another big advantage of living in Lake View was that we were only ten miles away from George and Thelma and their two children. Ellen was about seven when we moved there and Gerrit was five. We saw them frequently and it was great. I was in the third grade when George went to college. We always saw each other in Parkersburg through the years, but it was so nice to live close.

George was an excellent lawyer with a large practice.

Everyone trusted him and came to him with their problems even though he would bawl them out like crazy when they came with problems which could have been avoided if "they had used their heads." He used very colorful language and would really let them have it when they described some stupid mistake they had made. But they kept coming because they knew he would help them.

Stopping by his office one day I asked why he had a big stack of shoe boxes piled up in a corner. "When these G— D— farmers come in here and want me to do their taxes they'll have just a few seed corn receipts, a few machinery repair bills and then they want me to deduct hundreds of dollars of expenses. I tell them 'Hell, no,' and I give them a box. If they don't come back the next year with every single receipt I won't do their taxes."

A middle-aged farmer came to him once and said, "George, my son is running up and down Main Street in his car on Saturday nights just like I did when I was a kid. I'm going to send him in here and I want you to read him the riot act just like you did to me."

Another client called and said he was very sick and asked if George would come out to his farm so he could write a will. George went and took his secretary with him. The man started, "I want to leave 200 acres and $25,000.00 to my son, Edgar, 200 acres and $25,000.00 to my son, John, and my daughter should get…"

George interrupted him and said, "I've been doing your work for twenty-five years and you don't have that much land or that much money."

The farmer replied, "I know. Let them work for it like I did!" George had countless stories, but he also did a lot of serious work. He would sit on his back patio at night, smoke his pipe and figure out how he could solve some horrendous legal problem.

My Midwest Journeys

Parkersburg was 180 miles away so we could visit my parents especially on holidays. Gertrude, Mike and their three children lived in Waterloo, thirty miles from Parkersburg. Ed, Frannie and their three daughters lived in Cedar Rapids which was about 100 miles away. That five-year period in Lake View was the only time that we lived close to so much family and I really loved it. Mike took lots of hilarious home movies, which I still have.

Mama often made a rich, dense applesauce cake and I asked her to send me the recipe. A letter arrived in the mail that said, "Your father is fine. For the cake I use quite a bit of flour, baking powder, a little milk, eggs and butter, a dash of cream of tartar, and whatever applesauce you have in the icebox." At the bottom of the page she added, "This makes a very big cake. You can cut it in two if you like." Mama had memorized hundreds of recipes and her cooking was always good.

We had lots of good times and made many good friends in Lake View. The Women's Auxiliary had a fundraiser in the big room on the second floor of City Hall. We sold homemade cake, pie and ice cream, so everyone in town came. Amazingly, all seven of us who were serving the food were pregnant and we got hysterical with laughter as we bumped around the crowded tables.

I loved my babies and watched with great joy as they grew into toddlers. Norman loved them, but he never got very involved as a father. He thought they were "interesting" and he loved showing them off in public, but he never related to them much on a personal basis. He was more interested in the wedded bliss part of marriage. His two older sisters had spoiled him terribly and I think he missed being the center of attention. His attitude puzzled me but it didn't deter us from being a good family.

One day over a bridge game my friends decided that

I should run for the Lake View School Board. They were upset because their home economics kitchen only had one sink, a two-burner stove and a few cupboards. Besides, they thought a woman could make a big difference on the all male board. A woman had never been elected; the only woman who had served was the widow of a board member who was killed and she just finished his term.

It sounded like a good experience for the town to have a woman try, but I didn't expect to win. Much to my surprise I did win. We immediately updated the home economics kitchen. At that time the school board would come up with the budget and then the school taxes would be based on what was needed. Some of the farmers in the area weren't too happy with me because the taxes increased during my tenure.

I was only on the board for two years when we decided to leave Lake View. Norman was a great salesman and he could sell farm machinery like crazy. He was also good at supervising our mechanics because he knew a lot about machinery. Unfortunately, he had no business sense. He would give farmers way too much allowance for their used machinery. When he couldn't sell it he would haul it down to Des Moines and auction the equipment for so little money that we ended up losing money on the original sale. I was doing the accounting and my brother was pouring money into the business to keep us afloat.

Finally, we talked it over with George and decided we would leave. It was all very amicable. Alyce and Don had come up from Kansas a few years earlier to be part of the business and it was decided that he would run it. Norman got a job with a big construction firm which was building Fort Randall Dam in Lake Andes, South Dakota. We sold our house to Alyce and Don and moved on. Jon was eight months old at the time, Mary Pat was two and a half, and Nancy was four.

In South Dakota

It was 1953 when we left Lake View. South Dakota was not the best of times.

Norman preceded me to Lake Andes so he could find a house to rent. That meant I got to do the packing and moving! When the furniture was loaded a friend of George's who had a small plane flew me and the children to South Dakota. We landed in a field somewhere and Norman met us. The house Norman had rented was a large, old frame with a big front porch. As we walked up the porch a huge rat scampered right past us. I screamed and he disappeared down a hole next to the porch.

Shaking all over, I didn't even want to go in. Norman tried to assure me he had already spent two nights there and there were no rats in the house, but I didn't believe him. All of our furniture had been delivered there so I didn't have much choice. When we entered the house I looked out a window and saw a creek running across the far end of the lot. There was no fence and the prospect of three small children playing there traumatized me. That did it. I knew we were not going to stay there one minute longer than necessary.

Norman insisted that this was the only rental house available in the whole area. The few for sale were not suitable and had exorbitant prices. People from all over were moving in to work on the Dam and housing simply wasn't available. A lot of families were buying trailer houses (it wasn't until later they had more civilized names like "mobile homes" or "manufactured houses"). At that moment I wasn't in the mood to even consider such a possibility. I only knew we were not going to stay in this house.

We set up the beds in the living room. I had read books about how children had their noses gnawed off by rats in slum areas and I was not going to let mine out of my sight. I hardly slept a wink that night. Every few minutes I was up checking on whether or not there were any rats in the beds.

The next day I loaded the children into my car and we started house hunting. Lake Andes had a population of about 1,000 so it didn't take long to determine that there were no "For Rent" signs and the few "For Sale" signs were in front of shacks in bad neighborhoods. The only real estate office had no good alternatives to offer. I did notice several yards in good neighborhoods that had signs which said, "Trailer space available."

That night we talked it over. Norman's job paid well and he had a good chance of being promoted. As a supervisor of a group of welders, he enjoyed the work, and it would take five years to finish the dam. Along the way we might be able to find a good house. The alternative was to find a job in another location, and we probably would spend all of the money from the sale of our Lake View house getting relocated. If we spent at least a few years here we would be in a position financially to live wherever we wanted. Then we would make it permanent.

And so we went to Sioux Falls the next Saturday and bought a sixty-foot long and twelve-foot wide trailer house for $4,000, fully furnished. We splurged by also buying our first television set and paid extra for a gangly antenna which we would need out in the boondocks. (In spite of the antenna the only thing we saw on it was snow! Once in awhile we could dimly see Liberace with the candelabra on his piano!)

We sold our furniture for practically nothing to the people who rented the rat house. The trailer had two bedrooms, a bath, a kitchen and a living room with a dining area. The second bedroom had a full-sized bed for the girls, and Jon had the bunk bed on the top. We located it next to a house in a very nice neighborhood. It had a nice fenced-in yard and I was allowed to wash clothes in the landlord's basement and hang the clothes in their back yard. I wasn't thrilled but it was clean, snug and no little critters would be able to invade us.

We quickly made friends in the neighborhood since many of the families also had small children. We started attending a small church and I was even invited to join the Eastern Star, the highest social standing you could have in this community. The children happily played in the big yard, fascinated with the neighbor's chickens.

Soon it was fall and Norman loved the hunting in South Dakota, especially for pheasants. One of his friends at work was also an avid hunter and, like Norman, had been born and raised in Alabama. Glen had rented a farmhouse with his wife, Irene, and their two sons. One beautiful fall day the children and I went to their farm for the day while the men went hunting. They hunted by walking down through the cornfields a row apart and being careful to stay abreast of each other. We could hear occasional shots but we couldn't see them.

During lunch we heard a thud against the house. A wounded pheasant had flown into the side of the house and dropped dead just next to the porch. The men came home at dark terribly disappointed because they had not managed to kill a single bird. They were really surprised when we served them a perfectly roasted pheasant.

On another hunting trip Norman and Glen left early in the morning. Irene and the boys came over to our house about the middle of the afternoon and we cooked a big dinner for everyone. I still can't believe that we would have four adults and five children for dinner in that trailer house but we did it fairly often. They were a very nice family and we enjoyed it.

The men were to return about an hour after dark so we had our big dinner all ready to serve but they didn't come. It had started snowing earlier in the day and by mid afternoon the wind had increased and the snow was heavier so we started to worry. We fed the children because they were hungry but still Norman and Glen did not appear. About eight o'clock I put my three to bed and we sat and listened for a car in the driveway. Irene's boys were about seven and nine and we put them in our bed about nine o'clock.

The police had no news when I called, but said they would alert the Highway Department because they would be out clearing the highways. Unfortunately, we had no idea where they had gone hunting. So Irene and I sat there the whole night long waiting and worrying. We talked about everything under the sun but never mentioned the awful possibilities. We just couldn't go there. The snowy television shows droned on while we ate popcorn, drank cocoa and found ourselves checking on the children every ten minutes as if they were the ones in trouble.

It wasn't until eight-thirty the next morning that we finally heard the car arrive. Both men were fine and they had quite a story to tell. They had stayed in the field way too long. The Alabama boys didn't realize how quickly the roads could become impassable. When they returned to the car, parked on the side of a highway it was practically covered with snow. At first they tried to get the car up on the road but soon realized it was impossible.

They could see a farmhouse down a long driveway just opposite so they decided to go there for help before dark. It was tough getting through the snow banks on their way to the house. When they finally made it the farmer and his wife were very nice to them. Unfortunately, their telephone was "out" – not an uncommon occurrence in a snowstorm. They told them there was no way they could get that car out before morning when the snowplow would come through. They invited them for supper and told them they could spend the night sitting in some comfortable chairs by the fire in their living room

They had worried about us but there was nothing they could do. Their boots and jackets were frozen stiff, so they hung them near the fire and fell asleep. Sometime in the night a shotgun shell suddenly exploded and within seconds there were shells flying all over the room. They had forgotten the shotgun shells in their coat pockets. It was a miracle that no one got hurt. The farmer and his wife came flying down the steps and were understandably very irate. The wife wanted to throw them out immediately but the farmer said they could stay until the snowplow came through.

They assessed the damage and Norman and Glen agreed to pay for the needed repairs to the walls and replacements for the shattered vases and lamps. The farmer made some coffee for them but as soon as it was light he sent them packing. He gave them a shovel and told them to leave it next to the mailbox. They made their way down to the highway and found that the snowplow had been through. They shoveled the car out and drove home without any more incidents. Small wonder that I have very few fond memories of South Dakota.

Later that year we traveled through the Black Hills. Our newfangled camera took movies. I took lots of pictures of the scenic area, but they didn't turn out very well. When we showed the movies, it looked like the Black Hills were galloping across the horizon. Norman couldn't figure out how in the world I could have done that, but it had been easy even if I couldn't explain it. Soon after that trip we got holed up for the winter.

The trailer house was fine during the summer and fall when we could spend a lot of time outdoors but, boy, you haven't lived until you've spent a South Dakota winter in a trailer house with three small children! We made cookies or pie every day and read books until I was blue in the face. I can still quote *Peter Rabbit* almost word for word. But you run out of things to do in a hurry when you are confined in a sixty by twelve-foot closet. When they woke from their afternoon naps I would bundle all three of them up in their snowsuits, boots, mittens, scarves and stocking caps. After three minutes of playing, we would have to hurry inside again. It would take days to make a snowman. (I appreciate the Arizona sunshine so much today!)

But it wasn't all cookie baking, reading and making snowmen. Kids are kids and they whined and fought and cried. It was a good thing that I really loved these children and that I had taught first grade. I learned to just close my eyes for a moment or two and pretend we were flying fairies. Then I could carry on. And when the going got tough I always reminded myself that at least I didn't have to be on rat patrol!

We drove to Parkersburg for Christmas and had a perfectly marvelous time seeing all of the family and having the usual festivities. Driving back to the snow-bound trailer was tough. Then Jon got sick. He was about a year and a half and he was really sick. He woke up in the middle of the night with a fever, vomiting, diarrhea, the whole thing. I rocked him all night between his frightful episodes and by morning I had to get him to a doctor. There were no doctors in Lake Andes, so I had to take him to a neighboring town.

The doctor prescribed some medicine, but poor little

Jon's problems continued the rest of the day and another night. He couldn't keep the medicine down for two minutes. I was terribly afraid he might die; he just got worse and worse. The next morning we were back at the doctor's office. He listened to me and then said, "Are you giving him gruel?"

"What's that?" He explained that Jon was to have no milk, only a thin, watery cereal. With the gruel and medicine he did improve rather quickly but the poor little guy was so weak he couldn't even walk. He had to learn all over again.

Finally spring did come and we could see more of our neighbors. But I had already decided that Fort Randall and Lake Andes were not for us. There was no future here and we were not saving money like we had planned. We could do better and Norman agreed that it was time to go. I wrote to the U.S. Civil Service Commission for application blanks. This had been an interim situation for us, but it was time to look for something more permanent. I wanted to get into a better situation, especially before the children started school.

It might take time to find the right opportunity so my summer project was to find better housing. My children could not live through another winter caged up in that trailer. Our best bet was to follow through anytime Norman heard that someone was quitting his job. He posted a notice at the job site and I waited for clues. Then a totally unexpected disaster happened which changed everything.

One morning in July I was planning to go house hunting. The children were all in the neighbor's sandpile and everything was under control. Then I got a call that Norman had been in an accident at the Dam and was being taken to a hospital in a neighboring town. That was all they could tell me. I was scared to death, so afraid he was dead. Praying to stay calm, I collected the children and drove to the hospital.

I should have asked a friend to help but I just concentrated on getting there.

It seemed like an eternity but it probably took an hour to get there. I tried to concentrate on driving and keeping the children under control, but I couldn't help thinking about the horror I might face. It was all like a nightmare. Finally we were in the hospital room with him and learned that he had a badly injured right arm and shoulder. I could breathe normally again when I knew he would live.

It had been a freakish accident. The job site was in a large metal building, like an airplane hangar, open at one end. Huge cylinders were prepared for the dam site at one end and then rolled on a decided slope down to where they were to be attached. The release and rolling to the job site were carefully controlled. But on this morning one of the huge cylinders had broken loose and was rolling toward a group of unsuspecting men at the lower end. They could get killed.

Norman arrived on the scene just as this potential disaster was beginning to develop. He and other workers picked up pieces of metal and threw them under the cylinder to impede or stop its progress so the men at the lower end could escape. Horrifically, one of the pieces of metal caught on Norman's sleeve and pulled his arm under the cylinder up to his elbow. The doctor explained that his rotor cuff was badly torn and his arm and hand were crushed but they would be able to save them. I was so relieved.

We spent the next several months rehabilitating his hand, arm and shoulder. Ordinarily, Norman had very little patience but I had to admire his determination and dedication to making a full recovery. He spent about ten days in the hospital and then we started a regime of physical therapy at home. When we started, the arm, hand and fingers felt like wood and he had almost no feeling. The shoulder had to stay immobile while we rubbed and soaked the hand and arm in a strong liniment several times a day. In the fall his company, I believe it was Brown and Root, suggested we go to Minneapolis. Norman needed better therapy for his arm and shoulder than they could provide in Lake Andes; they promised to place him in a good job as soon as he was able to work again.

Minneapolis

And so we took off for Minneapolis. We decided to keep the trailer because the stay in Minneapolis might be very temporary and it did provide warm, safe housing which I could accept since it wouldn't last. I dreaded the trip but it all worked out. We owned two cars by then. Norman and a friend pulled the trailer, so I took the children and drove the second car. It was pretty scary. The whole way I could see that sixty-foot trailer in my rear view mirror going up and down the hills and around the corners. It wasn't quite as bad as the Lucille Ball movie, *The Long, Long Trailer,* but considering what we were putting at risk it was almost as bad.

We parked the thing in a court in a suburb called Robbinsdale and there we stayed for the next three or four months. Norman did get regular therapy and we continued the rubbing and soaking. He squeezed a small rubber ball almost constantly to improve the mobility in his hand. And gradually his efforts paid off. The company would probably offer him another job in construction, but he just wasn't strong enough. As soon as he was able he started looking for another job. I encouraged him to look at sales jobs because he was a natural for selling.

In the meantime Nancy started kindergarten in a nearby school and I ran a preschool for Mary Pat and Jon at home. Nancy wasn't crazy about her kindergarten so I let her stay home when she didn't want to go. I didn't want her to develop a bad attitude toward school. I wondered if our trailer court address had anything to do with it. We were not blissfully happy but we managed. We were all alive and Daddy was getting better.

It was about the middle of February when Remington Arms offered Norman a job selling Humane Cattle Stunners. He was quite fascinated by this new product. The usual practice in slaughter houses was to have the cattle go down a chute and a man would stick them in the throat. The animal would bleed until he fell over and then would be carted away on a conveyor belt. With the stunner the steer would be hit between the eyes and be immediately unconscious before he was killed. Certainly it was a better way and Norman was certain he could sell the Stunners.

He would be paid a very good salary – $600 a month and expenses but that was a lot of money then. He had a choice of going to Oklahoma City or Little Rock. We opted for Little Rock because there would be less travel involved although I was dubious about the schools.

And so we started to Little Rock with great expectations. Again we took the trailer because it would afford us housing until we could get into a real home. I was very hesitant because it was winter and we would be going through the Ozarks in Missouri and northern Arkansas. But Norman saw it as a big challenge and had no fear whatsoever. And so we started our two car caravan once again. The whole trip was a real nightmare, especially when the mountain roads were icy. I don't remember praying so hard anytime in my life, but miraculously, we made it. It was late in February in 1955.

CHAPTER EIGHT

North Little Rock, Arkansas

I had reservations about living in Arkansas. The redneck jokes as well as the poor schools were a concern, but it turned out to be a great place for us. We raised our children there and I spent years working with the PTA's at every level. We became very involved with the church and the community, and I got into politics in a big way. We made many life-long friends. But it wasn't all fun and games. It was also the place where I got a divorce and that was difficult.

The first order of business was to sell the trailer. Under the GI Bill we could buy a house with no down payment, so we just had to find one which had payments we could afford. We owed very little on the trailer so we figured we just needed money from it to buy furniture. A couple with a new baby and a thirty-foot trailer bought it in less than a month. They were ecstatic with the increased space, and we were delighted to have our trailer house living come to an end.

A real estate firm in the newspaper looked promising, and they were also builders. When we described the house we would love to have and told them what payments we could afford the young agent immediately said, "You should build in Lakewood." It was in North Little Rock just across the Arkansas River from Little Rock. He took us out to a beautiful development on wooded, rolling hills and we immediately fell in love with it. It had five man-made lakes, one with a swimming area and clubhouse. All of the lakes were stocked with fish. They also had tennis courts, ball fields and all the amenities available at the time. They showed us the Old Mill on one of the lakes. It is the Mill which is pictured in the opening scene of *Gone With the Wind*.

By the end of the day we had picked a lot at the end of a 200 acre lake, and signed a contract for a 3300 square foot house. The split-level, red brick house would have a kitchen, two bedrooms, two baths, and a living room with a picture-window to the lake and woods. The lower level had two bedrooms, a bath, a workroom, a laundry room – what luxury – and a spacious den opening to the back yard. All of this for the vast sum of $18,000 with a three percent interest rate and payments of $139 a month including taxes and insurance. We were thrilled, never dreaming we would be able to do so well with the resources we had. It was the best decision we ever made.

We were told the house would be ready by July first. What they didn't tell us was that the U.S. Air Force had recently established a base in nearby Jacksonville and houses were being built like crazy in the area, especially in Lakewood. Builders were running further and further behind in their commitments.

When we sold the trailer we had only a week to vacate so we found a rental duplex in the Park Hill area which was adjacent to Lakewood. It wasn't fancy but it was adequate. By July the house was barely started and it obviously was not going to be finished when school started in the fall. I did not want Nancy to have to change schools when she was in the first grade so I made a visit to the District School Administration Office.

When I asked if Nancy could enroll in the new Lakewood Elementary School they immediately informed me that she could not. They had so many new people moving into that area that they had no idea if they could handle all of the ones already living there. There were also problems at Park Hill Elementary where Nancy would be going – they still needed a first grade teacher.

Without really thinking I said, "I'm a first grade teacher, would that help?" I was immediately ushered into the Superintendent's Office and within minutes I was offered a Provisional Certificate and a Contract for the sum total of $1400 a year. I walked out in sort of a daze and in the fall I started teaching first grade again.

Our house wasn't finished in July or September or by Thanksgiving or Christmas or for my birthday in February. In fact, we moved in after school was out in May and they still hadn't quite finished it. But it was worth it. I loved that house every minute we lived in it.

Decorating it was so much fun. Pale turquoise carpeting accented a purple and turquoise striped divan with purple chairs and creamy wood tables made an elegant effect in the living room. The pink kitchen was ultra modern, with a built-in refrigerator that looked like the cabinets. It was beautiful. Everyone said so. And the lake was in the backyard.

We all loved Lakewood. We had great neighbors and most of them had young families. Some of them are still my best friends. The children really thrived. All three of them make friends very easily so they adjusted very well. Since Nancy had been two years old she had had a pretend friend "Karwol" whom we heard about constantly. It was rather unusual since she had a sister, but Karwol was soon replaced by a real friend, Carol. Mary Pat had a problem with our first babysitter. She was an older woman and she kept Mary Pat, Jon and several other children in her home while Nancy and I went to first grade. She had come highly recommended but I suspect she either shook her or hit her and Mary Pat started rebelling about going. We switched to a much better situation and everyone was happy.

We had many happy times as the children grew up in North Little Rock. Like all mothers I have forgotten the diapers, the toilet training, the carpooling, the constant "I don't care what the neighbors do, you can't do It," exhortations. Nancy was always a creative innovator. She would organize the neighborhood kids into performing plays and circuses. One time they raised money for South American flood victims and a local TV station came by. They were stars on the evening news. Mary Pat was put out because she was the back half of an elephant and no one could see her under the grey blanket.

Nancy loved dolls and played with them by the hour. She would use shoe boxes and make rooms, furnish them and sew curtains and blankets. She was ten years old when the first Barbie dolls came out. That doll had piles of pillows and clothes. Mary Pat had dolls, but she wasn't particularly interested in them. Books always fascinated her. Both of them loved their coloring books.

One morning I walked into the den where Nancy was sitting at the table with a coloring book. She heaved a big sigh as if she had all the burdens of the world on her shoulders. I said, "Honey, what's the matter?" and she said, "Oh, I have so much coloring to do today!" It's hard to take so much responsibility when you are seven years old.

My children were all very different and they still are. Nancy loved horses from her earliest childhood. When she was almost two years old we visited my brother George and his wife Thelma. One morning Thelma and I were doing dishes, baby Mary Pat was on a blanket on the floor and Nancy was playing with toys on the porch adjoining the kitchen. I glanced out to check on her and she wasn't there! Thelma and I ran out and found that she had gone to the end of the lot where they kept four horses. There was Nancy hugging the hind leg of one of those huge horses and the horse was standing perfectly still. That was our first clue that she loved horses.

When she was three years old I bought her a really fancy wooden horse for Christmas. When I unveiled it she just walked around it rather solemnly and I said, "Don't you like it, honey?"

"Well, yes but what I really wanted was a horse made out of horse."

She was in the fourth grade when she got her first horse made out of horse. She had been saving money and had almost twenty-five dollars.

She read an ad in the paper about a horse for sale for $100. She talked three of her friends at school into buying the horse – they would each contribute twenty-five dollars and share it. She was so excited when she came home from school but I knew that would never work. I got on the telephone and called the mothers and they agreed it was not a good plan.

Nancy was devastated. In a weak moment I said, "Honey, I'll buy you a horse." We couldn't afford it but I was desperate. Mary Pat and Jon felt so badly for her that they contributed their twenty-five dollar savings bonds. Mary Pat was a third grader and Jon was in the first grade. They didn't have much but they gave their all. Jon went to his room and came back with his little drawstring bag. He emptied it all on the table and said, "Here you are, Nancy." He had nearly four dollars. Mary Pat had more, and she, too, contributed until they pooled $100, with some help from Mom.

It took all summer to find the right horse, but we bought Rusty on Jon's birthday. We couldn't afford him because, in addition to the initial cost, horses are an ongoing expense – the barn rent, the saddle and all the gear, the hay which they eat every single day – but it was worth it because of the love Nancy has for horses even today.

Life for Nancy centered around her horse as she grew up. She had a series of them and became a trainer and horse-trader early on. At least three times a week we went five miles out to the barn so she could ride. She taught herself, entering all of the horse shows and parades in the area. I learned to pull a horse trailer although I never conquered my fear of doing it. Backing up was real trouble! She did very well in school and had good friends there but she never got involved in extracurricular activities. When she was a junior she joined the Spanish Club. I was surprised and asked her why she did it. She said, "Well, my picture will be in the Yearbook this year and I don't want it to just say 'Girl' under it."

We had one very horrible experience with the horse when Nancy was twelve. Late one Sunday afternoon Mary Pat and I went to pick her up at the barn. When we got there the horse was standing perfectly still near the barn and Nancy was lying on the ground under him. My heart stood still. I don't know how I ever got out of the car. She was alive but her face was smashed.

Later Nancy said that a neighbor boy had thrown a rock at the horse and she pitched off when he bolted. She had landed face first on a rock. I sent Mary Pat to get the farmer and he helped me get Nancy into the back seat of the car and we took off for the hospital. There were no 911's and no cell phones in those days. It was about ten miles away and to this day I don't know how we made it. I kept reassuring Mary Pat that Nancy would be alright and I kept praying that she would be. I hurt all the way through when she moaned but at least it told me she was alive. I had no idea how seriously hurt she was and I just prayed she would live.

Nancy's right cheekbone and her nose were badly broken. The surgeon went through her mouth to push the cheekbone back into place and straightened her nose. Norman and Jon came out to the hospital and we all survived the harrowing experience. She stayed in the hospital for about a week. As soon as Nancy could speak she said, "I want to go back out and ride."

I didn't think I could ever let her on a horse again but our preacher, Dr. Basil Hicks said, "Mildred, you must rethink that. Nancy really loves horses." I did and she did.

But she had many other interests too. From early on she was interested in cooking and I encouraged her. When she was about eight years old she made some chocolate pudding. Mary Pat and Jon watched intently while she dished it up for them. Jon said, "I want more."

"No," Nancy retorted. "Everybody gets three slops." She also loved to sew and her dolls had very stylish, creative gowns. When she was in the seventh grade she made a three-piece suit for Home Economics class and it won first prize in a contest. She is still an expert at cooking and sewing.

Mary Pat was very different. She was a very beautiful child with baby blond ringlets all over her head and later long curls down her back. She loved books from the time she was two years old. She could sit for hours with a few picture books. As she grew older she became interested in theater and the arts. My taxi service after school was unbelievable. Often I had to pick them up at maybe two different schools, get Nancy out to her horse and Mary Pat down to the new

Art Center in Little Rock which Winthrop Rockefeller had just built. Jon might just ride along or maybe he wanted to go to a friend's house or go fishing down at our lake.

Mary Pat loved all of the activities at the Art Center and she appeared in some plays which were really very good. She was also very active at school joining all kinds of clubs and was a cheerleader. All three of them were good students but Mary Pat was especially bright and had a great affinity for math. During an open house at the high school her geometry teacher raved about how Mary Pat could solve problems even she couldn't solve. She went on and on until I became very embarrassed. Since I was on the school board at the time, I was afraid other parents would think that that was why the teacher was carrying on so much.

When Mary Pat was a junior she was named as a prestigious National Merit Scholar finalist and her first reaction was, "Now the kids will know that I didn't get good grades just because my mom is on the school board."

When she was a sophomore a senior who was a BMOC (Big Man on Campus) asked her for a date and I was petrified. I wanted so much to go along. He was a real jock – on the football and basketball teams and I had nightmares about what could happen. I tried to tell her but she was so innocent and I didn't want to scare her. The best I could do was to give her a dime and tell her to be sure and call me if she needed me. It turned out that he too was interested in drama and in fact, I think he went to New York and studied acting when he graduated. My worry over their date was entirely unwarranted. He was really a nice kid.

One time when she was in college Mary Pat and I went to a show. There was a very vivid bedroom scene and I thought, "Oh, what in the world will I say to Mary Pat about this?"

About then she leaned over and said, "Mom, if it bothers you, just close your eyes."

Three of her friends died when she was a junior and it
was quite traumatic. One of them was a sixteen-year-old
boy, on his way to the Art Center after school and he was
killed in a car accident. Mary Pat and her friends who were
waiting for him to arrive were devastated. Sharon, a friend
and neighbor since Junior High, died ten days after she was
diagnosed with Acute Leukemia.

Susan was probably Mary Pat's very best friend. Her
family had just moved to Colorado, but Susan stayed behind
with us so she and Mary Pat could go to a Church Camp in
Montreat, North Carolina. Shortly after they returned in late
August Susan left for Colorado because school was starting.
A few days later we got word that Susan had dropped dead
at her locker on the first day of school. On the day of her
funeral, Mary Pat received a letter from Susan, written the
day she died. It was tragic. I wanted to explain to her and I
couldn't. You want so much to protect them from the hurt
but you can't.

The girls were both avid readers. We went to the library
regularly and they always found more than enough books
to interest them. And I never had to remind either one of
them to do their homework. Jon was always happy with B's
and C's although he always tested very high on the IQ tests
they occasionally gave at school.

Piano lessons for the girls didn't work. I was so disappointed that neither of them were even slightly interested
and I had to force them to practice. Their piano teacher was
a good friend of mine and she thought it was terrible when
I let them quit. But my experience with first graders made
me know that you only learn what you want to learn and I
just couldn't get them motivated.

Jon was always a special little boy. He wasn't typical because he never cared about participating in sports. He wanted to take part in Little League as soon as he was eligible because all of his friends were playing but it didn't work out very well. When he was young he was small for his age and from day one he was left sitting on the bench most of the time. I found myself mostly watching parents fight with the umpire or the coach. We stuck it out for one season but then we turned to swimming and fishing in the summertime. All three of them loved that. We could pack some lunch and go up to the swimming lake about four blocks away and spend most of the day when they were in the lower elementary grades.

One morning I came up to the kitchen table where all three of them were eating their breakfasts. Jon was probably four years old and the girls were six and seven. Jon was saying, "Guls, eat your breakfast or Mom will tell us about the Germany kids." I hadn't realized that I had talked about them so much although I still thought about how I used to put cans of soup on top of our garbage pail because it was so hard to see hungry children eating from our garbage.

On Halloween night when Jon was three years old we walked up and down the hills in Lakewood collecting goodies and he didn't want to quit. Finally I said, "Jon, aren't your feet getting tired?" and he said, "My feet aren't tired but my mouf is tired from saying "Twick or tweet, twick or tweet."

When he was in the second grade his teacher told me about helping the children learn to spell the name of their church. (You could do that in those days!) Jon was really struggling with Presbyterian. When she came by to help Jon looked up and said, "This is the first time in my life I wished I was a Baptist."

One Saturday morning I was on the telephone talking to teachers. As President of a teacher's organization, I had some business I had to take care of. Jon was four or five and he wanted me to take him somewhere. He kept tugging at my skirt and I kept telling him to "Wait a minute." He was pretty insistent so I finally said, "Honey, I have to do this."

"Why?"

I said, "Because I am the president."

When I finally hung up he said, "Mom, what is Mr. Eisenhower doing now that you are the president." I hated to tell him.

Another summer morning I went to the office to help Norman for a few hours. The children really didn't need a babysitter for a short period and Anna, the next door neighbor was "on call." I got home about noon and the girls were in the kitchen. I asked about Jon and they said that he was downstairs in the den. I went down and this poor child – he was probably ten – was sitting on the floor watching television and holding his left arm. It scared me to death. Just above the wrist the arm turned to almost a right angle. It obviously was badly broken.

We rushed to the hospital and after examining it the doctor told us that he could set it "right now" or we could go over to the hospital and put Jon under an anesthetic. He said the outcome would be the same. Before I could even think about it Jon said, "do it now," and with one quick motion it was done. The pain must have been excruciating for a moment. He winced but never cried out. I couldn't help but be proud of him although I felt like a terrible mother for having allowed him to suffer. He was one brave little boy.

Jon and his friend Jim went up to play on the Lakewood School Playground one spring afternoon, and a quick, violent thunderstorm blew through. I knew they could take cover and the storm wouldn't last long. A little later they appeared back at the house, thoroughly drenched and shaking all over. They were as white as ghosts and their eyes as big as saucers. They had taken cover under a big tree when it was struck by lightning. The whole tree was split in half and part of it fell over. The boys had been knocked to their knees, but they got up and never stopped running until they got to our house. My knees were shaking and I was as white as a ghost by the time they stopped talking.

Jon, too, had a friend who died during his childhood. When he was in the third grade one of the boys in his class went to visit his grandmother in Florida and he drowned in the ocean. I remember Jon and several of his friends gathered and silently rode their bicycles in circles in front of our house for hours. I watched them from my kitchen window and made cookies for them but they didn't want any.

In the sixth grade a nursery hired him to weed young trees they were growing from seed. When Jon got his paycheck for about thirty dollars he would cash it for all dollar bills. Then he would iron the bills and put them in his brand new billfold. Sunday afternoon Jon went fishing in the lake behind our house. We had a small boat tied up in our back yard and he used it frequently. He went to a spot in the middle of the lake which had a manhole surrounded by a circle of concrete, something to do with raising and lowering the level of the lakes. Jon liked sitting there because it was more stable than the rocking boat.

As he sat on the concrete circle fishing, he scooted back and his billfold fell out of his pocket and down the manhole. He could see it lying at the bottom which was probably about twenty feet down. There was a metal ladder built into the interior side of the manhole and Jon started down it. What he didn't know was that a lot of treacherous gas collected in those manholes. He made it to the bottom and retrieved the billfold but when he started back up he started to feel sick and weak. It got worse and worse and he really had to force himself to keep trying to pull himself up. He wasn't sure that he could make it but finally he emerged and fell in a heap on the concrete. I still shudder to think how easily we could have lost him on that day.

They watched all the TV shows for kids as they grew up and we sent off for all the trinkets Uncle Bob and others offered. *Howdy Doody, Captain Kangaroo, The Mickey Mouse Club* and *The Shari Lewis Show* were great favorites. Mary Pat loved Elvis and Jon could do a marvelous imitation of him when he was just five years old. He swung his hips exactly like Elvis. As they grew older they were all rabid Beetle's fans. The entire neighborhood came to watch the *Ed Sullivan Show* when they made their first U.S. appearance.

On Sunday nights I always made popcorn and we watched *Bonanza,* The *Jack Benny Show,* and *Edgar Bergen and Charlie McCarthy.* During the week it was Sid Caesar, Red Skelton, Jackie Gleason, Bob Hope and many others. Television was a real joy in those days and the comedians were really funny. Whatever happened? And there were great movies for children – *Lassie, National Velvet* and *My Friend Flicka* among them. And marvelous love stories and musicals for the adults. What happened?

We always had a dog and it was always a bird dog because Norman loved to hunt. Our all time favorite was a big pointer named Sport, who was quite a character. We had a large fenced in yard but Sport would jump the fence, take a swim in the lake and then come back via the fence again. We put electric wiring across the top of the fence but that didn't stop him. He would yelp as he crossed over, especially when he was wet on his return but the electric shock didn't stop him.

But every once in a while he would jump the fence and take off. He had a real sense of adventure and had some harrowing experiences. He might be gone for weeks. Sometimes we would come home from school and he would be lying in the carport. His feet would be all raw and bloody and he would be as thin as a rail but it was always a happy homecoming. One time when he was gone we got a call from a woman who asked if Sport was home. When we said he wasn't she said that there was a dog lying in the weeds next to the highway at the bottom of our big Lakewood hill. We went down and there was poor Sport. He had been hit by a car and was almost dead. We took him to the vet and he survived to run off yet another time.

Once we got a call from a friend who said that he had noticed several dogs penned up in a very small enclosure on a nearby farm and it looked like Sport was one of them. We went out and sure enough, there was Sport. He led a very adventurous life but developed heartworm and died peacefully at home.

Norman bought a big boat and a tent that would sleep all five of us and we did a lot of camping and fishing. The children loved it – mama wasn't so sure. It took all day Friday to get ready to go and all day Monday to clean up afterwards but I guess it was worth it. Out on Lake Maumelle once we were all in the boat and ran into a bed of crappies (that's a small fish – great eating). The kids were catching them like crazy and Norman was busy taking the fish off the hooks and baiting them again. They started counting to see who caught the most and after while Mary Pat said, "Daddy, you haven't caught any." He didn't think it was funny.

One time we were fishing and Jon announced he had to go to the bathroom. Norman drew up to the shore and Jon jumped out and took off for the woods. He kept running back and forth and finally I called out, "Jon, what are you doing?"

He stopped and shouted, "What tree shall I go behind?"

I remember the scary times and the more dramatic events but we had lots of ordinary good times too – Christmases, birthdays, and holidays were always big family celebrations. Unfortunately, we had some very bad times too.

Tragedy

The biggest tragedy of my life was divorce. Norman worked for Remington Arms for three years and then had the opportunity to take a franchise with General Electric to sell two-way radio systems. This was a great field for him because he had a brilliant mind for technology. He could foresee even then in the middle sixties the possibilities of what might happen with communications and technology in the future. He predicted even the Internet and he wanted to be in on the ground floor. (About this time I read a magazine article about a boy genius named Bill Gates.)

We set up a business called Communication Enterprises, Inc. I quit teaching because Norman really needed me in his office. I took care of the business end and did all of the paperwork to get the Federal Licenses the buyers needed to operate their two-way radio systems. Getting good frequencies was a must and a challenge. One of the items on the application for the license was to enter the elevation of the site where the needed 100 foot tower would be erected. Once I got a very nasty letter from Washington ridiculing me for recording that the 100 foot tower would be 90 feet above sea level. I used my best first grade school teacher skills to inform the writer that some parts of Louisiana are below sea level.

Norman's work meant he had to travel a lot because he sold systems to owners of large businesses or ranches. In those days you couldn't buy drinks in bars or restaurants in Arkansas or Louisiana. You could take a bottle of liquor that you bought in a liquor store into a restaurant and buy "setups" and mix your own drinks. It was a ridiculous arrangement.

For Norman it meant that he would often end up in a hotel room with half a bottle of liquor and it led to uncontrolled drinking for him. Sometimes he would call me from a hotel in Shreveport or Baton Rouge and say, "I've got this liquor and I'm afraid I'll drink it." I would beg him to throw it down the john but an hour later he might call me again. He would be very drunk and say, "I'm coming home," and he would. It was miserable.

Norman became an alcoholic and although I tried as hard as any human being could possibly try in the end I couldn't help him. Shortly after we were married I became aware that he liked to drink too much but it didn't become a serious problem until after we moved to Little Rock. Alcoholism is a terrible disease.

His was a sad story and I don't want to relive it, but the children were teenagers when it started to get out of hand. It was all so unfair to them and to this day I regret it. We never fought or argued but I listened to literally thousands of promises which I wanted desperately to believe and we lived through harrowing episodes when he would come home very drunk. I became the world's best enabler but finally I had to tell him that I would get a divorce if he didn't go to a three month live-in facility for alcoholic rehabilitation.

The psychiatrist who headed up the program told me after a few weeks that there was little chance for success because Norman insisted that he could handle his problem and that he was only there because his wife forced him. The doctor was a member of our church and I knew him well. I cajoled him into keeping him on the chance that he would become cooperative but he didn't.

He got very drunk the day he was released. The doctor and our preacher came to me and said, "Mildred, you have to think of yourself and the children," and I knew they were right. Because of his drinking we had been forced to have the business declare bankruptcy and he was not capable of getting a job. I was out of options. I had done everything I knew to do. I had no choice.

Feelings of failure overwhelmed me. The wife, the mother, the teacher, the nurse, the friend – everything in me longed to help him but I finally had to accept the fact that I could not. And so in the summer of 1967 I filed for divorce. He was such a tortured man that I didn't see how I could do it but I did. The whole thing was such a tragedy because he was brilliant, handsome and had an engaging personality. He knew he had a lovely home and a wife and family whom he loved. I think his addiction was in his genes because every time he promised to quit he would tell me how much he loved me and I knew he intended to keep his promise. Sometimes he would cry like a small child. I knew he meant it but he just couldn't handle it. His alcoholism literally destroyed him.

It had a lasting effect on the children. To this day they never want to think about him or talk about him. But they need to tell their own stories from their own perspective. Suffice it to say for now that all three of them turned out to be wonderful human beings and I am very proud of them. Sometimes when I worry about it I tell myself that maybe adversity helped them grow but I realize that maybe that is just what I want to believe.

Win Politics

But the entire time that tragedy was playing out other things were happening. We got very involved with the church, the community and politics. Politics was the most fun and being a part of it got to be a very big part of my life. Orval Faubus was the Democratic governor. About ninety percent of the people were Democrats and almost all of them thought Faubus "was a crook but he got things done." They kept re-electing him because there didn't seem to be an alternative.

Winthrop Rockefeller had built a cattle ranch and home, called Winrock, on Petit Jean Mountain near Morrilton, about fifty miles from Little Rock. Occasionally, we would read a little about his activities. We were surprised when Governor Faubus appointed him to the Arkansas Economic Commission. Later, he announced in the papers and on TV that he was hosting a series of dinners to promote a Two-Party System in Arkansas. He ran ads on TV showing two grocery stores and pointed out the advantages of having competition.

When a dinner was announced in nearby Searcy, I told Norman I really wanted to go. A neighbor couple went with us. The dinner was at the local Elk's Club, but when we found it I thought it must be the wrong place or the wrong day because there were very few cars in the parking lot. We went to the upstairs room and saw long tables set up for about 200 people. There was a dais at one end with a long table for the honored guests.

There were only seven or eight people in the room and one of them was a very tall man with a cowboy hat and boots. Winthrop Rockefeller was very friendly, yet he had a rather shy manner about him. I was so impressed. About twenty minutes after the scheduled start time Mr. Rockefeller invited all fourteen of us to sit down and we were served a very nice dinner. About twenty waiters and waitresses stood at the side of the room with rather incredulous looks on their faces.

After dinner Mr. Rockefeller stood up and asked us all to introduce ourselves and tell why we were there. One man was the Chairman of a local County Republican Party and his wife was with him. One woman was the Secretary of another County Republican Committee and her husband was with her. All of the rest of them were mail carriers on Star Routes with the U.S. Post Office. It occurred to me that they were probably overnight Republicans because Dwight Eisenhower was the president, so you had to be a Republican to get those jobs.

Mr. Rockefeller didn't seem to be disturbed at all. He just proceeded to describe the advantages of having two political parties in the same manner as if the room had been filled. He never mentioned Faubus or the Democrats. He talked a lot about the need to start at the grassroots level. Again, I was so impressed. I thought, "Here is this very wealthy man from one of the most prominent families in America and he is here in a small Arkansas town telling this handful of people that we can make a difference in this state?" I became his instant loyal fan.

I started rather slowly. It was hard even locating the small group of organized Republicans in Little Rock. I was appointed a County Committeeman almost as soon as I walked in the door. At the next public election I had to be formally elected and it was a landslide! I got all of the seven votes which were cast. I dutifully went to the occasional Republican County Committee meetings where the four or five of us talked about how bad Faubus was and how we desperately longed for someone who would come along and run as a Republican for any office at all.

This went on for a few years. Winthrop Rockefeller was still having his dinners and usually someone from his office would visit and encourage us. We were the grassroots in the largest county in the state. We were growing but very slowly. Then in the very early 60s Mr. Rockefeller became more visible because his efforts to grow a Party were taking hold. People came out of the woodwork. In Little Rock we began to realize that there were quite a few Republicans up in the northwest corner of the state. Fort Smith had more of them than we did and up in the Ozarks there were many retirees from the Midwest who were dyed-in-the-wool Republicans.

We started to get more publicity and began to make a little splash as a Party. Some prominent Democrats came to us surreptitiously to lend encouragement, but I was never privy to their involvement. They didn't like Faubus either. Most of the delegation in Washington – all Democrats – was sympathetic to our cause but their involvement was all under the table. Arkansas had some very influential people in Congress at that time – Bill Fulbright and John McClellan were our Senators. Brooks Hays was one of our Congressmen. He was a truly delightful man with a marvelous sense of humor and a great storyteller. He told about the time he was campaigning up in the Ozarks and he asked an elderly woman for her vote. She said, "Oh, I never vote. It just encourages them."

I wrote a letter to the editor of the *Arkansas Democrat* praising Mr. Rockefeller's efforts and several days later I had a visit from the State Republicans. They invited me to attend some special events they were sponsoring. The number of participants was rapidly expanding and we started encouraging Win (we were on a first name basis by now) to run for Governor. It was exciting to see the party grow.

Win's first run for Governor was in the 1964 Election. We worked so hard. It wasn't easy. The Democrats kept describing him as the "rich man from Madison Avenue who knew absolutely nothing about Arkansas." When it was publicized that he got a haircut in New York City one day our whole campaign almost collapsed. He took all kinds of abuse, but he never allowed us to reply with the same rhetoric.

We emphasized what we could do but we also talked about the abuse of government power and pointed out problems in many of the state agencies. We concentrated on the corruption at the Hot Springs Race Track and the illegal acts, especially at the State Prison, the Insurance Department, the Welfare Department, and others. We never made accusations that we couldn't prove.

We uncovered all kinds of wrongdoing. For example, the son-in-law of the director of one of the large agencies was from Florida and he was getting his Ph.D. from the University of Iowa. His expenses were all being paid with federal money which had been awarded to the State of Arkansas. We didn't publicize that particular one because we had bigger fish to fry. I could list dozens of examples. Faubus openly bragged that he would "get people beholden to him." If he built a concrete driveway for a farmer who was in the Legislature he had his vote forevermore. The whole system was a challenge.

The corruption at the State Prison in Cummings was rampant. Several State Legislators were involved. Torture which led to the deaths of some prisoners was proven.

The Insurance Department was another agency riddled with corruption. You could set up a bona fide insurance company with only $3,000 capital. Some agencies were run efficiently and honestly and there were a lot of good state employees who had nothing to do with corruption, but problems existed on a large scale.

Win may have been one of the first politicians to hire a consultant. A nice fellow came from the East and he taught us how to get organized. Computers didn't exist in the 60s but we bought a sorted telephone list which gave names and addresses of doctors, lawyers, and other businessmen statewide. This list enabled us to target specific mailings. We had a contraption that would fold letters and put them in the envelopes. It was a clumsy elongated piece of machinery that took up half of a large room, but it worked.

We had one of the first memory typewriters in existence –

at least in Arkansas. You could type one letter into it and it would type as many more as you wanted at the rate of 150 words a minute. The paper for each letter had to be inserted and the address had to be typed in. It took a full time clerk-typist to operate it, but it was like magic compared to the dirty carbon paper we used for duplicate copies prior to this new invention. And it was so fast, we couldn't believe it.

Our campaign also had its own printing machine – a huge outfit that had to be hoisted up to the fifth floor on the outside of the Tower Building and brought in through a window. By today's standards it was very primitive, but at the time it was state-of-the-art stuff. A group of teens, including my girls, designed and printed bumper stickers, posters, business cards, flyers and newspaper ads on this contraption. We provided services to anyone in the state who would run as a Republican.

Sometime in 1963 I became a paid employee instead of an almost full- time volunteer. I had personnel responsibilities and worked with the volunteers. Communication Enterprises, Inc. had its own office manager and accountant by then, but I still did the licenses at home.

As part of our campaign planning we decided that we needed as many candidates as possible on our Republican slate so we could have a Republican Primary for the first time in Arkansas history. This meant that the Democrats would have to have a primary, too. Previous to this, there was only one election and the top Democrat always won. No Republican had been elected Governor since the Reconstruction Days after the Civil War.

Footsie Britt, a War hero who had won the Congressional Medal of Honor and several other military honors was our candidate for Lieutenant Governor. He had lost his right arm in Italy during the war. He was a very friendly, likable man and a great campaigner. You couldn't help but love him. Like Win, he was about six feet three inches tall and weighed about 250 pounds. We called them our 500 pounds of leadership.

And I ran for the state legislature! I was the only woman candidate for the legislature in Pulaski County. I hadn't even thought about running and no one even suggested it until the day of the deadline for filing. My co-workers thought it would be a good way to encourage more women to be interested in politics. We worked hard to enlist candidates so we could have a decent primary and we succeeded in finding a few here and there across the State.

I had a ball running for office. My children and their friends did a lot of door to door campaigning. I was so pleased to learn that some of the kids I had taught in first grade organized themselves to campaign for me. Now they were in the fifth, sixth, seventh and eight grades. I did surprisingly well but I didn't win. A young lawyer was the Democrat incumbent, but he was one of the honest ones and a good Legislator so it didn't really matter.

The primary election was a hoot. People didn't understand what was going on. I was a poll watcher and voters would come in and vote on the Democrat side and then go over and vote on the Republican side. They would tell the election judge, "I want to vote for Rockefeller," and he would let them go. I certainly wasn't going to stop them if he didn't. It didn't matter since Win was the only Republican candidate for governor.

And through it all Win just kept working and "stumping" all over the state. He hated to make speeches, but he made them anyway, lots of them. He practiced in front of a mirror but they always came off rather stilted. He was obviously uncomfortable. People seemed to empathize with him. He certainly did not sound or look like a rich man from Madison Avenue in his cowboy hat and boots. Ordinary folks could relate to him.

One time we had a big rally in a pasture near a little town up in the Ozarks. I introduced Win to the surprisingly big crowd. Afterwards we were walking down the country road to the car and Win said, "I wish it were as easy for me to speak as it is for you."

"Oh well, it's because I'm from a big family and we were raised in a little town in Iowa."

"Well, I'm from a big family and we spent a lot of time in a small town when we were growing up."

I laughed and said, "But it stops there."

"No, Grandfather would give us a dime and we were expected to give ten percent to charity and ten percent to the church. My mother taught us that money was a responsibility." His mother obviously was a great teacher. He had a little book written about her – Abby Aldrich Rockefeller. I still treasure my copy. Win believed his mother.

Up at Winrock there was a large stone on the bluff overlooking the valley. On it was carved the Bible verse from Micah 6:8, "What does the Lord require of you but to do justice, to love kindness and to walk humbly with your God?" I believe Win tried to live that way. Life wasn't easy for him. He had many insecurities and he probably drank more than he should. I personally never saw him when he had too much to drink. I used to get really annoyed the way some of the workers would ply him with drinks when he was in the office, but I didn't pay a lot of attention to it because this was at a time when I was desperately trying to help Norman with his drinking problem.

We had a list of all the voters from the prior general election. A bank of telephones was set up and we had volunteer callers using them every afternoon and every night.

The callers each had a list of nineteen "Yes or No" questions and they recorded the answers. One volunteer laughingly told us about one call. The question was, "Do you have a Party preference?"

The answer was, "I like the evenings."

One day I went out to the State Capitol to cause a little stir. We heard that many of the employee's desks had Faubus stickers on them and I wanted to point out that their desks were owned by the public and they couldn't use state property to campaign. As I walked up the slope approaching the very beautiful Capitol, I saw a rather prim, middle-aged woman walking toward me. I thought I recognized her so I smiled and she said, "What are you doing here?" I blithely told her about my mission and she looked like she was going to explode. All of a sudden I realized she was Mrs. Faubus!

Another time we were at some big public gathering; my children and I were going around handing out Rockefeller literature. There were so many people and we were moving fast so I didn't realize that I had given one to Mrs. Faubus until she grabbed it, threw it down on the ground and drove it into the dust with her heel. I really didn't mean to pick on her.

In the summertime especially, I got my children involved. They would come down to the Headquarters and be "go-fers" and do all kinds of odd jobs. We organized several youth groups. The youngest group included kids as young as nine (Jon's age). We called them the YARS – Young Arkansans for Rockefeller. Jon told me about the first meeting they had. He said, "I was just sitting there looking around and all of a sudden they elected me Vice President."

Nancy was president of the TARS (Teenage Arkansans for Rockefeller) and we also had the CARS (College Age Arkansans for Rockefeller).

We had a big special day up at Winrock and invited all the kids in the state – about 10,000 of them came on chartered buses. There were kids all over that farm. They all wore big round pins which said, "Win with Win." Bob Hope was the special attraction and he wowed them all. Some popular rock band was there and tons of food and drinks were served. During the course of the day I went down to the playroom in the main house to write a Press Release. Nelson Rockefeller was down there reading the paper. There had been a lot of talk about his running for President. He was a very outgoing, charming man and we chatted for a bit and then I went to the desk in the corner to do my work.

Jon came down after a while and wanted me to take him over to the stables. I asked him to wait, but Nelson got up and said, "I'll take him."

Jon chirped, "Oh, thank you Mr. President."

Nelson laughed and said, "That sounds so good." Later young Jay Rockefeller drove me back to the party on the lake. I didn't even notice when we passed my girls, waving hysterically.

Arkansas was using voting machines for the very first time in this election. Prior to the election voting machines were put in business places all over the state so people could practice using them. Candidates like "Peter Rabbit" and "Mickey Mouse" were entered on the ballots and people could experiment with the machines. The night before the election hundreds of us all over the state made calls to prospective voters reminding them to go to the polls. One voter replied, "Oh, I don't have to. I voted at Kroger last Saturday." The beauty of a democracy.

I loved every minute of my politicking because I knew it was for a very good cause. Win Rockefeller would bring integrity to our state government and we desperately needed a second party. He would bring intelligent, experienced people with the right motives into our State house so I was willing to work my heart out for it. And I thought it was wonderful that my children and all of the children and youth in the State had the opportunity to learn about government and to take a part in this fight for good.

Win didn't win that first time but he came surprisingly close – only about 15,000 votes short. And the Democrats had to pull off some real shenanigans to keep him from being victorious. On election night boxes and boxes of late votes came in from the small town of Jacksonville. If every man, woman, child and dog had voted in one of their precincts they would not have as many Democrat votes as they reported.

But we did have one big winner in that 1964 Election. John Paul Hammerschmidt from northwest Arkansas was elected to be a U.S. Congressman. He had been the State Treasurer of the Republican Party and he worked hard to get elected but he didn't really expect to win. Election night we were all at Headquarters watching the votes come in on TV. John Paul was leaning back on two legs of his chair talking to someone. I kept noticing that he was doing very well and finally I said, "John Paul, you are going to win."

He looked at me and started paying attention to the TV. After a bit he got up and said, "I'd better go tell Virginia." His wife was not at all excited about going to Washington. He was elected and reelected until he voluntarily retired after 26 years in Congress.

We contested many of the votes that first time around. Win filed literally hundreds of law suits. In Fayetteville we were contesting the final vote in some of their precincts. The courtroom was filled with mostly Rockefeller supporters. The prosecutors alleged that a missing box of votes had been blown out of the poll worker's hands as he crossed a bridge and the box had floated away down the river. Our defense attorney presented the fact that there was practically no wind in the area on that night and the river had about four inches of water in it. Amazingly, the judge ruled that indeed the box of votes had floated away.

I was one of four Republican women who flew up to Huntsville in Win's plane. It was Faubus' hometown and we had received numerous complaints about irregularities in the voting. When we walked into the Courthouse in this small Arkansas community there were men sitting on the floor on either side of the wide hallway. Some of them were chewing on straws. We assumed at first that they were all Faubusites but later we learned they were all Rockefeller supporters. They had heard at the coffee shop that Mr. Rockefeller's plane had landed and they had come to see the excitement.

And it became very exciting. We were met at the courthouse by the County Sheriff who informed us "If you don't get out of here you'll end up dead under the Courthouse steps by night." (We reported that back to Little Rock and Win sent another plane with a lawyer who stood by us.) We argued, cajoled and begged all day to see the voting records which we knew we were legally entitled to see but they would have none of it. They had all kinds of excuses – the lock on the vault was broken and they couldn't get to the ballot boxes, the only man who could fix it was out of town. Finally, the local judge said we could see them the next day so we all called home and made arrangements with our families to stay overnight.

And this is unbelievable but true. When we arrived the next morning we were told that there had been a fire inside the vault during the night and the ballot boxes and the voting lists had been destroyed. They had just finished cleaning up the mess.

We never stopped working between the 1964 and 1966

Elections, following up on the voting problems and making plans for 1966. By the time the campaign started, we were ready and this time we won! Faubus had chosen not to run – he knew he couldn't win and he was not about to be embarrassed. Win's opponent was Jim Johnson, a political hack who had been appointed a judge by Faubus.

Election night was thrilling when Win, Footsie, John Paul and several candidates across the state won! Our campaign headquarters was jammed with people. There were reporters from all over the country and Win was interviewed almost nonstop. We celebrated until past midnight. I was too excited to sleep, so about five o'clock in the morning I returned to the office. The telephone was ringing and just off the top of my head I answered, "We have a Republican Governor!"

The voice at the other end said, "This is Richard Nixon and that is what I wanted to know." We had a nice chat.

The January Inauguration took a lot of planning but it was thrilling.

It was hard to believe that Win was actually Governor and Footsie was Lieutenant Governor. Several of Win's family members were there. I walked down the hall behind Win, John and Lawrence. Dad would have loved this day. He always admired the Rockefeller family.

And then it was time to govern. Several well qualified, campaign staff members were appointed to be agency directors, but we recruited nationwide for many of the top positions. Win wanted only the best qualified and experienced people. He subsidized many of the salaries because the existing salaries were pitifully low. I stayed at campaign headquarters initially and continued working on transition matters. My interest was in personnel and they didn't have such an agency, but plans were being made to develop one.

Before the inauguration, I had gone to the Secretary of

State's office and got a list of members of the various committees and boards that the Governor appointed, about six hundred. By checking on when various terms expired, Win would be ready to appoint new people to these agency boards. What I did not foresee was that someone would tell Faubus. As soon as he found out he immediately reappointed every single one of his appointees to new terms.

After a few months I got a call from Marion Burton, Win's Executive Director. There was a vacant position in the Comptrollers Office which we would be able to transform into a personnel position. He had told the Comptroller that I would be applying for it.

I'll never forget that interview. When I walked into the conference room on Friday afternoon, there were six old men sitting around the huge table. I recognized some of them as Faubusites. Obviously, their job was to scare me off. We chatted for a bit and then we chatted some more. "I understand you have a vacant position.

One of them said yes, and then we chatted some more. They didn't want me, but they didn't know what to do with me. I was afraid one of them would say, "Thank you for coming. We'll let you know." So I decided that this was one of those take charge moments for me. I got up and said, "What time do you start work in the morning?"

One of them said, "At 8:30."

"Fine. I'll be here on Monday morning." And so it was that I became a state employee.

Working for Win's administration was an exciting challenge. The first thing I told the comptroller when I reported for work was that I wanted some offices in the auxiliary building across the street. Nobody could say "no" to me so I got my way. I'm sure I was pretty obnoxious that first week or so but after things settled down we started building a good working relationship. A few of the old men couldn't face working with a Republican woman, and they retired.

The comptroller, who was technically my boss, became an important ally. He had been around for years and he knew exactly what was going on. He was quite a character – knew the entire state budget backwards and forwards. One day we were walking back from a legislative committee hearing where he had presented the entire budget.

"I'm so impressed with your detailed knowledge."

"Oh," he said, "I just confound them with the numbers." I have no idea what his relationship with Faubus had been, but my guess is that he probably just ignored him.

Understanding what was going on personnel-wise in more than sixty agencies was a daunting task. Their "system" was based on typical political patronage, where individual legislators filled the vacancies and decided on the salaries. If you wanted to work for the state, you went to your local legislator and he decided whether or not you got a job. Only the governor held veto power and it was strictly based on political considerations. Every legislator had his own little fiefdom and they were not interested in changing one bit. They were "ready for bear" when it came to this new Republican Governor and any ideas he might have.

Win was having the same problems with the legislature. They were not one bit interested in what he wanted and most of them were ready to fight him tooth and nail. He had to work mainly through the agency directors he hired. They were experienced and knowledgeable and slowly progress was made. Getting a decent budget from the legislature was the biggest challenge.

I was not afraid of the legislators, but I quickly realized that I did not have sufficient experience to set up an efficient Civil Service system. In Germany, the salary schedule was given to us by a committee of Americans and Germans. The employees who worked for the Americans had to follow the military rules and regulations, and the ones who worked for the German economy had to follow the German laws. Our office was primarily concerned with the employment process, training, and employee relations (they always sent them back to us if they got into trouble.) I didn't know much about classification or salary schedules and they would be the cornerstones of our system.

A nationwide search was made and Harold C. Bennett was hired to be the Personnel Director. A native of Louisiana, he was a Cajun and absolutely delightful to work with. He knew everything about personnel. He knew exactly what objectives we had to set to achieve our overall goal of having an excellent civil service system, and he knew how to reach those objectives. I learned so much from him. We hired more staff and went to work immediately.

Harold was very down to earth and I loved some of his Cajun sayings. Sometimes I would go into his office and tell him about some bright idea I had. He would lean forward in his chair, knock out his pipe and then lean back again and listen. When I got through he would say, "Are you sure it's not progress toward the ditch?" When something surprised him he'd say, "That's enough to hog-tie a pig." He had dozens of these ridiculous sayings.

The work seemed endless. We classified all the jobs, set up a salary schedule, wrote personnel rules (I was responsible for those and I collected state and federal rules from all over the country), we organized an employment process, an evaluation system, a training plan and we started an employee newsletter. We had to just limp along because most of our plans, especially the Salary Schedule had to be approved and funded by the legislature. It was very challenging.

We had very little budget for our new operation so we

mainly had to transfer or borrow employees from other agencies to work for us. This took a lot of diplomacy but the comptroller and the governor's office were very supportive, so we were able to cobble a staff together. Sometimes we just had bad employees dumped on us but we were pretty much able to convince the agencies that our efforts were going to be helpful to them in the long run.

Classification was the biggest challenge. Win hired a firm from out of state to help us. They sent in a team of experts who had every state employee fill out a job description and each job was assessed separately. They were assigned to one of twenty-six grades, the basis for a salary schedule.

The governor's office told me about a well-qualified black girl who was available for employment and they had the funds to pay her. Win had just appointed her husband as the head of the new Civil Rights Office, the first Negro agency director in state government. I told them to send her over. I was working late and no one else was around when she came in. She was very attractive and very personable. She was really over-qualified for the clerk-typist opening we had, a college graduate with secretarial experience. She had glowing letters of recommendation and I was pleased to hire her on the spot. We arranged for her to start the next Monday morning. I told her that it might be a difficult situation and she said, "I know."

Knowing it was going to be traumatic, I waited until late Friday afternoon before I called my clerical staff together. There were about ten of them. I told them I had filled our vacancy and they all breathed a sigh of relief because they had all had to do extra work. I described all of her qualifications and then I dropped the bombshell. "She happens to be a Negro." From the reaction you would have thought that I had announced that a nuclear bomb was going to explode in the office on Monday morning.

There was dead silence and then one girl stood up and said, "I won't work with a nigger," and the rest of them all mumbled under their breaths.

I just said, "Well, it will be your choice."

The girl who threatened not to come was the daughter of an assistant director of the State Police. He called me at home that night and informed me that he was going to see to it that I didn't hire any niggers or no one would work for me. I replied, "Well, I've already hired one," and he just hung up. His daughter didn't show up on Monday and I got a call saying she had transferred to another agency. I was glad to be rid of her and I hoped it meant that the father wasn't going to do anything drastic. He didn't.

I was embarrassed for the entire white race because of the way my staff treated Wanda. They wouldn't speak to her. If she went to the copying machine they would all flee and when she would go into the bathroom they would all vacate immediately. She didn't even try to go into the lunchroom. But she just kept plugging away. It had to hurt but she just pretended she didn't notice. I really admired her. She became the most productive, efficient worker I had and gradually things changed. It took months but finally they started speaking to her. And finally, they began to accept her. It was a banner day when some of them suggested she go to the lunch room with them and when she wasn't welcomed by everyone, they actually defended her.

It worked but it wasn't perfect. When I resigned two years later to go to Phoenix the staff planned a going away party for me. Wanda was confident enough by then that she suggested they have the party at her home. But this was too much for them. We were having a staff meeting and everyone just froze. I could tell by the looks on their faces that they couldn't do this even though she lived in one of the best areas of the city and undoubtedly had a very nice home. I quickly invited them to my home and that is where we had the party. I was disappointed but at least we had made a lot of progress in the workplace.

Integration

Other things were going on in my life simultaneously. Racial tensions in Little Rock resulted primarily from the 1954 Brown versus Brown decision. Under this Supreme Court decision, all students were to have an equal opportunity to be educated. There would no longer be all white and all black schools, and that's all we had in Little Rock. Negro students who actually lived across the street from the all-white Central High drove several miles to a run-down school that was flooded half the year.

My first brush with segregation had occurred when Alyce and I went to Miami. We were in a department store and I saw a water fountain with a "Whites Only" sign above it. Thinking it was a practical joke, I had looked around in horror for fear some black person might see it. Our Miami principal had said at a staff meeting, "The day a Negro walks in the front door is the day I will walk out forever." I couldn't believe it. What about my dad's big "melting pot?" But that had been the closest I had been to segregation problems.

When we arrived in Little Rock in 1955 I never realized how involved I would get in the integration problems. I became very active in AAUW (American Association of University Women) and we worked to make integration possible. Some of our members were black school teachers. One of our actions was to sponsor a Panel of American Women comprised of four women of differing ethnic backgrounds. Sometimes I was a substitute for the Anglo woman. We went around to various clubs and churches and presented a discussion of how we had been discriminated against. I could tell stories about how I had sometimes been badly treated as a member of the Occupation Forces in Germany simply because I was an American.

A personable, young black woman on the panel was the wife of a professor at Philander Smith College, the all-black college. She had a four-year-old daughter and would describe simple incidents which always were effective with the all white audiences. Her little one would ask, "Why can't I play in the park across the street with the other kids?"

"Because only white children can play there and you are not white."

They were standing on a street corner downtown waiting for a light to change. A white child about the same age was standing next to them with her mother. The white girl offered the black child some of her popcorn and the white mother yanked her child away saying, "You can't do that!" Very simple stories, but very thought provoking.

A white friend told me that her six-year-old daughter was being ostracized by her friends because she always talked to the Negro man who took care of their yard. "I'm so proud of my daughter. When her friends asked her why she talked to that 'nigger' she said, 'He's not a nigger, he's my friend.'"

Most surprising to me was that some of my best friends at church tried to convert me. They would say, "Mildred, you just don't understand. These people (Negroes) can't take care of themselves. We have to help them." They really believed that. Ministers were in a quandary. Only a small handful of them in the entire city had the courage to even mention integration. But miraculously very few of them actually fought for it. I was so disappointed. I thought we were all the children of God. But I couldn't blame the preachers. Ninety percent of their congregations would have disappeared if they had even mentioned that it might be time to think about integration.

Jon and I were downtown shopping once when he was about five years old. At lunch time we went to the counter at Woolworth's Dime Store to eat. While we were eating five or six black students from Philander Smith came in. One of them took the only vacant seat at the counter and all the white people, except Jon and me immediately fled. The other black students sat down but none of them were served. The press arrived within minutes and the next morning our pictures were in the newspaper.

I became a member of the Urban League Board and we were able to do some good social and political work because Winthrop Rockefeller supported us financially. He was on their national board. I met some wonderful Negroes (this was prior to when they were called "Blacks"). Some of them were schoolteachers and I really admired their courage and their wisdom. In this connection I also met Daisy Bates, the State President of NAACP (National Association for the Advancement of Colored People) and her husband L.C. Bates. Martin Luther King was their inspiration. I valued their friendship.

And then in 1957 the Little Rock Central High School drama took place. Nine very intelligent, personable, courageous young Negro students attempted to integrate the all white high school. They were a group of six girls and three boys and they were all fourteen or fifteen years old. This didn't just happen. The Negro community led by Daisy and L.C. Bates had been working with Virgil Blossom, Superintendent of Schools, the Little Rock School Board and others for probably two years. They thought they had a very workable plan, but they did not foresee the unbelievable response they got from Governor Faubus and the white community.

Everyone in the state was aware that the attempt to integrate was going to be made when school started in September 1957 so they were ready. Faubus got on the radio and

TV on Sunday night before school started and riled up the entire state. There was an actual mob of angry, screaming, pushing citizens from all over the state filling the streets surrounding the school the next morning. Faubus had the National Guard at the doors to keep them out but federal officials forced him to withdraw them and the City Police took over. Some of the people in the crowd had lynching ropes. Not a single one of the students got even near the building. They fled for their very lives, but they didn't give up. They went to federal court and won their right to attend Central High.

Three weeks later they tried again. This time some City Police helped them get past the angry mob. Other policemen threw down their badges and joined the mob. Again, they could not get into the building. It wasn't until President Eisenhower sent in the 101st Airborne Division that the students finally, on the third try, got into the building safely. I took my children over to Central High one day that week. I just wanted them to see what was going on because it was an historical event. Nancy was eight years old, Mary Pat was seven and Jon was five.

Many of us breathed a sigh of relief and assumed that things were pretty much under control when the 101st Airborne took over. I didn't realize until I read Melba Pattillo Beals' book published in 1994 just how horrible the whole year was for those brave nine students. Her book, *Warriors Don't Cry*, gives a detailed account of the terrible cruelty they endured not only during the school hours but around the clock. Sadly those nine students never knew that there were a considerable number of us on the outside who sympathized with them and tried to do what little we could. It will forever be a blot on the history of Little Rock. And the Little Rock Nine will be heroes forever.

I was still teaching first grade in 1957, so I attended the

State Teacher's Meeting in Robinson Auditorium. The president of one of the state colleges made a speech. The Central High situation was raging at the time and he was suggesting privatization of schools. He said, "We may have to abolish our public school system as we know it." I was sitting in about the fourth row and I suddenly felt one of those big moments coming on. I got up out of my seat, marched down the aisle, and went up to the stage. My school superintendent was sitting on the stage and he looked horrified. I took the microphone and said simply, "The public school system is not expendable." It took down the house.

Elizabeth Huckaby was Vice Principal for Girls at Central High, a member of AAUW and another heroine in the story. By her own admission she couldn't do nearly as much as she wanted because she had to work with the white students and their parents, too. And she couldn't talk much about what was happening. Virgil Blossom and Eugene Smith, Chief of Police, also worked valiantly to make it work but the school board was divided and the public was vigorously anti-integration so it was an almost impossible situation. One of the students gave up in February and went to a high school in New York City, but the others stuck it out and they all eventually became successful, contributing citizens in our society. At the end of that 1957–58 school year Ernest Green became the first black student to graduate from Central.

In September 1958 Faubus closed the high school so the turmoil continued. He tried to use public funds to open a private high school and got by with it briefly until the courts stopped him. Then in May of 1959 the school board attempted to fire forty-four teachers and administrators suspected of being sympathetic to integration. Elizabeth Huckaby was one of them. That's when all of us who were trying to accomplish integration peacefully went into high gear.

We planned a huge rally called STOP (Stop This Outrageous Purge).

Hundreds of people worked on it. By now the business community was realizing that we couldn't continue on Faubus' path, so they cooperated. The primary purpose of the rally was to get people to sign petitions to recall the three school board members who were still fighting for segregation. Winthrop Rockefeller was one of the big contributors so we could afford to rent the large Robinson Auditorium in downtown Little Rock for the event. This was prior to Win's advent into politics, so I didn't know him then but we were all so grateful for his contribution.

STOP was a huge success. People were tired of the whole situation. We were getting national and even international bad publicity and most people realized it was time to quit fighting. There was no way they could win. Late in May the recall election was held. Those of us in North Little Rock couldn't even vote because we had our own school district but the three segregationists on the board were removed by a narrow margin and were replaced by moderate members. Finally, finally, things calmed down. However, the schools still had not been fully integrated when we left Little Rock in 1969. It was very slow and it didn't come easy.

Another School Board

Sometime in 1964 some businessmen in North Little Rock approached me about running for the school board. I wasn't sure I could win because they had never had a woman elected to their board and besides I was a Yankee and a Republican. However, I had done unexpectedly well in my run for the Legislature the prior year, and I still had a following from my four years of teaching. At the time I was working for Win Rockefeller and his cause was really drawing a lot of attention. So I accepted the challenge.

Time and money were in short supply to spend on my campaign, but again my former students got organized. Friends, neighbors, church members, and others backed me and I campaigned hard. I spoke to any group who would have me and I visited the black churches, telling them about my father and his "melting pot" philosophy. A black man was running against me, but he was a good candidate and I promised to help him get elected if he would run for the next vacancy that occurred. He withdrew and I gained more Negro support. Then I WON! (At the next election, I did help him and he was elected.)

Unless you have served on a school board it's hard to understand what a big responsibility it is. This was especially true in North Little Rock at that time. We were working under fourteen court orders pertaining to integration. I was glad they existed because they were a mandate to work for integration. The only one I hated was the one about busing. It was necessary for the junior and senior high schools but I hated it for the elementary students. I shuddered to think of little black children getting on a bus all alone, riding for maybe an hour across town, and walking into a room with all white children and a white teacher who didn't like them. These little children had probably seldom been out of their black neighborhoods before. It was brutal but we were forced to do it.

Everything about being on that school board was hard. Besides the integration problems, we were about to lose our national accreditation and we were grossly underfunded. We had some excellent teachers but we also had many poorly trained teachers in the schools. They were all underpaid and as a group were very unhappy. Superintendent Bruce Wright was very competent, but constantly in trouble with most of the board over integration. One night the other four board members called for a private personnel meeting and they tried to fire him. Probably the thing I am most proud of is that I talked them out of doing it. It wasn't fair.

I also worked at consolidating the three school Districts in Pulaski County – the North Little Rock District, the Little Rock District and the County District. Little Rock had by far the best tax base because most of the businesses were there. The County had the big Air Base at Jacksonville, so they got a lot of federal money to educate the children of military personnel. North Little Rock was the bedroom city for Little Rock so they were on the short end of the stick when it came to school tax money.

Dealing with the problem students was always difficult. They were brought to the board for a decision on expulsion. I would have preferred giving every sixteen- or seventeen-year-old kid another chance, but you had to respect the rules or they would become meaningless. You couldn't rule with your heart so it was hard.

But I only lasted one term. The segregationists and the anti-tax people ran six people against me in the next election. I only lost by thirty votes so some businessmen called me and said they would pay for a recount because it was so close. However, that turned into a disaster. On the recount I lost by 68 votes but the tax increase of three mills which had narrowly won, lost on the recount. I didn't mind losing my seat so much but I was devastated to see the tax increase go down. They needed it so badly.

But the school board experience was a good one. It was entirely different than the experience on the board in Lake View, Iowa but I was proud of a few accomplishments. We did build the Rose City Elementary School, bought land and started building a new high school, and we set standards for hiring new teachers. These standards brought about some changes in the nearby State Teachers College which had long-term benefits. Years later when Bill Clinton was

Governor he made all of the teachers pass a written test in order to retain their teaching certificates.

Actually, I have some fond memories of this experience. The school board members took part in the high school graduation ceremonies and I really enjoyed those. Jones High was the all-black high school in North Little Rock and only the superintendent went to those graduations. I told Mr. Wright I wanted to go along. He was surprised but was glad to take me.

We were sitting on the stage of the auditorium which was filled with parents, relatives and friends. The principal read the names of all of the students who had won scholarships at Harvard, Yale, and Princeton and the audience clapped politely. They knew these universities were handing them out only because of Brown versus Brown but everyone knew the students couldn't possibly take advantage of them. They needed a lot more money than just their tuition to actually attend.

But then the principal read the name of a girl who was going to work for a large insurance company downtown. He said, "She is not going to clean the floors. She is going to be a clerk-typist!" You can't believe the cheering and clapping that went on. It brought the house down!

The 60s were a tumultuous time in the history of our country. President Kennedy was killed on November 22, 1963 and for four days the whole country was in limbo. Thankfully, the assassin, Lee Harvey Oswald, was captured. Everyone was just numb for days.

I first heard the news at a friend's house because her husband had dropped dead of a heart attack that morning. Several of us were in her kitchen when another friend arrived and told us. From then on it was like a nightmare. Nancy and Mary Pat were in the seventh and eighth grades and Jon was in the fifth grade at the time. They were told about it at school. There was no way you could explain it and the horror continued.

On Sunday we witnessed the unbelievable scene on television when Jack Ruby shot Lee Harvey Oswald. The next day was the President's funeral with the riderless horse and little John-John saluting his father's casket. Then in April 1968, Martin Luther King was killed and just a few months later in June, Bobby Kennedy was killed. You felt like the whole world was falling apart. It was out of control and you couldn't do anything about it.

Our Busy Life

But life went on. Like everyone else in the state of Arkansas we were rabid Razorback fans and in the fall our life revolved around their games. All year long we were involved in school and church activities. I was President of the PTA at Lakewood Elementary, then at Ridgeroad Junior High and then at the North Little Rock High School as the children advanced through the grades. I can't tell you how many carnivals and fundraisers I was involved in during those years.

And there were always the political events – Lincoln Day dinners, inaugural balls, committee meetings and rallies. I met lots of prominent people at these events. At one of our events I met Richard Nixon. He was living in California at the time. It was after he had been Vice President but before he was elected President. At another, I had a long visit with a young Congressman from Michigan, Gerald Ford. Another time I chatted with a young Congressman from Texas named George H. W. Bush. Pretty cool stuff for a gal from Iowa!

Sometimes Jeannette Rockefeller had teas up on the mountain top at Winrock. She always wanted yellow tablecloths and fresh flowers on all of the small tables that were set up all over their beautiful yard. At a Winrock cattle auction I sat with Greer Garson. I told her I had attended my first Sunday movie when I was a critic for her *Goodbye Mr. Chips* – she laughed. Her husband, Buddy Fogelson, and Win both raised Santa Gertrudes cattle. I nearly fell over when Buddy bid $25,000 for a quarter interest in a bull. Bob Hope and Johnny Cash were visitors sometimes at Winrock.

In the early sixties we went to a Central High School football game. We usually attended just the North Little Rock High school games, but Central was playing the black Horace Mann High school at Central for the very first time and I knew few white people would show up. However, by now Central had a black player on their team and he was very good. I was pleasantly surprised to find a decent crowd when we got there. When the Central team came out on the field some man in front of us got up and yelled, "Get that nigger out of here."

A white woman behind us stood up and hollered, "He's not a nigger, he's our black boy." I thought that was real progress!

After our divorce I had to sell the big house I loved so much. But fortunately, we were able to buy a much smaller one in the Lakewood area which was just blocks away. By then Nancy had married a neighbor boy and had a little girl, Andrea Sha. I didn't think much of my son-in-law but I loved my precious little grandchild. Mary Pat was a senior in High school and Jon was a sophomore.

My work at the state continued to stay busy. In late 1968 Harold and I presented our big personnel plan to various legislative committees. Early in 1969 we were sitting up in the balcony of the House Chambers waiting for them to pass the bill we needed to implement our plan. It was a disaster. The legislators realized that this was going to take away a lot of their powers, so their little fiefdoms wouldn't even exist. They wouldn't be picking out employees or deciding on salaries. It was too much for them and they just passed bits and pieces, but wouldn't go along with the classification and salary plans. They made drastic changes which gutted both of them.

Harold and I were just sick as we watched the wrangling. Just off the top of my head I said, "I won't work in a system like that. I'll quit!"

Harold said, "I won't either, but don't you get another job until I get one." I was just frustrated and didn't think much more about it until some weeks later I happened to read an ad in a trade magazine for a Personnel Director for the State of Arizona. I took it down to Harold and he tapped out his pipe and said, "Hmmm."

Harold applied for the job and was invited to Phoenix for an interview. When he came back he was very excited. He said they had already passed a law which allowed them to do exactly what we had wanted to do in Arkansas. A week later he was called for a second interview and this time he was offered the job. The second interview was a dinner meeting at the home of the only woman on the Arizona Personnel Board – Sandra Day O'Connor. When he left, Harold told me that if he could work it out he would be offering me a job with the State of Arizona.

After he left I started thinking seriously about whether or not I would want to leave Little Rock. Win was in his second term as Governor and he had always said that he wouldn't serve more than two terms. I knew there were plenty of Legislators who would want to get rid of me as soon as he was gone. I was divorced but Norman kept coming back home and it was very difficult to deal with him. He needed money to live and I didn't have any extra. Even if I did, I knew he would buy liquor with it. It was especially hard for Jon because Norman wanted to do things with him and Jon felt very sorry for him. It was summertime and Jon had just finished his junior year in high school. I would hate to take him away from the school where he had been since first grade. He had so many good friends.

Mary Pat had just finished her first year at Washington University in St. Louis. She had gone there because they had made her a fabulous offer since she had been a National Merit Scholar. But they did not have a very good drama or dance department – medicine and law were their strong points. Now she was interested in the University of Utah because they had an excellent Modern Dance program.

Nancy was expecting a second child. She and her husband and little Sha were living in the town of Harrison in northwest Arkansas where her husband worked for Frontier Airlines. I didn't want to move far away from them. And I did not want to leave all my friends and connections in Little Rock.

When I heard from Harold he said that he could only offer me a provisional appointment to the vacant position he had. There were a lot of personnel people in the agencies who wanted the job and I would have to compete for it. He said all the applicants would have to take a Civil Service test and he would have to choose from the top three scorers on the test. He warned me that the potential applicants all had a lot of experience. I knew he wanted me but he was being very fair. I would have to earn the position.

What a quandary. I had no idea what this test would be but I realized that if I didn't score high enough I would be in Phoenix with no job. I decided that I would put my house for sale and if it sold quickly I would take it as a sign that the Good Lord wanted us to go west. If it didn't sell in three months I would take it off the market and stay put. It sold in six weeks, so after a big round of farewell parties and lots of tearful goodbyes, Jon, Mary Pat and I were off to Phoenix. We hated to leave but there were lots of challenges ahead for us. By then I was comfortable with my decision. We drove away from Little Rock the first of July in 1969.

CHAPTER NINE
And So It's Phoenix

*O*ur trip was uneventful except for seeing the Rehoboth Mission. We left Interstate 40 at Flagstaff and headed down Black Canyon Highway for Phoenix. We were about forty miles along on the 110 mile trip when I noticed that the fuel gauge was almost on empty. I thought we'd just stop at the next gas station when I realized that there were no signs about any towns or gas stations on this beautiful winding, mountainous road. Mary Pat and Jon were snoozing and there was no point in rousing them.

Flagstaff has tree covered mountains, everything is green and there is an abundance of pine trees. But as you go south everything changes. The trees get smaller until they are just shrubs. Then there is a mixture of small shrubs and cacti and the elegant saguaro start to appear. The black soil disappears and the terrain is very sandy. There are still mountains, but they are barren – just rocks – a most phenomenal drive.

I started coasting down the hills and watched closely for signs of civilization. The gauge was already on empty when we saw a sign pointing to a gas station a quarter of a mile off the highway. Fortunately, it was all downhill so we coasted to the edge of the station and were about fifty feet from the gas pump before the car came to a halt. I decided the Good Lord did want us to get to Phoenix.

We arrived in Phoenix about three o'clock in the afternoon of Friday, July 4, 1969. It was 112 degrees. I located the State Capitol Building and the little dinky Personnel Building first of all because I wanted to know where to report on Monday. We found a small hotel nearby and when we got out of the car it was like an oven. We looked at each other in utter disbelief. What had I done?

After getting settled in the hotel, we had dinner and recovered enough to go to a ball game which included fireworks – the extent of our fourth of July celebration.

The next day I studied the ads in the newspaper and found an apartment in Scottsdale which sounded interesting. We drove out and liked it so much that we rented it for a month on the spot. It was a long way from the Capitol complex but I was more interested in where Jon would attend school for his senior year. My plan was to buy a house or condo during the next month.

Neil Armstrong made his walk on the moon on July 20 and it was a memorable occasion. The apartment manager arranged for several TV's around the pool area. All of the residents brought food and we had a big potluck and then watched in awe when Neil Armstrong stepped on the moon and said, "One small step for man, one giant leap for mankind."

I bought a six-month-old, three-bedroom, two-bath condo for $23,000 and we were all set. Jon went to the new Saguaro High school in the fall and Mary Pat returned to Little Rock for a year and then entered the University of Utah in Salt Lake City to major in modern dance. Nancy and her family were still in Harrison, Arkansas.

Working with Harold Bennett again was great. And this time it was more satisfying because the law authorizing a comprehensive Civil Service had already been passed the previous year and the development of the new system was underway. Personnel had previously been decentralized to the agency level and now all of the separate systems were being centralized and forged into something new. Harold inherited a lot of staff from the agencies and many of them fought for what they had always done. All of them were very wary of me especially since they all wanted the Assistant Director position, which I was now holding on a provisional appointment. Now I had to pass the test.

The test was administered about a month later. Harold was terribly nervous. The test was to be at two o'clock in the afternoon and he spent the morning walking the halls and smoking his pipe furiously. He didn't say a word to me. I wasn't terribly worried since there were a lot of ads in the newspaper for teachers. They paid just a little less than the salary I would be getting so I figured that if I didn't pass the test, I would go back to teaching.

The test was given by the same woman who supervised testing all day, every day. She kept the tests under lock and key. About ten of us took it and most were long-time employees who felt they deserved the job. As soon as I looked over the test I knew I could pass it. It covered a lot of material which I had learned when I took the personnel training in Frankfurt for my Arbeitsamt job. And I learned more from Harold in Arkansas when we developed a state of the art system.

Two days later I learned that I had made the highest score on the test so Harold could appoint me to the job with no problem. Some of the other applicants still thought there was something suspicious about my score but over the next few months we worked together very well and over time we became very good friends.

After I had been on the job for a little more than a month my secretary told me that the Governor was on the phone and wanted to talk to me. I was puzzled. I had only met Governor Jack Williams once very briefly. Why would he call me? I picked up the phone and the voice said, "This is Governor Jack Williams and I have just returned from a Governor's meeting and I bring you greetings from Governor Winthrop Rockefeller." He went on to tell me nice things Win had said. Just like Win. He would go out of his way to be kind to his friends.

One of my responsibilities was to develop rules for state employees. This was not terribly difficult because I had done so much research in Arkansas and had kept a copy of that work. Getting consensus from fellow workers and Harold, especially, helped build support for the new rules. Harold presented copies of the new rules to the five members of the personnel board. He asked them to review them because they would vote to adopt them at the next board meeting; they could call me if they had any questions.

The only woman, Sandra Day O'Connor, called and said she would like to go over them with me. We met for two full afternoons in our small conference room and went over every single rule. I was so impressed. She was so friendly and kind but asked very good questions. With extensive notes she had questions about the promotion procedure, the grievance and appeals systems, the amount of leave employees earned and other topics. At the time she was Assistant Attorney General and represented state employees on the Board.

It was not surprising when she went on to serve as State Senator and Majority Leader, then as a judge in Maricopa County Superior Court and later on to the Court of Appeals. I was thrilled when we turned on the radio one morning in 1981 to hear President Reagan appoint her to the United States Supreme Court, where she served with distinction for twenty-five years. From a personnel standpoint she had it all. Not only was she well educated and brilliant, but she worked so well with other people. I was privileged to have had that brief encounter with her and will always be her biggest fan.

The classification system was partly developed when Harold arrived in Phoenix but there was a lot of work to be done. The inequity in pay that existed was astounding. Each of the seventy agencies developed their own pay schedules and what the Legislature approved depended pretty much on how well the agency director got along with Legislators on the appropriations committee. The agencies who were eligible for federal money had by far the highest salaries.

The Welfare Department had a large group of women who worked with the public and assisted them in filling out applications for aid. In the Health Department there was a large group of men who did almost exactly the same thing, except that the questions pertained to health. The men were paid exactly twice the amount the women were receiving.

One of my least favorite assignments was to go around to the agencies and explain to some of their employees that they were being paid more than the top step of their new salary grade so their salaries would be frozen until the pay schedule caught up with them. Not fun. I became known as "the hatchet woman."

I seldom went to lunch in those hectic days. Often I would go over to the Twin Barrels next door and get one of their big juicy hamburgers. One day I ran over and a new waitress reached into a freezer and got out a little dinky frozen one. I said, "Oh, I'd like one that you make."

"Oh, we just bought the place and there were so many

bugs and mice and rats in the kitchen that we are going to completely redo it before we make any." I couldn't throw up retroactively.

Every change we made was a mixed blessing. Some of the agencies allowed more sick and vacation leave than the new rules provided and some allowed far less. The new grievance procedure ended with the Agency Director as the final decision maker but the Appeals system could go all the way to the Superior Court. Equalizing the rights and benefits was a very good thing but some people were always unhappy.

Feminism was a big deal at this time. In 1963 Betty Friedan's book, *The Feminine Mystique* came out and women took it very seriously. And the Civil Rights Law of 1964 had a big impact especially when they later added "Women" to the mix. Many women were working for men who weren't nearly as bright or as capable as they were and some began thinking, "Hey, maybe I should be getting ahead in this world of work. Maybe I should be given a fair opportunity to earn more money." And even if they had a good, fair boss they still wanted an equal chance for promotion and recognition.

Some people reacted rather foolishly. Arizona State University started offering courses in Assertiveness Training for Women and a host of other institutions, public and private followed suit. I didn't think that was productive at all. A lot of people – men and women – would never make good bosses because they had no interest in planning other people's work or dealing with other people's problems; they could care less about budgets. That group would include many of our leading scientists, musicians, artists, surgeons and a host of others with specialized skills. Being a man or a woman had nothing to do with it. Leadership qualities were a part of your personality – some people would never acquire them, certainly not with just an "assertiveness" course.

I didn't think that was the way to go. If you worked hard and produced a good product you would get ahead. Confrontation was not the answer. However, I recognized that if you had a boss who thought "women should stay in their place" you would never make it. Get out of there. Also, you had to be completely asexual. You could be very friendly but you couldn't come close to flirting. It was proven over and over through the years that sleeping with the boss brought only temporary rewards. You had to work hard and be brave enough to speak up and present your ideas but you couldn't be brash. A sense of humor was a must.

We developed a course for state managers and supervisors and handled the problem very differently. We included both men and women in the classes and decided that, assuming you met the basic qualifications, the most important factor was how you related to your staff. We based our class on Peter Drucker's *Management by Objectives,* which he was promoting nationwide. We divided "bosses" into various categories – the Theory X'ers who were the very dominant top down people who said, "This is what you are going to do." They did all of the planning by themselves and everybody was at their mercy. Staff members were like robots.

And we had the Theory Y's who were the weak wimps. They never had a plan. They bumbled along from day to day and the workers each did the best they could. Each of our classes developed their own categories – the Superbs, the Lookers, the Bests, the Honeys.

We videotaped a lot of role playing, and then evaluated the interactions. It was great fun. In the end we always decided that practically no one was all of any category – everyone was more or less a cross breed but that sex had practically nothing to do with it. And we always decided that

attitude and competence were the really meaningful qualities. Those qualities had to be assessed on an equal basis.
An intelligent, qualified person with the necessary experience and human relations skills could be a good manager
regardless of their sex.

A perceptive woman in class observed, "Some men think
of women in the same way they think of computers. They
don't understand them and they don't want to learn. They
hate to change and they'd prefer maintaining the status quo."
I liked that. Computers were new then and it was true that
men resisted them more than women did.

And the federal government imposed more changes on
us in order to comply with the Civil Rights Law. We were
told to delete "Sex – F or M" from all of the application
forms. We did it knowing that it had not been completely
accurate anyway. You would be surprised how many people
wrote in "Sometimes" or "Twice a Week." After we deleted
it the feds asked us for monthly reports on how many men
and women we had hired!

On a personal basis, I never dated anyone I worked
with and when I went to lunch with a male fellow worker I
always insisted on paying for my own lunch. Once I went
out to Arizona State University to conduct interviews with
about fifty students who had applied for summer intern
positions with the State. We usually just had funds to hire
eight or nine and we chose them primarily through personal interviews.

A professor conducted the interviews with me; he was
not married and about my age. Obviously, his clerical staff
decided we would make a good pair. I didn't pay any attention to them but one day when we went to lunch I discovered that I didn't have any money with me. He paid and I
told him I would reimburse him. When I got back to my office I realized that I didn't have the belt to my suit. So I put

the money in an envelope and added a little note, "Thanks and here is your money. And I lost my belt. Did you find it?"

He called me and said, "Mildred, do you realize the excitement your money and note caused? My staff can't wait to see what happens next."

Another time Harold sent me over to talk to a new agency director who had a lot of questions about his relationship to our Personnel Division. Taking my book of rules, I sat down across the desk from him and started earnestly explaining the rules. After a while I glanced up, and he was leering at me with a silly grin on his face. He said, "Do you see that couch over there? It has never been used. What do you say we use it?"

I looked in the other direction and said, "Do you see that door over there? If you say one more word like that, I will walk right out of here right over to the Governor's Office and tell him exactly what you said." The grin disappeared in a hurry and I resumed my explanation of the rules. We got along fine, but a few years later he got fired. I could half-guess the reason, but I don't know.

Mary Pat came home one summer from the University of Utah and worked as a waitress at Coco's, a popular eatery. One Sunday afternoon she waited on a middle-aged woman who was crying. Mary Pat asked if she could help her and the woman said she and her husband were from Iowa. She said they were on their way to California but stopped in Phoenix to see a man and his wife who were former neighbors. When they arrived they were surprised to learn that they were divorced and only the man was living at their home.

The man told them that he had to go to Tucson on business all week but that they could stay in the house as long as they liked. But on Sunday morning her husband had a heart attack and he was now in the hospital. The house was up on the desert and she was afraid to stay there alone and she was in a quandary.

Mary Pat told her, "I'll call my mother. She will help you." So I went to the house up on the desert and stayed with the woman from Iowa. She was very nice and we had a pleasant evening. I told her I would go back to my house and shower and have breakfast the next morning so she wouldn't have to worry about me. And so I got up early, put my clothes over my arm, carried my shoes and walked out to my car in my robe and bedroom slippers.

I walked around the back of my car and a man across the street was just picking up his morning newspaper. We were both completely stunned when he stood up and we recognized each other. He was the Director of Finance for the state and we worked together frequently. I knew exactly what he was thinking. I should have explained, but I was so confused I just said, "Hi" and got in my car and drove off. After that, whenever I saw him there were other people around and I couldn't explain. I thought about calling him, but the longer I waited, the less likely he would believe my story, so I said nothing. To this day he probably thinks I am more "interesting" than I am.

We made a lot of progress and kept improving the system for a number of years and then the Legislature created a new Department of Administration. It improved the coordination between finance and personnel, but it took away our independence and made us much more political. Harold became the Assistant Director of the Department of Administration so now he was responsible to the Director of Administration and the Governor as well as to the Personnel Board. It really messed up the authority of the Personnel Board which is bound to happen when you interfere with the line of command.

A series of bosses who were not professional personnel people diluted the effectiveness of personnel. Our division was reorganized every time we had a new boss. All of them were more political. I ended up spending a lot of my time on grievances, sexual harassment cases and appeals. We had a lot of very interesting cases.

The most bizarre occurred when a man came in and told me he was undergoing a sex change and he wanted to know when he should start wearing dresses. My very first thought was, "He can't do that. The computer won't allow us to change the sex." He came from a very small agency which had a preponderance of women employees. I told him it simply would not work. It didn't matter when he started wearing a dress, he was never going to share the bathroom with those women. I advised him to go to the city or the county because they both needed people with his skills.

One time a girl called me and said that her boss was constantly chasing her around her desk. "I can help you, but I need to know who you are and where you work."

"I'll ask my husband if he thinks I should tell you." I never heard from her again. She may still be running around her desk.

Another woman came in and complained that her boss used horrible language which really offended her and her co-workers. "He keeps saying 'shit' right in front of us." Later I mentioned to her boss that some of his subordinates objected to his language and he said, "Oh, shit."

We hired a Park Ranger for the State Parks Department and the first day on the job they informed him that he would be wearing a uniform. He didn't object to that except that he did not want to wear the hat because it was a Lord Fauntleroy type that he thought was ridiculous. I checked and found that the Uniform Rule was not in writing and he had not been told about the uniform as part of the job interview.

His only alternative was to file a grievance but the agency suspended him for insubordination. It went through the appeal process and ended up at a hearing before the Personnel Board. They held in favor of the Parks Board. He would have to wear the hat. He took it to Superior Court and they reversed the Personnel Board ruling because the agency had nothing in writing and he was not informed during the interview. This whole procedure took more than a year. He came back to his job and worked as a Ranger for one day without the hat and then quit.

A sad case which bothers me to this day concerned a maintenance worker. The director of buildings and maintenance called me and told me about a man who had been sent to the dump with a load of old scrap iron. These trips were made whenever the state couldn't use or sell furniture, supplies or equipment they no longer needed. On this trip the worker passed a store with a sign which said, "We Buy Old Iron" so he stopped and sold it for forty dollars. He came back to the office and bragged to other employees about what he had done.

When the Director told me about it, I said, "Oh, no. I"ll have to tell the Attorney General about this." Our office handled any infractions against the rules, but if an employee broke the law we were to advise the AG. The Director agreed I should do this because his employees all over the state would be selling surplus goods and in effect they were stealing from the state.

I had a good relationship with the Attorney General and he had used good judgment in settling a lot of cases for us. I gave him all of the facts and he asked what I thought should be done. I thought a three day suspension without pay would take care of it. Several weeks later I realized that I had never heard about what happened to the maintenance worker, so I called the AG. I was horrified that he had turned it over to a new Assistant AG just out of college who apparently thought he would make a name for himself by pursuing it vigorously. He had taken it to court downtown. Later I learned the man had been sentenced to two years in jail. I still worry about that.

One time a Corrections Department supervisor fired an employee and the employee appealed to the Personnel Board. There had been a prison break in the middle of the night so employees were brought in to try and find the prisoners. This prison was out on the desert in the middle of nowhere. The employee was responsible for a trained dog who would help in the search. The dog started out riding in the back of the truck but when it started to rain the employee said that the dog should be brought up into the cab. They argued. The supervisor insisted that he wouldn't allow the dog into the cab and the employee insisted that he had been taught that the dog should not ride in a cold rain. His ability to smell would be affected. The supervisor got so upset that he fired the employee on the spot.

The Personnel Board listened to the entire case and announced that they would make their ruling at the next monthly meeting. At the second meeting the employee brought the dog with him and he jumped up on a chair right in the front row and looked around as if he were as interested as any of us in what the verdict would be. When the personnel board chairman announced in favor of the employee I swear that dog held his head high and looked all around the room as if to say, "I won, I won."

Sometimes whistle blowers would bring us very serious problems about top echelon managers who were usually Governor appointees. Governor Babbitt always encouraged us to investigate further even when they were people he thought he could trust completely. Three appointees actually ended up in jail. I was terribly shocked about two of them but I learned that "power corrupts" sometimes.

Money is terribly important to a lot of people. Three other top people were fired – all because of sexual harassment. Everyone in the general public should admire whistleblowers because very often they are the only ones who know about wrongdoing. It takes a lot of courage to do it. The investigations were team efforts, often complicated and very challenging. I enjoyed being a sleuth.

Computers started to be available in the middle 70s. We realized how valuable they could be to us. The population of the state was growing and the number of state employees grew commensurately. We realized how great it would be if we could computerize our personnel actions which were the basis of the state payroll. They could handle our employment process and any number of transactions we took on a regular basis.

Computerization was entirely different in those early years. We hired keypunch operators who typed information onto cards which we sent to the mainframe. A new agency building was especially designed with a very large room in the basement which held this huge mainframe. The temperature was controlled 24/7. Each agency had a time schedule when they could input their punched cards and a schedule when we could get information out of the mainframe. Word processing wasn't available until 1979. We also hired a flock of programmers and system analysts; unfortunately, not all of them were of the Bill Gates caliber. The good ones were in high demand.

Governments can't operate like businesses. The private sector can take advantage of changes as quickly as they can afford them or can borrow the money to make them happen. State agencies have to go to the Legislature and it can take years to convince them to spend the money. They thought that you should give up some employees if you wanted to use computers. And technology changed so fast that when you did get the money the equipment you asked for was already outdated. Such a struggle! But it was worth it. It was amazing how much needed information you could get and how quickly routine matters like payroll could be processed.

Harold sent me to Chicago for a course on what managers could expect from computers. Their main message was that you could get any financial or statistical reports you wanted if you had good programmers and systems analysts. The course designers knew that because they didn't have them. They kept trying to demonstrate what they were telling us on a monitor down in front, but nothing ever worked. They were so embarrassed. And it was there that I first heard the phrase, "Garbage in, garbage out" and it became a cliché in the computer world.

Our computers didn't always work smoothly either. I could relate to those poor guys in Chicago. One Friday the computer paid about 400 employees at the State Hospital the amount of their retirement deduction, instead of the amount of their pay. It was discovered in the middle of the afternoon and we had to tell all of those people they could come by our office and pick up a handwritten check for the correct amount. A group of us from Personnel and Finance sat and wrote checks until about nine o'clock that night.

There was no Internet or e-mail and so agencies couldn't relate to each other. Our Personnel Division kept track of all 25,000 employees through a Personnel Action Form which had all of the pertinent data about employees including Social Security Number, Job Title, Classification, Grade, Step and Pay. We processed every single change – new hires, promotions, demotions, resignations, etc. etc. The finance division required detailed payroll forms from every agency every two weeks. In those days you needed five copies of everything.

Harold and I talked about how great it would be to combine all of the information we needed from personnel action forms and payroll forms and computerize it. We drafted a form to cover everything and he sent me over to the Finance Department to discuss it with their computer gurus. We spent an entire afternoon going over all of the information and they agreed it was a great plan. They assured me it could be done so I was very excited when I reported back to Harold at the end of the day. He talked with the Finance Director the next day who agreed it would be a big improvement. So Harold asked me to order 30,000 of the new forms so we could implement it.

Just after the new forms were delivered, Harold had a call from the Finance Director. After reviewing our plans again, the systems analysts had decided that it would be too difficult for them to develop a new program. Software didn't exist yet and these un-Bill Gates types simply didn't know what to do or how to do it. It was almost a year later that we implemented the plan and by then our forms needed updating. The ones I had ordered were useless. Entering computer land was not easy but after just a few months we began to wonder how in the world we had ever managed to operate without it.

Bruce Babbitt, the Attorney General, suddenly became governor when Governor Wes Bolin died of a heart attack. Fortunately, he did not make many political demands on us. But after about three years we had a second Director of Administration and one day he called Harold over and fired him. I couldn't believe it. I felt terrible. But Harold got plenty of job offers and ended up going back to his native Louisiana in an even better job. They bought the house near Baton

Rouge his wife Elaine had been raised in and they continue to live there. We still keep in touch.

In early 1983 Governor Babbitt came up with a plan which enabled older employees to retire with benefits which were almost equal to what they would get if they waited until they were 65 years old. He realized that he had some dead wood in state government – employees who were just hanging on for their retirement pay but were contributing very little. He wanted to replace them with younger more productive employees. The plan was tied to age and time in service. I was sixty-three years old and I decided to look into how it would affect me.

I visited the Retirement Division and had them figure out exactly what my situation would be. I was pleasantly surprised to find that it would be more pay than I expected and I could continue my health insurance. It would be equal to what I got if I worked another two years. I would not be able to collect Social Security for those two years, so I called their office to determine what benefits I would have from them when I became eligible. That turned out to be a ridiculous call.

The girl I talked to at the federal office tried first of all to get me to consider using Norman's Social Security, because we had been married for almost twenty years. I didn't want to do that but she kept asking more and more questions until I finally was telling her all about my divorce and the fact that he was an alcoholic and anyway I had been making a very good salary for many years. She then looked up my financial record and ended up telling me, "You know, my husband is an alcoholic and I think I will get a divorce and do what you have done." I couldn't believe it.

I decided to retire. I still enjoyed my work, although we had lots of problems under our succession of directors. After Harold left we weren't moving ahead like we had been and politics were playing a bigger part. The traffic coming and going to work was a big factor, too. This was before we had any freeways going north and south in the east part of the Valley. Even with air conditioning in the car, my right arm would get sunburned driving a long way north every afternoon.

And there were lots of things I wanted to do besides work for the state. Maybe I would get a different kind of job. And so in May 1983 I retired. By then we had computerized almost everything we did. I wondered where Personnel would go in the future. Would supervisors and managers be lying home on their couches pushing buttons to tell the robots what to do? Would they be sending faxes and e-mails to their fellow managers on Mars? Your imagination could run wild thinking about what might happen in the world of work. Maybe everyone would have a mini car on their back and traffic wouldn't be a problem.

Retired

And all of the time I had been working I had a life outside of work which was good too. Jon finished high school and attended Scottsdale Community College for one year. He became an activist – where did that come from? The college was brand new and he and some friends decided that having another football team in the Valley was not nearly as important as lecture programs, drama, music and other fine arts. They lost their campaign but did succeed in getting the student body to vote "pink" as the school color and "artichokes" as the name of the football team.

After a year of college Jon and a friend made a trip all over the country in an old car. When they ran out of money they would stop and work. Their first job was at a Big Bob Restaurant, a well known chain specializing in hamburgers. When they left the manager gave them a wooden coin which was their recommendation for a job in any one of the Big Bob's in the country. They used it repeatedly and had a wonderful trip.

When he returned he took a job in Arizona's first resort – Castle Hot Springs located up in the Bradshaw Mountains about forty-five miles from Phoenix. It was a beautiful, green oasis on pristine desert and featured natural hot springs cascading out of surrounding cliffs. The lovely old resort had been built in the 1890s and now it was operated by Rock Resorts, which was owned by Lawrence Rockefeller. Jon loved it there and talked one of the local ranchers into selling him twenty acres of land which adjoined the Castle.

He planned to just spend the summer there but it unexpectedly led to a career as a chef for him. The Austrian chef who was the director of all of the Rock Resort chefs visited Castle Hot Springs during the summer. He was very impressed with the figures carved from butter which Jon had created for a buffet table. He offered Jon the opportunity to join a new apprentice program he had just established which was to train the participants in the European tradition of preparing food instead of having them become "American fry cooks." Jon accepted the offer and completed the seven year program and then stayed on with Rock Resorts for several more years. He worked at Caneel Bay Plantation on St. Johns Island in the Caribbean, at Kapalua Bay on Maui in Hawaii, at Mauna Kea on the big island Hawaii, at Woodstock Inn in Woodstock, Vermont, at Jenny Lake Lodge in Jackson Hole, Wyoming, at the Grand Hotel on Mackinac Island in Michigan and finally at The Boulders in Carefree, Arizona. The land Jon had purchased adjoining Castle Hot Springs was fully paid for by now and it was about thirty miles from Carefree. He put a small mobile home on the land and started building a permanent home. Although part of the road was pretty horrible he drove back and forth to Carefree for his job. One day he was working on his land and a man stopped by. When he confirmed that Jon was the owner of the five acres on the top of the mountain he asked, "Would you sell it for $8,000.00 an acre?" Jon had paid $300.00 an acre for it so without hesitation he said "Sure," and they made the deal. After several years, Jon quit his job at The Boulders. It was very stressful and he didn't need the money so he decided to spend his full time building his home. He thought getting the well dug, the septic tank buried and electricity to his land was difficult but it was even harder and terribly expensive to get all of the building materials brought all the way from Phoenix, especially since the last six miles were on a really bad road. It didn't take long for him to decide that buying a manufactured home was the way to go. Miraculously they delivered the whole thing comprised of 1600 sq.ft. fully furnished. It even had a Roman tub. It appeared to be split down the middle and arrived on two trucks which went up and over the mountains, around the treacherous curves and through some creek beds without any trouble at all. The crew set it in place, put it together, hooked it up and took off. Jon built decks on the front and back and there he was snug as a bug in his own home in his own beautiful canyon. He could climb up the mountain right behind his house and see all the way to Phoenix. Jon stayed there several years but then sold another parcel of land and bought a place in Phoenix. He chose not to go back to the cuisine world but now works mainly in construction. Some summers he works as a chef in a camp for underprivileged children and occasionally he will go up to Las Vegas to help a friend who has a catering business. He keeps busy in the enviable state of being able to make choices about his employment. Just now he is in the process of selling the last of his land holdings and will remain in Phoenix. Jon has never married but we all like Pam, his girlfriend.

And Mary Pat was at the University of Utah dancing for hours every day and working hard at a local restaurant to pay her way. She was an excellent student and did very well. One summer she came home and worked at a restaurant named Coco's. She cleared $1,000 and bought a used Volkswagen which she kept until after she graduated. She would drive all the way from Salt Lake City to Phoenix and back for holidays and occasionally, we would all drive up there.

When Mary Pat graduated from the University of Utah she took a summer job as Dance Instructor at Interlochen Academy in Michigan. There she met Peter Bankoff who had just graduated from Indiana University with a major in Music. He played the piano brilliantly and was teaching Jazz that summer at Interlochen. Peter played with Henry Mancini's orchestra as their "keyboard man" anytime they were east of the Mississippi. Mary Pat and Peter fell in love and a year later on August 18, 1974 they were married, on her twenty-fourth birthday. The traveling lifestyles of musicians and dancers was not what they really wanted. Peter decided to go into medicine like his father and brother. They lived in Indianapolis. Mary Pat worked but decided that she would also go to school since Peter was studying every evening and she enjoyed learning.

She entered Law School partly because they only had one car and it was close to the University of Indiana Medical School. She had their first child, Amy, on her graduation day and passed the Indiana Bar Exams the next month. And she had a full time job during all of this. Peter graduated the next year and they came to Phoenix for his residency. They had two sons, Michael and Ben in addition to daughter Amy and they still live here.

We were in Phoenix for less than three years when

Nancy got a much needed divorce. She and her two girls, Sha, who was four, and Shelby, who was one and a half, came out to live with me. Nancy worked in a restaurant and started college. She went to the nearby Scottsdale Community College and then to Arizona State University where she graduated with a major in psychology. It was a lot of hard work but it was well worth it. I loved having them with me. The girls were just precious and I didn't have to worry about them anymore.

When we decided that Nancy and the girls would come to Phoenix I realized that I needed a bigger house. In two days I sold the townhouse I had bought for $23,000 for $28,000 and bought a two-story, four bedroom condo for $32,000. A few years later when Nancy was at ASU over in Tempe I made a down payment on a condo over there for her and I sold the big condo to buy a fix-up house.

Nancy had called to tell me that she had met Kathy Miller's father at work and he had asked her to go to lunch. Almost everyone knew about Kathy Miller. She was twelve years old when she was hit by a car while crossing Scottsdale Road. She was in a coma for about three months and her condition was reported almost daily in the newspaper. When she recovered she was on a lot of TV shows, a book was written about her and she won an international award for courage. The book was made into a movie. Her parents had been divorced during her recovery time.

Larry came to dinner about two weeks after they met and I liked him immediately. He had been born and raised in Topeka, Kansas and I am always inclined to trust Midwesterners. He had graduated from the University of Kansas (he's still a Jayhawk fan). As a college baseball All-Star, he was drafted by the Los Angeles Dodgers. After a stint with the Army during the Berlin Wall crisis, he played for the Dodgers, the Orioles and the Mets before being sent down to Phoenix. He has hundreds of crazy stories about his baseball career. Did you know that baseball is in the Bible? It starts, "In the big inning..."

Larry was a left-handed pitcher but his name was never a household name. He played for the Dodgers when Sandy Koufax and Don Drysdale were on the pitching staff and they were always described as "Sandy Koufax, Don Drysdale and the others." He was one of the others. Nancy and Larry were married on May 5, 1984. We were happy to welcome him into our family. I couldn't possibly have better sons-in-law than Peter and Larry.

Operation QT

While I was still working, I learned that some carpeting, paint, decorating and yard work could do wonders for a house.

I turned the trick nine times – always buying in a good neighborhood but always buying low and selling high. Those fix-ups became a money-making hobby, which was very challenging. I would stay in a house an average of three years and then look for another fix-up. I had invested $3,000 in the first condo I bought and I walked away with a check for $68,000 from the last sale. And every house I lived in was nicer than the last one.

My kids worried because my last house was in a new development way up north, 20 or more miles from where they lived. And so I accepted an offer from Mary Pat and Peter and built a house on their property in beautiful Paradise Valley. It is a small incorporated town nestled behind the mountains between Phoenix and Scottsdale. Technically my house is a guest house and I built it in their horse corral but it's a great 1400 sq.ft. house with a marvelous view of the mountains and I love it.

When I retired Mary Pat and I decided that we would

get real estate licenses and get serious about buying and selling houses. Amy was a toddler and Michael was a baby and she wanted work she could do out of her home. She would concentrate on the paperwork and I would do the running around. It was a great plan but it all changed the last week of real estate school. I was returning home on a Friday night when I was hit from behind by a drunken nineteen-year-old man. I had a compressed fracture in my lower spine and it took more than a year to recover.

While I was recovering I read a lot of magazines and watched a lot of TV. Drugs were becoming a bigger and bigger problem for our youth. It worried me. And every afternoon I would see a young girl with green hair go by my house on her way home at about 2:30. I wondered what she was going to do the rest of the afternoon and what was her green hair saying? I decided that with my background and interest I ought to be able to do something. I enlisted the help of my son-in-law Larry Miller.

And it was Larry who drove me around to help me research what I wanted to do to help our youth with the growing drug problem. Because of my back injury I couldn't drive. He was doing research of his own to develop seminars he later built into a successful consulting career. We visited twenty-six different agencies – rehabilitation centers, law enforcement agencies, and state agencies. I asked everyone, "Why do kids get into drugs?"

I almost always got the same answer – kids have too much time, too little supervision and low self-esteem. I used those reasons to develop an after school program. I founded Operation QT (Quality Time) a non-profit corporation in March 1987 which is still going to this day.

We devised a program which impacts the students directly. Our thinking was based on the philosophy the columnist Jimmy Breslin expressed when he said, "You can't make people be good. You can only put them in an environment where they want to be good." Our program puts them in a productive, supervised environment during the critical non-school hours when most juvenile crime occurs. It is an alternative to bad behavior because it keeps the students out of the malls, away from gangs, off the streets or from being home alone. But more importantly, it gives them motivation toward higher goals.

Our program is very cost-effective because the schools provide the facilities, equipment, utilities, insurance, accounting and auditing. QT pays the teachers who staff the programs. We buy all of the program materials, mainly by writing grants to government agencies and charities.

Our main goal is to help overcome the hopelessness too many young people feel today. Our society is not kind to our youth. They have more temptations and turmoil in their lives than probably any generation in the history of our country. Drugs, alcohol, teenage pregnancies, suicides and dropouts are all happening at alarming rates. Our children and our youth need to be motivated toward seeing a brighter future. After doing our original research I talked with school administrators at all three levels – elementary, middle school and high school.

The program we came up with was originally for just the after school hours but evolved to sometimes include evening hours, time in the morning before school starts and summer school. It is unique because it is school based. We choose schools which are in economically deprived areas and have a lot of minority students. We fund programs which are planned by our executive director and the school principal. Each one is tailor-made to meet the needs of the particular school. Some of the programs include parents as well as students. The staff is made up of the professional teachers who know the students and their individual needs.

QT may include tutoring in reading, computers, English or chemistry as well as recreational and cultural activities.

We are proud of our many diverse accomplishments but we are constantly striving to raise money so we can provide more programs. The need is so great. Lots of good people have served and are serving as board members. The one who has helped the most is Congressman Ed Pastor, a board member since 1988. He was elected to the U.S. Congress in 1991 in a special election to replace Arizona's beloved Mo Udall, who had to resign for health reasons. Ed has been instrumental in getting federal grants which have helped us tremendously. Now because of recent legislation he is an "Honorary" board member.

Our friendship goes back to the early 1970s when Ed worked in the Governor's office and he would come over with personnel problems. We discovered that we were both former school teachers and shared many visions for education.

I could write a book about the schools and the individual children and youth who have been a part of our program. One is an alternative school for students who have been remanded back to school by the courts or have been expelled for a semester or more. This particular school was for students in the fifth through the eighth grades and they were limited to twenty-two students at a time. The students are each interviewed by the staff when they are enrolled. One of the questions they asked was, "What do you want to be when you grow up?

Without exception every child answered, "Alive." What a challenge for us.

The second is a middle school in one of the poorest school districts in the state. For economic reasons and the demands of Bush's unfair "No Child Left Behind" program, the school board had to eliminate all but a minimal amount for music, arts and drama. We provided them with the funds to buy instruments and music so now they have two bands and two choruses. We are told that these additions have changed the atmosphere of the entire school of some 1200 students.

A fifteen-year-old girl is a QT student at one of our high schools. I was talking to a QT teacher when the door to her room opened and this girl appeared. She said, "Oh thank you, thank you, thank you a million times." She was obviously very elated.

The teacher said, "Oh, you're welcome," and the girl left.

"What was that all about?" I asked.

"Oh, yesterday in QT she told me that her mother's boyfriend had moved in with them. She said, 'He has this thing about toilet paper. He won't buy any and he says that if we want some we can steal it at work or at school.'" The teacher continued, "I went out and bought some for her last night and put it in my room closet where she can get it anytime." I was so pleased because that teacher would never have had the opportunity to listen to this girl, and give her hope, if it had not been for QT.

The second girl was ten years old when she wrote a poem which keeps me going when I get discouraged about our fundraising efforts. The staff passed it on to me.

DOES ANYONE CARE?
Would anyone care if I said
I was in danger?
Would you laugh at me if I was dead?
If I would cry, would you be there for me?
No, I guess not.
If you were there, I would feel better
But all these problems come back,

317

Would you care if I had a disease?
Does anyone know how I feel?
Does anyone understand how I feel?
Would anyone care for me?
Please, anyone tell me
For in this world, I do not know if
anyone cares for me.
Would you yell at me if I had a disease?
Every question comes to me,
then I start to cry
Thinking, no one cares for me
Or does not even care if I die.

I love visiting the schools and seeing the students participating in the programs. It is so rewarding to see rows of
children sitting in front of computers at elementary schools
working on their reading skills. The schools have software
that enables children to progress through reading programs
at their own pace. The reading materials are written at half-
grade levels. The children can read as much as needed at
one level and decide when to self-administer the tests on
the computer. If they pass, they can go on to the next higher
level. The children love it and they make an unbelievable
amount of progress. It is so great because there is never
enough time during the school day to allow all of the children the time they need on the computers.

Middle or high school students often used computers for
interactive work or playing games. The rooms will be filled
with more students than there are computers. I observed
one high school group writing the life story of John F. Kennedy. Each student was concentrating on a different phase
of his life and then they put it all together. The ones without
computers supplied ideas and facts. This was all after school
during time when these same youth might have been out

on the streets with gangs or hanging out in the malls. Some of them might have been having sex when their parents are gone. It is so good that instead they were making friends and building support systems at school.

Carl Hayden High School in west Phoenix has a great, very popular program to teach English to the parents. They improve their skills by also speaking English in their homes so the whole family makes progress. The program enables many of these men and women to get better jobs especially when some of them are able to take advantage of the help they get in reading and writing English as well as speaking it. Often we forget that those are entirely different skills. Speaking is just the beginning.

Language is such a huge problem. Some of our sixteen QT schools have as many as ninety-five percent of the students who have English as a second language; another high school has students who speak fifty-nine different languages. In these cases assimilation simply doesn't work, so QT is very valuable. Teachers are overwhelmed. There is not enough time in the day to meet the needs of each student.

I hope Operation QT, Inc. will be my legacy. I hope it will continue as long as there are children in this country who feel hopeless. Since 1986 it has been a very big part of my life.

Through the years we heard from Norman periodically. At first he called every three or four days but the calls dwindled down to fewer and fewer as the years went by. He left Little Rock and went to Houston. He took jobs in Saudi Arabia and in Vietnam. He would return to the States with lots of money but he always ended up drinking until the money was gone. He spent a lot of time in Veteran's hospitals. On July 16, 1988 his cousin called from Montgomery, Alabama to tell me he had died in the Veteran's Hospital there.

They needed money to provide him with a decent burial

which I certainly wanted him to have. He had just a graveside funeral and was buried next to his parents in Ramer, Alabama where he had been born and raised. It was so sad. The children did not want to go and I decided I would not go either. We arranged for flowers to be sent and Nancy and Mary Pat went with me to pick them out. We decided on a very nice bouquet that looked like autumn because he spent so much time hunting in the woods. The girl helping us said, "Do you want the card to say 'With love from his children?'"

The girls looked at each other and at me as if to say, "Why should we say that?"

I quickly told the girl, "Just write 'From Nancy, Mary Pat and Jon'." How very tragic.

The flowers didn't even arrive in time for the funeral. The funeral director called and said they had decided to make the trip from Montgomery to Ramer earlier than they had originally planned so the flowers were not there when they left. He wanted to know what he should do with them. I grieved over Norman's wasted life. He had so much going for him. If only I could have helped him. I tried to remember only the good times. But I moved on knowing that I had three wonderful children.

About a year after his death I heard a man on TV. "I am a college professor and I don't know how to read." That intrigued me so I sat down to listen. The man talked about how he had successfully deceived everyone. He had numerous tricks for how he could get information without having to read it. He told about how he would get knowledge from his fellow students or fellow workers. He had a great memory so if he listened carefully he could always get by. It had become a game for him to always get ahead and still not know how to read.

As I listened to this college professor his story began to

remind me of Norman. It slowly dawned on me that Norman had done all of the things this man was talking about. The tricks he described were astonishingly familiar. I remembered the many times he would tell the children, "Mom will read to you." Saturday mornings Norman would ask me to come to the office so we could dispose of the mail that had arrived during the week while he was gone. I would read it and he would say, "Tell me about it." He would go back to the shop and the men would read the new General Electric Instruction Books while he actually made the changes on the equipment. They greatly admired his talent and his ability to solve any technical problem. I'm sure they never even noticed that somebody else always read the instructions.

I could recall hundreds of times when he cleverly avoided reading but I had never recognized his problem. It was so sad – he was so smart. I could have easily taught him to read in maybe a month or two. Hundreds of times he promised he would never drink again. Maybe it was at those times that he wanted to tell me he couldn't read but he was too proud to admit it. Surely he knew I would understand. I never suspected. It makes his life story even more tragic.

I made lots of trips after I retired. I visited my Dutch relatives in The Netherlands twice, I went to London with my grandson Michael, I went to Israel with my sister Frannie, to Germany with my daughter Mary Pat and to New Zealand where my granddaughter Amy lives. I went on a hostel trip to Salt Lake City, I visit Los Angeles and San Diego and I have often taken friends and relatives to the Grand Canyon, Sedona or Mexico. And every summer I make a trip to Iowa.

Now I only have two sisters left – Frannie in Cedar Rapids, Iowa, Edene in Grand Rapids, Michigan and my sister-in-law Thelma in Des Moines, Iowa. The four of us are the lone survivors of the seven siblings and our spouses.

And I've kept up with technology. I have a new forty-inch LED TV, the newest Bose radio and CD player, my computer, a cell phone, but no iPod. My coffee pot and toaster and my car are computerized and I have a microwave which makes good popcorn!

I have decided that enough is enough. There is no end to what I could write – something new happens every day. All in all, life is good. I guess my only regret is that I never had a good marriage. I envy married couples that love each other and are real partners. But I don't spend time worrying about it. The best thing I have going for me is that I have a very loving family and hundreds of good friends. I'm very happy being independent because I can do whatever I want whenever I want to do it. I've been blessed with excellent health. Besides that, I can go over to Trader Joe's any time I like and buy their divine chocolate-covered Bing cherries. How could anything be better!

Mildred Norman
July 2006

EPILOGUE

I'm proud that in America we eventually do solve our problems. Immigration over the Mexican border is currently a big, complicated issue and the approaches many people take are very discouraging. However, I'm hopeful that it will be like slavery, suffrage, civil rights, integration and all of the social problems we have endured as a nation. We will work our way to doing the right thing, but changes are never easy. I continue to attend rallies and carry posters, I write letters to the newspapers that are never published and I respond to all of the requests for votes on the Internet, but I wish I could do more.

And I must admit that not all of the changes I have seen in my lifetime have been for the good. As Harold Bennett would say, some have been "progress toward the ditch." The prevalence of sexual assaults, pornography, the thirty percent dropout rate in our high schools, the teenage pregnancies, the illicit use of drugs and alcohol, the crime rate – the problems in our society go on and on. There are plenty of challenges for my descendants to tackle.

Goodness will prevail. People like our past Presidents

Jimmy Carter and Bill Clinton are working on problems like wiping out worldwide poverty and disease and are making a difference when disasters occur. Al Gore just made an outstanding documentary film on global warming, which, hopefully, our populace and politicians will take seriously. I am very proud of my grandson, Michael Bankoff, who majored in International Affairs at the University of Colorado and now aspires to make a difference in the economies of emerging nations. And I'm proud of my granddaughter, Amy, who lives in New Zealand and works to improve health and the environment in her surroundings. In fact, I'm proud of all members of my family.

Because I feel so strongly about keeping peace in the world, it is a bitter disappointment to me that as I write this our country is at war and we have the whole Middle East riled up. And it was a preemptive war based on lies. The United Nations has actually admonished us as violators of human rights because of how we are conducting the war and we have lost the respect of much of the world community.

Currently, our education system is being dominated by President Bush's – "No Child Left Behind." It is based on negativity and testing, and seeks to homogenize our children, when we should be inspiring and motivating them! It will pass and we will return to educating children, instead of training them to pass tests. A good education system is a must, but it is always a challenge.

As for my religious beliefs, sometimes the more I learn, the less I know. In our little church in Parkersburg we all believed whatever the preacher said and whatever he said sufficed. We never questioned anything. Now as I look back I wonder if my father did. I wonder what he and the Catholic priest discussed over the kitchen table those long winter nights. But I just accepted and believed whatever I

heard at church. And I attended many churches throughout my life.

It wasn't until I went to Germany that I began to have
lots of questions. That visit to Dachau, seeing the DP camps,
hearing the stories of my Dutch relatives, all had a lasting
effect on me. Later in life I began to read more and question more. Today I still have an abiding faith in God and I
believe that Jesus is his Son sent here primarily to show us
how to live. But I also realize that the Old Testament was
written 500 years after it supposedly happened and I certainly don't believe that every word is literally true or that
every word is "the inspired Word of God" as I was taught
as a child. The New Testament was probably written only 50
to 70 years after Jesus died but the various books certainly
don't always agree with each other and a lot of it has to be
fiction. And King Constantine actually chose the 52 books,
which would be included in the Bible, and he had hundreds
to choose from.

Dr. Duane Holloran, an excellent Bible teacher and a
former minister at the church I now belong to taught us
that when we read the Bible we should know when it was
written, who it was written for and what was the situation
at the time it was written. That is very good advice. It gives
you an important perspective and a better understanding
of the Bible.

We would get into fascinating discussions during Dr.
Holloran's classes. I remember once he had a Jewish Rabbi
come and talk to us and afterwards we got into a discussion about whether or not Jews would go to heaven. That
seemed idiotic to me. They laughed when I spoke up and
said, "Well, I have a wonderful son-in law who is a Jew and
if he can't go, I'm not going."

I still worry about World War II. We had to stop Hitler

but my experience in Germany had a huge effect on my religious beliefs. It broadened the scope of my thinking. I wonder if Uncle Willem prayed in his cage at Bergen-Belsen. And why weren't his prayers answered? When I was in Germany I was told six million Jews and five million others – gypsies, communists, trade unionists, Christians, and others, including thousands of children, were killed. I don't know if anyone knows the exact numbers but it is pretty scary when you have to round them out in millions. Think of the number of prayers that must have been offered. You can't just brush it off.

I came to the conclusion that God created the earth, set it in motion and pretty much turned it over to us. He is in control but He gave us the "free will" which Presbyterians talk about so much. We can do good or we can even destroy the whole planet if we choose to. He doesn't stop us. I have learned through my trials and troubles that it is meaningful for me to pray for wisdom and the courage to handle whatever may befall me. And I pray for my relatives, friends, the problems of the world and always for peace. And I always throw in "all of the children of the world." When I worry about all of the unanswered questions I have, I rely on my "faith." To me "faith" means I don't know and I never will – I just have to trust God. That has meaning for me but everyone has to find his or her own way.

I read a very intriguing book several years ago. The book is *The Dead Sea Scrolls Deception* by Michael Baigent and Richard Leigh. Their postscripts written in 1991, end this way and I quote:

"The Dead Sea Scrolls offer a new perspective on the three great religions born in the Middle East. The more one examines those religions, the more one will discern not how much they differ, but how much they overlap and have in common – how much they derive from essentially the same source – and the extent to which most of the quarrels between them, when not precipitated by simple misunderstanding, have stemmed less from spiritual values than from politics, from greed, from selfishness and the presumptuous arrogance of interpretation. Judaism, Christianity and Islam are all, at present, beset by a resurgent fundamentalism. One would like to believe – though this may be too much to hope for – that greater understanding of their common roots might help curb the prejudice, the bigotry, the intolerance and fanaticism to which fundamentalism is chronically prone."

Think about it. Could we stop fighting and become one? Or at least couldn't we learn to be tolerant of each other and our differing beliefs?

Throughout history so many wars have been started because of religious intolerance. For starters, all three of those religions go back to Abraham. And Jesus was a Jew. If we now have three or more separate Gods out there then we are all in a mess. Will they duke it out? And what about the religions of the Far East? I don't have the answers but I am convinced that there is only one true God of the entire universe.

Wouldn't it be great if we could all accept one God even if we didn't agree on Jesus, Mohammed or Buddha? Are we humane enough to ever get our act together and develop some tolerance and understanding or will we just keep fighting each other? Hopefully my descendants and their fellow human beings can do a better job than we have. It's my nature to think positively, but I wonder. My advice is, "Go for it!"

Mildred Norman
June 2006

Printed in the United States
67773LVS00002B/190-258

9 781589 850569